Won't You Join the Dance

OSHO FROM FULL CIRCLE

- Inner War and Peace
- Die O' Yogi Die
- Behind A Thousand Names
- Meditation: The Only Way
- Freedom from the Past
- Ah This!
- The Way of the Sufi
- The Silence of the Heart
- The True Name
- The Secret
- Truth Simply Is
- In Search of Celebration
- From Sex to Superconsciousness
- Never Born, Never Died
- Walk without feet, Fly without wings...
- Won't you Join the Dance?
- Priests & Politicians — The Mafia of the Soul
- My Diamond Days with Osho
- Tantra — The Supreme Understanding
- The Goose is Out
- Sex, Money and Power
- The Rebel
- A New Vision of Women's Liberation
- I Teach Religiousness Not Religion
- Words From A Man of No Words

Also in Hardcover
- The True Name (HC)

Won't You Join the Dance

OSHO

FULL CIRCLE

WON'T YOU JOIN THE DANCE
Copyright © 1983 Osho International Foundation, All rights reserved
Osho ® is a registered trademark of Osho International Foundation, used under license.

Editing & Commentary by Ma Prem Maneesha
Coordination by Swami Amano Manish
Poem adapted from *Alice's Adventures in Wonderland* by Lewis Carroll.

This Edition, 2001
First Reprint, 2006
Second Reprint, 2009
Third Reprint, 2011
ISBN 81-7621-037-4

Published by **FULL CIRCLE** *PUBLISHING*
J-40, Jorbagh Lane, New Delhi-110003
Tel: +011-24620063, 24621011 • Fax: 24645795
E-mail: contact@fullcirclebooks.in • *website:* www.fullcirclebooks.in

All rights reserved. No part of this book may be reproduced or transmitted in any form or by any means, electronic or mechanical, including photocopying, recording, or by any information storage and retrieval system, without prior written permission from OSHO International Foundation.

Typesetting: SCANSET
J-40, Jorbagh Lane, New Delhi-110003

Printed at Nutech Photolithographers, New Delhi - 110020
PRINTED IN INDIA
83/11/04/01/20/SCANSET/DE/NP/NP/OP195/NP250

"Won't you join the dance?
What matters it how far we go?"
his scaly friend replied.
"There is another shore, you know,
upon the other side.
The further off from this shore,
the nearer to the other...
Then turn not pale, beloved snail,
but come and join the dance.
Wil you, won't you, will you, won't you,
won't you join the dance?"

Bhagwan Shree Rajneesh
is now known simply
as Osho.

Osho has explained that
His name is derived
from William James' word
'oceanic' which means
dissolving into the ocean.
Oceanic describes the
experience, He says,
but what about
the experiencer?
For that we use the word 'Osho'.
Later He came to find out
that 'Osho' has also been used
historically in the Far East
meaning
*"The Blessed One, on whom
the Sky Showers Flowers."*

INTRODUCTION

Osho. He has received many different accolades, among them 'a gem of a man', a poet-philosopher of the highest degree', 'one of the most important educators and religious leaders' and 'a twentieth century Buddha'.

The breadth of his vision is matched only by the depth of his wisdom. His fine perception of who we think we are, and the tender good humor with which he nudges us towards our real potential, makes this collection of talks from his evening 'darshan' — meetings with seekers — a must for all of us.

Many of those present when Osho spoke these words were there to experience the 'energyfield' of an awakened one and his commune. Some to ask for his insight on a host of issues from their meditative practice to relationships and work.

The majority, from all corners of the globe, came — knowingly or not — to be initiated into Osho's revolutionary sannyas. Into a way of living built on the cornerstones of love and awareness. A way that encompasses the outer and inner worlds in all their dimensions. That embraces the Zorba and Buddha, as Osho puts it, that resides within all of us.

The receiving of a new name or prefix as part of his sannyas worked then, as now, to support the conscious intention to discard worn-out, uncreative patterns of thinking and to start afresh. In darshan this came gift-wrapped as Osho addressed each seeker individually, indicating their particular direction through the meaning of their name. His ability to communicate across cultural, gender and generational differences was radiantly evident in the faces of those before him and in their subsequent transformation.

Our lives are becoming increasingly complex and stressful. Insecurity, uncertainty, and ambiguity are now unavoidable components of each waking moment. It is all too easy to lose sight of what we came here for.

Now more than ever the guidance of an enlightened consciousness of Osho's magnitude is needed.

Now more than ever we need to know how to contact our unchanging reality. To have the centering of a meditative consciousness as our touchstone of sanity.

Ma Prem Maneesha
Editor

1

We are still and snugly-robed in the crisp night. A child-voice wonders aloud 'Where's Osho?'

Then he is here, and the child, Karuna, with her mother, Yatra, are before him. While he bends to write her sannyas name, Karuna points excitedly at him, then on top of that discovers, and with appropriate amazement exclaims 'His toes! His toes!' and trots over to gently touch them. Osho does not pause in his writing, but a beautiful smile spreads over his face so we chuckle and enjoy her.

Osho : Good! Come here... your mala.

He pops the small mala over her head.

Just look at me.

But the camera has caught her eye and she points at it intrigued.

(to Yatra) Her name is good : Ma Deva Karuna. Deva means divine, karuna means compassion — divine compassion.

> *Yatra :* She told me she was going to say to you that she wants to do some groups. She said she wants to do some groups.

Osho looks at Karuna.

You have something to say to me? You want to do some groups?

She nods to gales of laughter.

That's good! You go to the school!

> *Deva Karuna :* I got my mala! And I met Osho! (much laughter)!

Won't You Join the Dance?   1

Osho chuckles, then talks groups with Yatra and Sangito while Karuna announces to anyone who cares to know that her mala 'isn't bwoken'. The trio are replaced by Christopher.

This is your name: Swami Anand Christopher. Anand means bliss, christopher means Christ-bearer. The story is that Saint Christopher bore the Christ child across the river. But it can become a tremendously significant metaphor for the inner journey. The meaning that I would like to give it is that each person, man or woman, is a Christ-bearer in the sense that everybody is pregnant with Christ, that we are carrying the child in our womb.

This is the whole dilemma of human existence, because if Jesus lives then Christ cannot live; if Jesus dies, only then can Christ live. By Jesus I mean the ego; by Christ I mean the egoless consciousness. Jesus and Christ cannot be together. When Jesus dies on the cross, then Christ is resurrected: the death of the ego is the birth of god. The majority of people have chosen the ego, they cling to the ego, and the Christ child remains suffocated, un-grown-up, like a seed — heavy, ready to be born, but finding no opportunity.

Sannyas is nothing but an opportunity for Jesus to die and for Christ to be resurrected.

Anything you would like to say to me?

Anand Christopher: I'm grateful to be here.

Alessandra is before him now.

This is your name: Ma Prem Alessandra. Prem means love, alessandra means a helper of mankind. The full name will mean: love, the helper of mankind. And this is something very important to be remembered, that unless you love you cannot be of any help. Help cannot be a duty. If it comes out of duty it is ugly, egoistic; it humiliates the other. When it comes out of love it obliges nobody; it is for the sheer joy of sharing. In fact you feel thankful to the person who accepted your help, because he respected it, he welcomed it — he could have rejected it.

People also become helpers without love — they become great public servants, missionaries, etcetera. These are the most mischievous people in the world : in the name of help they dominate, in the name of service they are on a power-trip. The service is nothing but a camouflage. They don't love; and without love whatsoever they do, harms —because this is the observation of all those who have known, that only love is nectar, everything else is poison.

So let love become the centre of your existence, your very being. And if out of the pulsation of love, service arises, it is beautiful; if you can help somebody out of love it is a tremendous joy. But it is not service, it is not duty, and you are not earning virtue. You are simply sharing your life as god has shared his life with you.

Jerry now.

This is your name : Swami Anand Jerry. Anand means bliss; Jerry comes from Jeremiah, the second greatest Biblical prophet. The literal meaning of Jeremiah is : god is exalted. That is the basic flavour of prayer — that god is great, that god is exalted, that god is supreme, that god is holy. The moment we say that god is exalted, automatically the whole existence is exalted, because god is not a person but another name for the totality of existence. It is all inclusive : men, women, trees, birds, rivers, mountains, stars, all are included in it. God simply means the whole, the total, all that is.

There is an ancient tradition which says that god is a code word. 'G' stands for 'that', 'o' stands for 'which', 'd' stands for 'is' : that-which-is. God is not a person, but all that which is, all that exists, all that has been.

'God is exalted' means the whole existence is sacred. Wherever you are moving you are on holy ground, and whatsoever you are doing is as significant as any prayer. Then the small acts of life are no more small, the ordinary is no more ordinary, everything becomes suffused with extraordinariness. Then even the smallest contains the greatest, and the atom in itself is a universe.

To feel this, this utter exultation of existence, is to be prayerful. Jerry is a beautiful name, the very essence of prayer. Become a blissful, prayerful yea-saying, a total yes — unguarded, unconditioned. And feel in everything the beauty of god, the expression of the divine. Slowly slowly, one becomes suddenly aware one day that we are like fish in the ocean of god. There is no need to go to seek and search for him : he is *here*, he is *now*.

Dara is in front of Osho now.

This is your name : Ma Prem Dara. Prem means love, dara is Hebrew; it means the heart of wisdom. Knowledge is of the head, hence it has nothing to do with love; in fact basically it is anti-love. Love plays no part in the growth of knowledge. Knowledge is the accumulation of dead facts, information, but those facts are not beating, they are not alive, because love is missing.

Wisdom is of the heart. It has nothing to do with fact, it has something to do with truth. And that is the difference between truth and fact : fact is only a corpse, truth is alive. The fact appears *like* the truth, but it is not — because the heart is beating no more, it is breathing no more; life has left it.

When the scientist dissects a body, whatsoever he comes to know about life is not the truth. It is certainly factual, but the moment you dissect the body you kill it, and whatsoever you know is about the corpse, not about the aliveness. When you dissect a flower you will know many things about it, but something will be missing : the spirit of the flower will be missing.

Facts can be known by the intellect; the spirit can only be contacted by the heart. Information is easily possible through the head, but wisdom only grows in the deepest recesses of the soul.

Love is the very nourishment for truth to live. Remember it : a Buddha may not know more than you, but he *is* more. A professor of philosophy may know more, but he is not more. Buddha, Jesus or Zarathustra have more being, not more knowledge; more heart, more love, more wisdom, not more information. The professors, the scholars, the pundits, have more information. Quantitatively they are very well-informed; qualitatively they are just empty.

Sannyas is the search for the heart, the search for wisdom — because it is wisdom that liberates. Knowledge binds you, wisdom liberates you. And love is the *most* essential ingredient in wisdom, the very heart of it.

Diwani is going back to Italy. She's discovered since the Primal group that she doesn't feel good with people.

It will change; all that is needed is awareness, more awareness. Almost everybody is trapped in the same situation, and those who become aware are fortunate, because from awareness, transformation starts. In the name of love, people are trying to dominate, to possess, to be powerful. Love is just a bait to be powerful. It is a strategy — the so-called love is just a very cunning strategy to dominate the other in such a way that the other never feels directly dominated; it is an indirect way. But the other is also doing the same with you, so there is necessarily conflict. Both are on power trips, and both clash.

Out of one hundred, ninety-nine point nine percent of couples are continuously fighting. And the reason is simple : each wants to be powerful over the other. Clash is inevitable; and in this clash all possibilities of love are destroyed. The whole situation becomes ugly, nauseating, sickening.

But once you become aware of it, then things can never be the same. Just watch and see that power is anti-love; power and love can't go together. If you are loving, you cannot seek power — hence all politicians are unloving people; if they are loving, they cannot be politicians. And lovers cannot be politicians, because who cares? — When you love, love gives you such fulfilment that who cares about power? Love makes you so high that no power can give you anything compared with it. And love gives you such contentment that all power trips look poor, beggarly, unhealthy, pathological.

So you have to watch and become aware; whenever you move into the next relationship with somebody, any friendship, any love, be watchful. Love is a totally different dimension. Love wants to share, love wants to give, and is not worried about what comes in return. Whether anything comes in return or not, that is not the concern of love. Its joy is in giving — and it is so fulfilling to give.

Then slowly slowly the old strategy, the old power-trip, will start disappearing from your mind. It is just a programme that has to be de-programmed. The beginning *has* started: just pour more attention into it. Whenever you see yourself playing old games, stop immediately, because they are suicidal. Whenever you catch yourself playing some old power-game, *immediately* stop. Don't wait even for a single moment, don't say 'tomorrow'.

Come back, because much has to be done. The journey has started; now much more work....

Keep it (a box) with you, and whenever you need me just put it on your heart.

She nods and smiles, Italian warm, then kisses her hands to him and is gone.

Hello, Sandipo. When are you leaving?

Radha (translating) : On the fifth of February.

When will you be coming back?

Sandipo : I just know that I will be coming back.

That's perfectly true — you *are* coming back. Time is not the question, mm? any day will do. There are only seven days!

2

Now Sue, a German group leader.

Osho : This is your name : Ma Anand Sue. Anand means bliss; sue is Hebrew, it means white lily. The full name will mean a blissful white lily. The lily is a strange flower, the poorest and the richest at the same time. Hence Jesus' statement to his disciples : Look at the lilies — even Solomon was not so beautiful, attired in all his grandeur, as these poor flowers are. And the reason for their beauty is that they think not of the morrow; they live in the moment.

To be in the moment is to be beautiful. To miss the moment is to fall into anxiety.

The only anxiety, the only anguish, is not to be herenow. The whole existence, except for the human mind, is herenow. Drop the human mind and you are a white lily, and as beautiful as even Solomon was not, attired in all his grandeur.

Hanneke sits silently. She's a nurse.

This is your new name : Ma Prem Hannah. Prem means love, and hannah is the original root of hanneke. It is Hebrew; it means grace, mercy, prayer. Your full name will mean : love and grace.

Love brings its own grace.

The moment one is in love, one is surrounded by grace. And that grace is not cultivated at all, it is spontaneous. Because it is spontaneous it is beautiful, and because it is spontaneous it is divine. It is something from above, as if the beyond has penetrated into the world.

To be in love gives you only a glimpse of grace, but to *become* love is to become grace itself. Start by being in love and end in becoming love.

His hand upturned, the thumb taps the root of the little finger as he says 'start' and moves onto the next finger as he says 'end'.....

Ingrid is a German physiotherapist.

This is your name : Ma Prem Ingrid. Prem means love; ingrid comes from Norse mythology, it means the god or goddess of fertility. Your full name will mean : love, the god of creation.

It is love that brings creativity to existence. It is love that tries to beautify it. It is love that is a constant urge to explore, to invent, to discover. Love is creativity, and it is only through creativity that one comes to know the creator.

The best way to come close to god is to participate in some creative act, whatever it is — painting, poetry, dance, music. Whenever you are bringing something new into existence you are close to god, because the new is born only when god is close to you.

But in the past, religion became very uncreative, very inactive, unfertile. It has made the whole world almost a wasteland; it has been anti-life.

We have to change it. We have to create a new concept of religion : a religion that does not renounce but celebrates, a religion that is not against life but for life, a religion that worships life *as* god.

Something to say to me?

Ingrid : I'm just thankful!

Danielle.

This will be your new name : Ma Prem Taro. Prem means love, taro means a star — a star of love. Love is the only light in the dark night of the soul, the only star; otherwise everything is dark inside. Those who don't know how to love remain afraid of going inwards, because the very idea of going in means going into a dark night of the soul where not even a distant star exists. It is frightening, the inward journey.

So Buddhas go on saying 'Go in.' Nobody listens. Socrates goes on saying 'Know thyself'. Nobody wants to know, and the fundamental reason is : it is so frightening to go in. Then what has to be done?

My approach is that before you can go in, you have to go out in love. It is paradoxical, but the inward journey begins with an outward journey.

If you can love, if you can start feeling love-energy, then going in will be a totally different phenomenon. You will have a distant star of love there in the dark night, and that light is enough to take you to the ultimate goal.

So your name is a message to love so that you can meditate. Let love become your meditation.

Next time come for a longer period.

This is just the beginning of the beginning.

Alexis is a French businessman.

This is your name : Swami Anand Alexis. Anand means bliss, alexis is a form of Alexander. It has two meanings : one, the helper of mankind; the other, one who drives evil away. Both are beautiful meanings.

Bliss can do both. The blissful person is naturally a helper of mankind, and only a blissful person can be a helper. In fact he never thinks of helping people; he helps just out of his blissfulness. It is not a deliberate effort, it is not a contemplated act; it is as natural as the fragrance of a flower.

And the blissful person naturally drives evil away. It is only in misery that evil can get roots; misery is the right soil for evil. It is impossible for a blissful person to be evil; out of bliss no evil can ever happen. Evil is a negative phenomenon, evil is destructive. And bliss cannot be destructive, bliss cannot be negative. Just as in the light there can be no darkness, so when you are blissful there can be no evil; they cannot co-exist.

So both the meanings are basically connected. The man who cannot do evil is the man who helps; the man who helps is the man who cannot do evil. But both arise out of a blissful state of consciousness.

Anne Dorte comes from Denmark via London's meditation centre, Kalptaru.

This will be your new name : Ma Deva Punit. Deva means divine, punit means purity — divine purity. By purity I mean innocence. Ordinarily purity means something that is against the impure — good against bad, right against wrong, moral against immoral. That is the ordinary meaning of purity, but the true meaning is innocence.

Innocence means one who is unaware of good and bad, unaware of right and wrong; one who is like a child, one who has not yet chosen, one who is in a kind of choiceless awareness — just like a mirror reflecting whatsoever is, with no judgment, no evaluation. That is true purity, that is divine purity.

If we cultivate purity, it is something human. It makes you moral, it can even make you a saint, but it will not bring you close to god, it will never make you a sage.

The saint is constantly struggling with his sinner; he is not innocent. He is in a constant civil war, he is divided. He is living in a nightmare. Each moment is a struggle : he is fighting with his body, he is fighting with his mind, he is fighting and fighting. His life knows no peace, no silence, no harmony. This can make a man very respected, it can be a very ego-fulfilling trip — that's why so many people have tried it — but it does not bring you close to God; in fact it takes you farther away.

Sometimes sinners are closer than your so-called saints, because they are more innocent.

The true saint has the quality of a child. That is the meaning of the word 'sage': one who has gone beyond duality, one who makes no distinctions, one for whom the whole of existence is beautiful. He denies nothing, rejects nothing, condemns nothing. He has no will of his own to impose on anything. He is just a dry leaf in the wind, and wherever the wind blows, he goes with it; he resists not. That is true purity.

Anything to say to me?

Punit: I'm happy!

Doris is a German nurse.

This is your name: Ma Anand Doris. Anand means bliss, doris is Greek. In Greek mythology, Doris is the goddess of the seas, of the oceans. So your full name will mean: bliss, the oceanic goddess. Bliss has the quality of the ocean in it.

Man can exist in two ways — either as an ego ... then he exists as a small wave and thinks himself separate from the ocean. He lives in an illusion, because that is utterly false — the wave cannot exist without the ocean. The ocean *can* exist without the wave but not vice versa. The idea of being separate from the ocean is the root cause of all misery. We are not separate, we are one with the ocean.

That is the other way of life, the way of a sannyasin: to live as the ocean, to cease being separate, to drop the idea of any identity, of any ego, of any definition, to just dissolve into the ocean and be one with it. And that's how we really are. Only the illusion is there; once the illusion disappears, the wave finds itself as the ocean. And that is the beginning of bliss.

The more you expand, the more blissful you feel. When you become one with the infinite, your bliss is infinite. The smaller you are, the more suffocated, the more confined, imprisoned, the more miserable you feel. And the ego tends to become smaller and smaller and smaller. Ultimately it becomes so tiny, so small, so atomic, that to live in it is to live in hell — that's what hell is all about. And heaven is to have no limits, to have no boundaries, to live unbounded.

Swami Prem Madir comes up with Nartan.

Hello, Madir. Something to say to me?

>*Nartan:* He's wondering whether it would be right for him to go into something traditional like Buddhism, in Japan, rather than coming back and forth between Japan and Pune, because he feels very frustrated because of the language problem.

Mm mm mm. Good — you can do something traditional like Zen, it will be very helpful. You can start; that's perfectly good.

>*Nartan:* He said Zen is not the only sect in Japan. There are many many other wonderful sects.

So you can choose any! If you already know, perfectly good, mm? If you feel that anything is good, do it, and when you are frustrated with all of them, then come!

That will be helpful, mm? First you have to be frustrated there!

Hello, Kovida. When are you leaving?

>*Kovida:* In two days.

Something to say to me?

>*Kovida:* I'm sad to leave. Stay with me and help me to come back as soon as possible.

I will. You will be coming back soon!
Then are you coming forever?

She nods a yes.

Good. You will be back soon! Keep it (a box) with you. I will be with you!

Hello, Gambheera. When are you leaving?

Gambheera : On Sunday.

Something to say to me?

Gambheera : This time I feel very much attracted to being here.

That's good! When will you be back?

Gambheera : Soon.

Come back soon, Gambheera, and help my people there. Each time it is going to become deeper and deeper. It just takes a little time, then things start happening....

Oma is an older, stocky Italian mamma.

Hello, Oma! When are you leaving?

Oma : In two days.

And when will you be back?

Oma : Soon.

Soon? Come back.

Oma : Before Christmas.

That's good. (A pause.) Whenever you come here it is always Christmas! (chuckling). There is no before, there is no after; it is always in the middle!

Ma Anand Salila is a cook from England. She's just arrived and wants to know the meaning of her name.

Anand means bliss, salila means a river. Life has to have a river-like quality, flowing and flowing, never getting stuck

---

14 *Won't You Join the Dance?*

anywhere, never becoming stagnant — because the moment life becomes stagnant, misery arises. If life remains a flow, a constant flow, bliss surrounds it. Bliss is a by-product of flow, and misery a by-product of becoming stagnant. People have become reservoirs of water, they are no more river — that is their undoing.

Your name has a message for you : remain like a river, always moving into the unknown, never looking back, never clinging to anything, enjoying the moment that you are passing through — the banks and the trees and the sun and the birds and the people — but only for the moment; not getting attached.

That is the greatest secret to learn in life — not to get attached to anything. Then one is always available to new things, to new openings; then the doors are never closed. Life *can* become such an incredible experience of ecstasy if one only remains in a flow.

So become a river and you will be blissful.

Niraj : Can you tell me the meaning of my name?

Prem means love, niraj means cloud — a cloud of love. Love is not anything solid. Everybody wants it to be solid, but the moment you make it solid it is no more love. Love can only exist as a mystery — vague, like a cloud. You cannot hold it in your hands, you cannot close your fist on it. The moment you do that, love is lost; and then you go on carrying something else in the name of love.

Love is as fluid, as formless, as a cloud. One moment it is one thing, another moment it is another thing. It is never the same; not even for two consecutive moments is it the same. It is a flux. And that's the beauty of it : it is alive, hence it is a flux.

Love is without roots, as is a cloud : it floats in the sky, it has no roots anywhere. It is a miracle; it exists without any roots. And also, love means tremendous trust, so it does not plan. It moves like a cloud, wherever the winds take it; it has no programme, no expectations. Love cannot be frustrated. If it is frustrated, then something else was there hiding behind the love. Love is always surprised but never frustrated.

So learn the ways of love — and the cloud is one of the most symbolic expressions of it.

3

Osho : This is your name : Swami Anand Raphael. Anand means blissful; raphael is Hebrew, it means healed by god, or a divine healer, or a medicine of god. Raphael is also the name of one of the angels, one of the four angels that surround god's throne. He represents one dimension of god's being.

Existence is four-dimensional. Three dimensions are very visible, the fourth dimension is invisible. Modern physics calls it time, the fourth dimension, but all the ancient mythologies have something to say about it — the fourth dimension.

Raphael represents the fourth. Gurdjieff used to call his way 'the fourth way' because his whole work consists of transforming time into timelessness, mind into no-mind. Time and mind are synonymous, two aspects of the same phenomenon. The East, Yoga in particular, divides human consciousness into four parts. One is waking, the second is dreaming, the third is sleeping, and the fourth is simply called the fourth — turiya. No other name is given to it, just 'the fourth'.

Raphael represents the fourth, turiya — entering into timelessness, mindlessness, entering into no-thought. And that's what meditation is all about.

Waking is full of thoughts — too full; one is crowded, there is no space for god to be. So is dreaming — too full of imagination, fantasy, pictures. The third, sleep, is better than both waking and dreaming, because one is not crowded; no thought exists, no dream. But then another problem arises : one becomes unconscious. We know only one way of being conscious, and that is continuously remaining occupied. Our consciousness is a by-product of occupation. The moment we are not occupied we start dozing, falling into sleep. If you have nothing to do, you will suddenly start feeling sleep overtaking you.

The greatest problem that all meditators face is that when they watch the mind, and through slowly watching it thoughts start disappearing, the first thing that becomes a problem is sleep. Hence the Zen master with his staff, moving around the meditators, watching who is dozing, hitting him hard on the head and waking him up. To move from waking consciousness into sleep is easier for the mind; it knows the way. But to move from waking consciousness, from thought to no-thought, and still not fall asleep, is a totally new phenomenon.

Sleep is far better still than waking and dreaming, because it is empty. But the emptiness is a negative state. Emptiness is not a fulfilment and cannot be. Unless this thoughtless state of sleep becomes suffused, permeated, with consciousness, unless this emptiness of thought becomes fullness of awareness, meditation has not happened.

When sleep is transformed into meditation, this is the miracle that happens : there is no content in the mind, yet the consciousness is there. There is no occupation, no object, yet one is fully alert, aware — aware, not of something, but simply aware. Or we can say aware of awareness, attentive to attentiveness, conscious of being conscious — that's all. This is the fourth stage.

In Christian mythology, Raphael represents the fourth state. All the three meanings are beautiful : healed by god — healing is a process of becoming whole. Not to be whole is to be ill. To be part is to be sick, to be whole is to be healthy. The moment the ego disappears and one joins the whole, healing happens of its own accord. It has nothing to do with physical illness; I am talking about metaphysical sickness, the sickness of the soul — that we have become uprooted, that we are feeling undernourished, that we are shrinking, that we are feeling very alone, meaningless, that there is great anguish inside. This is the sickness unto death. That's exactly what Soren Kierkegaard calls it : sickness unto death. But if we can relax into the whole, the healing happens.

Loredana.

What is the meaning of your name?

Radha (translating) : She doesn't know.

And you know?

Radha (laughing) : No!

That's going to be difficult! But it sounds beautiful! Close your eyes....

This is your name : Ma Anand Loredana. Anand means blissful; blissful Loredana. It doesn't matter what Loredana means (much laughter)! If you are blissful, that will do!

Good, Loredana!

Metella is also Italian.

What is the meaning of your name?

Metella : I don't know, either.

Mm?

Radha : She doesn't know, and I don't know.

When nobody knows you can always invent (chuckling) and nobody is going to catch you! Be a little inventive! If you cannot find any meaning....

Everyone laughing...

Close your eyes.
Good. Come close to me.

Won't You Join the Dance?

This is your name : Ma Prem Metella. Prem means love, and love is my whole teaching. If love is understood, then all is understood — god and all. If love is not understood, then everything is simply gibberish, with no meaning, with no significance. People can use very high-sounding words, theological jargon, and they can go on fabricating beautiful systems of thought, but they are made of dream-stuff and nothing else. Only love is substantial; all else is dream.

Love is the stuff that the existence is made of. Hence, whenever we are in love we are close to existence. A great intimacy arises, not only between two lovers; when love is there, a great intimacy arises between you and the whole existence — with stars, with trees, with birds. Suddenly there is communion. Even with mountains, rocks and oceans, you start feeling a kind of dialogue, an 'I-thou' relationship. Love is magical, miraculous.

Learn to be loving. And finally, learn to be love! The day your whole being has bloomed in love, that is the real day of sannyas.

This is just sowing the seeds : that day you will reap the crop.

Ronit is an Israeli art student who lives in Holland.

What is the meaning of your name?

Ronit : To sing happily.

To sing happily?

Ronit : Yes.

Very good (much laughter)! Close your eyes.
Good. Come close to me.
So this is your name : Ma Deva Ronit.

Deva means divine, and if ronit means happily singing, then it will mean divine singing. Singing is divine, one of the most divine activities. Only dancing is a competitor with it, it is only next to dancing. And why are singing and dancing divine activities? Because these are the activities in which you can be utterly lost. You can drown yourself in singing — so much so that the singer disappears, and only song remains, or the dancer disappears and only the dance remains. And that is the moment of metamorphosis, transfiguration. When the singer is no more there and there is only the song, when your totality has become a song or a dance, that is prayer!

What song you are singing is irrelevant; it may not be a religious song, but if you can sing it totally it is sacred. And vice versa : you may be singing a religious song, hallowed by the ages, but if you are not totally in it, it is profane. The content of the song does not matter; what matters is the quality that you bring to singing — the totality, the intensity, the fire.

Sylvia is a German teacher-therapist with abundant dark hair.

This is your name : Ma Prem Sylvia. Prem means love; sylvia is Latin, it means a forest-dweller or a forest maiden. It is a beautiful word. The full name will mean : love that dwells in the forest, love that dwells in nature, love that is courageous enough to be wild.

Man has become very ugly through civilisation. Civilisation has not really been a blessing; it has proved a curse. We will have to try another kind of civilisation sooner or later, and the sooner, the better — because this civilisation that we have tried up to now is doomed to fail. It has already failed; it is just taking time to collapse. It is a big edifice, so it will take time to collapse.

This civilisation has failed because it has been against nature. Man has tried to be very arrogant with nature; he has been trying to conquer nature, which is utterly ridiculous. We are part of nature! how can we conquer it? We *are* nature; to fight with nature is to fight with oneself. It is so foolish and so suicidal that later generations will not be able to believe how man committed such a crime.

Man has to learn again how to come closer to the trees, to the forest, to the mountains, to the oceans. We have to learn how to befriend them again — and my sannyas is an effort towards that great goal.

Man can live joyously only with nature, not against nature. The moment we are against nature, our love energy, turns into hatred. If we flow with nature in total harmony, love grows, matures, becomes more integrated. And the maturing of love is the greatest gift of life. To know a mature kind of love is to know god, because it brings joy, it brings freedom, it brings blessings.

Swami Anand Ananga is leaving for Europe.

Hello, Ananga. When are you leaving?

Anand Ananga: Next Sunday.

Something to say to me?

Anand Ananga: With you in me I have learned such beautiful things, such different things.

That's true!

Anand Ananga: Everything becomes love.

Very good. It is!

Anand Ananga: And life is so full of love. I am in the beginning.

Mm?

Anand Ananga: I am in the beginning so... you know everything that I can say to you.

When will you be back?

Anand Ananga: In a few days.

In a few days?
Mm, good (with a chuckle)! That's good. Just come back!

4

Osho: This will be your name: Swami Anand Tim. Anand means bliss, tim is a short form of Timotheus. It is a Greek name; it means worshipping god, honouring god. And bliss is possible only if you become related with the existence in a personal way. That's what the word 'god' implies — a personal relationship with existence.

The person who does not believe in god does believe in existence but there is no personal bridge, there is no love affair. He cannot address existence as thou; existence remains 'it' — dead.

Love is not poured on it, worship does not arise. And without love, without worship, you are bound to live in a dead existence. To live in a dead existence is to live in a dead way, because if you are surrounded by this immense existence which is not alive, which has no soul to it, how can *you* have a soul? The 'I' arises only when in deep love you have called somebody 'thou'. Thou is first, I is second. This is corroborated by modern psychology too, that the idea of thou arises first in the child's consciousness, and only later on comes the idea of I, as a by-product of thou.

The person who has never been in love is not really a self. He has never looked in the mirror of love: how can he see his face? He has never called somebody with tremendous joy. He will remain asleep himself.

Even in ordinary love affairs you become awakened: life starts burning in an intense way, you start vibrating, you have a new flair, there is a new gust, a new wind. So what to say about when a person falls in love with the whole existence?

And that's what sannyas is all about — falling in love with the whole existence, being able to call the existence thou in a personal way, being able to address existence, being able to write love letters to existence, being able to be in a dialogue.

And that is the basic meaning of Timotheus. Tim is a short form of it.

Become a blissful worshipper!

Marco is Italian.

This is your name: Swami Veet Marco. Veet means beyond; marco is Latin, it means god of Mars or god of war. Your full name will mean: one who has gone beyond war and war gods.

Man has lived under the calamity of war too long. We have to destroy all gods of war; instead we have to create a temple of love. We *should* kill all gods of war, because only through their death — the god of war dead, all gods of war dead — will the god of love be born.

War exists, not because there are warring groups outside in the world; fundamentally war exists because man is in conflict. The root of war is within; on the outside you only see the branches and the foliage of it. After each ten years, humanity needs a great world war. In ten years' time, man accumulates so much rage, madness, insanity, inside him that it has to erupt.

Unless we transform the very script of man, unless we give him a totally new programme of living and being, we can go on talking about peace but we will go on preparing for war. That's what we have been doing for thousands of years: talking of peace and creating war. The absurdity is that even in the name of peace we have been fighting: the greatest wars have been fought in the name of peace. This has been a sheerly destructive past. With the same energy, man could have created paradise on earth; and all that we have done is to create a hell instead. But it is not a question of changing the political ideologies of the world, it is not a question of teaching people to be brotherly, because these things have been done and they have all failed.

Something more basic is wrong. Man is split, and the same people who talk about peace are the cause of the split. They have divided man into good and bad, the lower and the higher, the earthly and the divine, the material and the spiritual. They have created a rift inside the human soul, and there is a constant war inside. Everybody is fighting with themselves, and when it becomes too much they start fighting with somebody else.

That's why in times of war, people look happier. Their faces shine with enthusiasm, their step has a dance to it. They are thrilled, because at least for a few days they will not need to fight with themselves; they have found a scapegoat outside. It may be the Fascist, it may be the Communist, it may be the Mohammedan, it may be the Christian — it doesn't matter, but somebody is there outside. It is an escape from the inner fight; in a very sick way it is relaxing. But one cannot go on warring continuously; sooner or later man has to turn inwards again. The politician creates war without, and the priest creates war within. This is the longest and the greatest conspiracy against humanity.

My vision of a sannyasin is that of an integrated soul. The body is respected, not denied; it is loved, praised, one feels grateful for it. Matter is not condemned, it is enjoyed; it is part of our spiritual growth. There is no duality : it is a dialectics of growth. This is how we move on two feet, the bird flies on two wings. Matter and spirit, body and soul, lower and higher, are two wings.

What I am trying to bring here is something utterly new, something that has never existed before on the earth : a man who is at ease with both the worlds, this and that; a man who is as worldly as one can be and as other-worldly as one can be; a man who is a great synthesis; a man who is not schizophrenic, a man who is whole and holy. That's what my sannyas is all about.

Ursula comes from Switzerland.

This will be your new name : Ma Anand Ursula. Anand means bliss; ursula is Latin, it is the name of a constellation of stars. Your full name will mean : a blissful constellation of stars.

Man is multi-dimensional. Man is not one star but a constellation of stars. Man is not finite, man is not limited. Man appears limited, finite, but that appearance is only an appearance. The deeper we go into man, the more we become aware of ourselves, and boundaries start disappearing. And to know the unbounded in oneself is to know God.

It is not something that we have to seek and search for; it is already there. We have only to uncover it. It is veiled : we have to remove the veil.

Sara is Italian.

This is your name : Ma Anand Sara. Anand means bliss, sara is Hebrew. It is the name of the wife of Abraham. The original name was sarai; sarai means the quarrelsome. The story is : god took pity on poor Abraham and changed the quality of his wife and she was no more quarrelsome. So her name was also changed, from sarai to Sara. Sarai means quarrelsome, sara means a princess. But this is the story of almost every woman — all are quarrelsome!

These stories are really parables; and it is not only so about women, the same is true about men. It is very rarely that a woman becomes a princess and a man becomes a prince. They remain wild animals at each other's throats. The so-called marriage is nothing but a constant quarrel; it certainly is not a communion. It is not a true marriage. The true marriage will make two persons so *one* that there will be no possibility of any conflict. They will understand each other so deeply that that very understanding will create the quality of being a princess and a prince. They will not be ordinary mortals any more; they will become part of immortality. They will not be mundane, they will be royal.

So this is a beautiful story. Your name will mean : blissful princess. But the word 'sara' in Sanskrit also has a beautiful meaning. It means the essence, the very essence of a thing, the perfume of a flower. Then anand sara will mean : the essence of bliss, the perfume of bliss.

Let bliss become the very centre of your life. Do whatsoever makes you more blissful, and avoid all that disturbs your bliss. And you will be surprised : we go on throwing our bliss to the dogs for such silly things, but this remains so because we are not aware. All our activities in life are so stupid, and the reason is that we never look at what we are doing to ourselves.

If one can remain a little alert and watchful and constantly judging whether this is going to give one more bliss or not, then that single criterion can become a transformation. And when one is blissful, one cannot make others miserable; that is impossible. A blissful person naturally creates bliss in others, and the same is true about misery too.

So to me, to be blissful is the greatest virtue. The blissful person slowly becomes a saint, a sage.

Good, Sara.

Nico does office work in Holland.

This is your name : Swami Anand Nico. Anand means bliss. Nico can have two origins, either from nicholas or from nicodemus, but both mean the same : both mean victory. So your full name will mean victory over bliss — and that is the true victory. All other victories are just plastic toys, substitutes for the real victory.

To conquer others is just an escape from conquering oneself; it is a strategy of the mind to make you go astray. But no victory over others can ever fulfil you, because deep down you will remain a beggar, you will never be an emperor.

In life, things are very complicated : when you become victorious over others, when you enslave others, in a subtle way they also enslave you. No slavery can be one-sided, no slavery can be one-way traffic; each slavery is a double-edged sword, it cuts both ways. If a man tries to make a woman a slave, the woman also tries in every possible way — of course her ways are feminine — to make a slave of the man. If you look at the total result, you will find two slaves, not two masters.

That's what goes on happening in all relationships, wherever the desire to conquer, to dominate, to be powerful over the other, is there. In fact the very desire is ugly; it comes out of an inferiority complex. The true desire is not to conquer the other; the true desire is to know oneself, who one is. In knowing oneself, the victory happens of its own accord, because knowledge *is* victory. The moment you know yourself, you have become the master of yourself.

This is your name : Ma Prem Liesbeth. Prem means love. Liesbeth comes from the Hebrew, elizabeth. El means god, elizabeth means godly, divine. Elizabeth is also the name of the mother of the master of Jesus Christ, John the Baptist. But the root, el, is tremendously beautiful; from the same root comes the Arabic Allah.

Your full name will mean love divine. Love *is* divine. If anything is divine on the earth it is love, and love makes everything else also divine. Whatsoever is touched by love becomes divine. Love is the alchemy of true life, because it transforms the lower metal into gold.

There are ancient stories, many stories, in almost all the languages of the world, that somebody kisses a frog and the frog becomes a prince. The frog was cursed : he was simply waiting for some kiss to be showered on him, he was waiting for love to come and transform him.

Love transforms : that is the message of all those stories. Those stories are beautiful, very indicative, symbolic. It is only love which transforms the animal into the human, otherwise there is no difference between other animals and man. The only difference, the possible difference, is that of love. So those who live without love, live without being human beings. And the more you live through love, as love, the more humanity is born in you. The ultimate, the omega point, is when one has become just love. Then not only is the animal transcended; even the human is transcended. Then one is divine, one is god. The whole of growth is love's growth. Without love : animals. With love : man. And when love has become your natural being, your very flavour : god!

This will be your name : Ma Prem Elysia. Prem means love, elysia is the root from where your name Elly, comes, but elysia looks more musical, more beautiful.

Elly comes from elysia. The meaning of the word 'elysia' is : divinely happy. Your full name will mean : love that brings divine happiness.

The ordinary happiness can come without love; it can *only* come without love. You can have money and can have a certain pleasure in having it; you can be successful, famous, and can have a certain happiness in having it — but love is not involved. In fact if you are very loving, it will be very difficult to accumulate much wealth. If you are really loving, it will be very difficult to become politically powerful because politics needs a stubborn struggle. One has to be hard, one has to be like a dagger. One cannot afford to be a flower, one cannot be loving.

There are pleasures which come without love; they are worldly pleasures. Their value is nothing. Their price may be much but their value is nothing. The only thing valuable that can happen, happens only through love. Then one moves in a totally different dimension: the dimension of grace, the dimension of empathy, compassion, love, sharing, prayer.

They all belong to one dimension, they are members of a single family. Then a happiness descends which is not of the world, which nobody can give you and which nobody can take away from you. It is a gift from god — but that gift is available only to those who prepare their heart in tremendous love and prayer. Those who purify themselves through the fire of love, only they will be blessed by divine happiness.

5

Osho : This will be your new name : Swami Anand Arno. Anand is Sanskrit, it means bliss or blissful. Arno is Teutonic, it means the eagle. Your full name will mean : the blissful eagle. It is a message.

Plotinus says : The search for god is a flight of the alone to the alone. It *is* a flight, and it is the greatest flight there is, because you are not simply changing one place for another, you are changing one space for another. You are not covering a physical distance, you are changing the very dimension of your existence.

To feel yourself as the body is one space, one dimension; and to start feeling as the spirit is another dimension, another space. And the gap between the two is infinite — logically it is unbridgeable. But it is good that logic is not all : there are ways to bridge it.

Sannyas is the way to bridge the unbridgeable. From matter to consciousness, from earth to heaven, from the outer to the inner, the gap *is* really big. And if one wants to bridge it gradually, it is impossible; one can only have a quantum leap.

That is the message, the symbolic message, in your name : become a blissful eagle so that you can go to the farthest corners of the sky.

This is your name : Swami Prem Simon. Prem means love, simon is Hebrew and also Greek, and in both languages it means the same : gracious hearing, one who is capable of hearing the truth. This great experience of being capable of hearing the truth is possible only through love. It is only through the heart that truth is heard; it is not through the mind. The mind can hear only the words — and the words are empty; their meaning can be heard only through the heart.

The moment a word enters your ears, it is divided into two parts : its body moves into the head, its soul into the heart. The soul is its meaning, the body is just a corpse. The head goes on dissecting corpses — analysing, philosophising, guessing; it does great work, but it deals with death and it knows only the dead.

The real spirit moves into the heart, it stirs the heart. It is not a question of analysing, dissecting, arguing; it is simply a question of gracious hearing.

That is the meaning of simon. And that is one of the greatest qualities for the seeker, because there are things of which the mind can never be convinced, but they *are*. They are the most important things in life : love, beauty, truth.

If you depend only on the mind, then all that is great is debarred; then only trivia is left for you. You can sink into the trivia but your life will not have grandeur, your life will not have significance, your life will continuously remain a wasteland where nothing grows — no foliage, no greenery, no flowers, no fruits, nothing that grows; everything dead, dull, boring, stale, stagnant.

To open yourself to things of which the mind cannot be convinced, is the meaning of simon. It is the very meaning of being a disciple.

Listen lovingly. Don't decide for or against; just let it in. If it is truth, without any of your effort it brings its own evidence. Truth is self-evident, self-authenticating; it has its own authority. It is not authoritative, but it has its own authority, its own validity. It needs no other proofs.

If it is not truth and you hear silently, lovingly, you will immediately know that it is not truth. This knowing will not be a conclusion; this knowing will be immediate. And when knowing is immediate, it is liberating. It never becomes a dogma, it never becomes a belief, it never becomes Christianity, Hinduism. It simply becomes your wisdom, your intelligence.

I open my eyes to watch as he speaks with Erich about his new name: Prem Elisha.

Prem means love, elisha is Hebrew, it means god is salvation.

Salvation is not something that man can do; it can only descend as a grace, it can only come as a gift. Salvation is so vast and man is so small that it is not possible for man to manage it. The more man tries to manage it, the more entangled he becomes in new kinds of chains, in new imprisonments. He moves from one cell of the prison into another cell, that's all.

To be really free, to be totally free, to be absolutely free, can only be a gift from god. That is the meaning of elisha: god *is* salvation.

Then what should *we* do? We cannot attain salvation on our own, but still something is expected of us. We should become receivers — not doers, but receivers. We should be on the receiving end. And that's what love is, to be receptive. Man can be loving, and then god descends as salvation. In the womb of love, the child of ultimate freedom is conceived. Man has to become a womb, a receptacle.

All that is needed on our part is to drop all armour, to drop all defences, to open all the doors and all the windows so that the wind can come, the rain can come and the sun can come....

What is the meaning of your name, Mihoko?

Nartan (translating): The one who maintains beauty.

One who maintains beauty?

'Good!' he murmurs.

This is your name : Ma Prem Mihoko. Prem means love, so your full name will mean : love that maintains beauty. In fact love not only maintains beauty, it creates it. Love is the alchemy that creates beauty. It is only through love that people become elegant, graceful; it is only through love that they start having something mysterious about them — because through love, poetry is born in their hearts. Their very bodies start pulsating with a new rhythm. They are no more alone, they are no more unneeded, for the first time in their life they start feeling a significance; and the feeling of significance is the most beautifying thing.

If you are loved and you can love, that means that the existence needs you, that you are not unwanted, that without you there will be something missing in the world. You may be a small song, but still the great universe will miss that small song. You may just be a small flower that grows by the roadside, but still without you the world will be a little less.

That feeling that 'I am an essential part of existence' imparts beauty. Beauty is not something that can be imposed from the outside; all those efforts of beautifying are really uglifying. Real beauty arises from the innermost core and spreads outwards. It is like a lamp burning inside you, and your whole being becomes luminous. Love is the flame that can make you luminous.

Prem Anand.

Hello, Anand. When are you leaving?

She is naked, exposed in the vulnerability love bestows on us, as his first question evokes the tears that look as though they were just waiting for an excuse to be released.

First, go into it. Close your eyes and let it happen.

Her tears are wept so totally that I feel the pain of leaving too.

Good. Now come back!

So let me ask the right question: when will you be coming back?

Her laughter is as total as her weeping.

Prem Anand: Soon!

Soon? (chuckling). That's good! Come back soon. Then are you coming forever?

Yes, she nods.

Finish things and come forever.
Something to say to me?

Prem Anand: Oh, my mind feels stupid.

Mm?

Prem Anand: My mind always feels so stupid.

Minds are all stupid!
You need not worry about it; the mind as such *is* stupid. Go, leave the mind there, and...

The rest of the sentence disappears into his chuckle and her laughter.

6

Osho is speaking to Leon...

Osho : This is your name: Swami Prem Leon. Prem means love; leon is Latin, it means lion, or lionlike.

Love is the greatest courage because it needs total sacrifice. It wants you to die so that you can be reborn. It is a death and the beginning of an eternal life; but death is first, hence the courage needed. One has to be really lionlike, ready to take the risk.

Millions of people live without love for the simple reason that they cannot gather themselves together to take the risk. It is safer to be unloving; secure. The moment you move into love you are moving into an uncharted sea, without any map. To love basically means to disappear as an ego.

For another reason also, love is lionlike, because if one wants to be loving, one has to drop out of the crowd psychology, the sheeplike mind, the imitative mind. One has to assert one's individuality. It is not the same as one's ego, it is just the opposite.

The ego can exist only in the crowd. The ego needs others to exist, it needs others as props; the ego cannot exist in aloneness. The ego is a social by-product. It will look very paradoxical, but the sheep has more of an ego than the lion, because the sheep lives in the crowd, as part of the crowd, inseparable from the crowd, and the lion lives alone, moves alone.

To be alone is to be egoless. To be alone is to be an individual, certainly; one has a tremendous, powerful, authentic, individuality. But when individuality is there, the ego is not needed, because the ego is a substitute for individuality; when individuality is not there, the ego is needed.

Love demands the sacrifice of the ego; only individuals can do it, only lions can do it. Once one has gathered courage enough to evaporate as an ego, a miracle happens : one disappears, and for the first time one is. That is-ness has tremendous beauty and benediction in it. That is-ness is god.

Alberto crouches before Osho.

This is your name : Swami Deva Alberto. Deva means divine. Alberto is Teutonic; it means noble, illustrious, brilliant, intelligent. It is a beautiful word. All the meanings are significant, and they are all joined together, they are interlinked.

Intelligence is brilliance, brilliance is noble. But remember : intelligence is not intellectuality. Intellectuality is pseudo-intelligence. It pretends to be intelligence; it is not. Intellectuality is borrowed; it comes through education, culture, it comes through others. If one is capable of having a good memory one can become a good intellectual. That's what the scholars in the universities are. They have good memories, but memory is not intelligence, memory is a mere mechanism. Any computer can have it.

Intelligence is a totally different thing — the spark of genius, the capacity to have new insights, the capacity to be creative. Intellectuality always remains repetitive. It can repeat beautifully, skilfully, accurately, but it can only repeat; it is a parrot.

Intelligence creates. It brings into the world something new which has never existed before. It makes the world richer, it makes it more beautiful, it brings a few more truths into existence. The ultimate act of intelligence is to create god.

God is not something there that you have to just uncover; god is not a thing or a commodity. God has to be created in the innermost being. The intelligence of a Buddha or a Jesus is needed. Unless one can be so creative, so totally creative, that one can give birth to god within oneself, one is not religious. And wherever there is intelligence, there is bound to be nobility.

So remember it : drop intellectuality and become more and more intelligent. It is in seeking the new and searching for the new that one becomes intelligent. It is in moving into the unknown that one becomes intelligent. It is in living dangerously that one becomes intelligent. Intelligence is sharpened when there are great challenges around you. And that's what sannyas is all about.

I am not here to console you, I am here to create as many inner challenges as possible. That is the only way to awaken you : the deep sleep can be broken only by a great penetration of challenges.

But once you are awakened, the dark night of the soul is over. And to know the morning is to know god. To see the sun rising in the inner horizon is the beginning of enlightenment.

(to Florian) This is your name : Swami Deva Florian. Deva means divine. Florian is Latin; it means flowering — divine flowering. Just as trees flower naturally, spontaneously, so can man flower. All that is needed is the right soil, the right nourishment : the seed is there at birth. It is really a miracle how we go on missing growth.

Man has done great harm to himself. The society makes a tremendous effort to create barriers, barriers so that people cannot flower. The society that has existed up to now is very afraid of flowering. It depends on immature persons, it requires immaturity — because only immature persons can be turned into slaves, only immature persons are ready to be dominated. Not only are they ready to be dominated; they seek their tyrants. They cannot live without tyrants, they feel very alone. They need to depend on someone, they need father-figures, they need authorities. If somebody authoritative is there they feel at ease. If there is nobody who is authoritative they become very hesitant; they don't know what to do then. They always wait for orders and commandments.

Because of this, the society does not allow people to mature. The average mental age of human beings is not more than twelve years; it is very close to the time of sexual maturity. By the time a boy is sexually mature the society kills all possibilities of more maturity in him, of other kinds of maturities — of intelligence, of love, of creativity, of freedom. That's why you see so many people without any flowers and without any of the fragrance of life.

My work here is to help you grow, to destroy all the barriers that hinder growth, to undo all that the society has done.

Once the barriers are removed, life energies start flowing of their own accord. Then nothing else has to be done : one has simply to trust one's own nature, and one day flowers are bound to happen.

It is very unfortunate to die without flowering, because that means that one lived in vain. And to die with flowers is to die joyously, because with the flowers one has arrived home.

(to Roberto) This is your name : Swami Anand Roberto. Anand means bliss. Roberto is Teutonic; it means bright or shining fame — which naturally happens to people who are bright. It is a by-product of brightness; their brightness makes them shiny, their brightness declares them to the world. They cannot remain hidden, it is impossible for them to hide.

Your full name will mean : blissful brightness that makes one shine. Misery needs no brightness, no intelligence. Any stupid person can be miserable; in fact only stupid people can be miserable. Unless one decides to remain stupid, there is no need to remain miserable. Misery is utter stupidity; you are doing something absolutely wrong with yourself. Misery is only symptomatic : it is simply a signal that you are doing something wrong with yourself, that's all. It is a cry from your innermost core, of 'Stop! You are doing something wrong, you are going against your nature. You are falling away from the harmony of existence.'

Misery is nothing but a cry to stop. It is not a disease, it is only a symptom; and it can be used in a very creative way. If one starts understanding one's misery, one will start moving into the direction of bliss. That's what intelligence is.

Nobody is born stupid, remember. People become stupid, people learn stupidity from others. Stupidity is something imbibed from the atmosphere, it is a learned phenomenon. Intelligence is inborn, stupidity is imposed. Hence stupidity can be dropped any moment, and can be dropped in its totality any time, whenever one takes a decision to drop it; there is no need to postpone it for tomorrow. The very moment of understanding that this is stupid is the beginning of a revolution; the very understanding is transformation. And the only proof of one's being intelligent, bright, wise, is blissfulness; there is no other proof.

Unless you are as blissful as a Buddha or a Krishna, remember, somewhere stupidity is lurking. Some shadows of foolishness are still within your being; in some deeper layer of unconsciousness, something still goes on being wrong. The moment all is put right, the moment all is in tune, the moment one is full of understanding from one end to another end, life becomes a shining star. You cannot hide it, it declares itself; it is self-evident.

Remember : one can be very skilful at creating machines, one can be very skilful at earning money, one can be very very efficient at becoming politically powerful, but none of these things prove that one is intelligent. Only one thing proves it : if one is blissful. There is only one criterion of intelligence, that one is blissful — as blissful as the flowers, as blissful as the stars, as blissful as the streams and the mountains.

Unless that bliss happens, don't rest : go on working, go on moving. Nothing less than that can ever fulfil you.

(to Noeleen) This is your name : Ma Deva Noeleen. Deva means divine. Noeleen is Latin; it means Christmas, a song of joy. Your full name will mean : a divine song of joy.

Life is a constant search to become a song, to become a dance, to become a celebration, a Christmas. Every form of life is searching to become a song of joy — birds, animals, trees. It is not only man who is in search of bliss; the whole existence is moving in millions of forms towards the same goal. The goal of all life is bliss. When one bursts forth into millions of songs, one has arrived. One has achieved the goal, one has become one with god.

Unless that happens we will have to be born again and again and again, because the search cannot be terminated before its ultimate goal is achieved.

Hence the Eastern idea of rebirth is tremendously significant. Christianity, Judaism, Islam : all these three religions which were born outside India have missed the point of it. These three religions think there is only one life, *this* life, these seventy or eighty years. Then what about those who will not be able to attain in these seventy or eighty years? Are they doomed forever? They will not have another chance, another opportunity, another challenge? That will be too cruel; that will be very unfair. If they have failed in this life, they should be given another chance. Why not? This was their first life, so it is more relevant to give them more chances — because if one fails in the first attempt, that does not mean that one is incapable of succeeding. It may be because it was so new and there was no opportunity to learn.

The Eastern idea is significant, more scientific, more human, more compassionate — that we have been here millions of times, we have been searching for the same goal, and we have not yet arrived. But we can arrive any moment if we understand the whole process, if we become more aware in our search. Any moment — and this moment is as good as any other — it can happen. It can happen instantaneously. It needs no time, because it is not a gradual process, it is a quantum leap. But if one misses in this life, then one is back again. God gives infinite opportunities: God is compassion and love. This existence cannot be so cruel that because you missed once, you have missed forever and you will be condemned to hell for eternity.

But remember, we can go on missing for millions of lives. In fact if we don't start becoming aware of our life, its processes, its inner mechanisms, there is every possibility that rather than reaching to the goal, in missing again and again we may learn the habit of missing. That danger is always there. And that has happened to many people: they have missed many lives, and now they have learned the trick of how to miss. They have become very very skilful and efficient in missing.

This is the problem that I have to face with every disciple, with every sannyasin: he has missed so many times that missing has become his second nature. Now to drag him out of that is really arduous work. But if the disciple co-operates, then it is simple. With his co-operation the miracle is possible.

Sannyas simply means that you are surrendering yourself for the transformation — that you are ready to go with me, that you will not hinder me, that you will co-operate; that you will not be constantly resisting me, but that slowly slowly you will grow more and more into trust, more and more into love. Only love and trust from your side will make you a real sannyasin; nothing else is needed.

Elisabeth is a psychologist from Switzerland.

This is your name : Ma Prem Elisabeth. Prem means love. Elisabeth is Hebrew, it comes from el; el means god. Prem Elisabeth will mean : love is god.

That is the most fundamental fact of all the religions that have existed, and of all the religions that will ever exist in the future. If they all agree on any one thing, that thing is the quality of love. They may not even agree on the existence of god. Buddhism does not believe in god, but Buddhism believes in love — more so : because there is no god, love takes absolute possession of the Buddhist mind. Jainism does not believe in god, but love becomes equivalent to religion.

Whether one believes in god or not does not matter; the only thing that matters is whether one believes in love or not. I call the person religious who believes in love, and the person irreligious who does not believe in love. That should be the only defining factor. Then you will see many religious people as irreligious, and you will see many irreligious people very religious. Then your total vision will change.

My approach towards life is that of love. All else is secondary, irrelevant, all else is nothing but ideology. Only love is truth. And those who live love, they attain to the ultimate. They can call it god, they can call it nirvana, they can call it enlightenment or whatever they wish; those are all names.

Love brings ultimate freedom, because love helps you to become one with the whole. It helps you to disappear as a separate part and to appear in the harmony of the totality of existence, as part of it; not apart, but as part of it, not as an island, not separate.

And once that happens, you start feeling as a wave in the ocean. Nothing more is needed. Then whatsoever you do will be right, and whatsoever you are will be good.

Moses has been back a week and hopes to stay three months.

> *Anand Moses:* When I was here last, in December, and took sannyas, about ten days afterwards I quit my Centering group and fled and flew back to New York in terror. I found that everything there was different, everything inside me was different, and all I felt was dread.

Mm mm.

> *Anand Moses:* I saw that what I wanted to do was come back here and spend more time here.

It happens: sometimes when people escape in the middle, then this is bound to happen! When some process of change starts, it is better to be here and to finish it; then you will go with a new integrity. Otherwise the old identity is lost and the new has not arrived, and there will be simply dread and terror and nothing else. You will be lost in a no-man's land.

But sometimes it happens. Nothing to be worried about. You are back home!

What groups have you done? Just two?

> *Anand Moses:* I had done Intensive Enlightenment and then dropped out of Centering.

And have you booked for other groups yet?

> *Anand Moses:* I haven't booked for anything yet.

Do a few groups.

Start with Centering again (chuckling), and don't escape this time! If one escapes from Centering, then I don't know what groups to give (much laughter) because that is the simplest, the least dangerous!

So start with Centering — there is no other way! The second group is Massage, the third group is Body Awareness and the fourth group is Satori. Then I will see.

But don't be worried at all. Something really beautiful is going to happen. Some door is opening — but whenever a new door opens, fear arises; and whenever something important is going to happen, the mind becomes a coward, because the mind always wants to live in the known. That's the obsession of the mind — with the unknown it starts trembling, because it does not know how to tackle the unknown; it has no know-how. With the known it is perfectly at ease, it knows what to do with it.

Even if it is very miserable, the mind is perfectly in control; it knows how to deal with the situation, how to encounter the misery. Even if something blissful is going to happen, but it is new, the mind says 'Don't go there because then I am at a loss; I don't know what to do.'

And the whole effort here is to drag you out of the known, somehow or other, into the unknown. All these therapy groups are nothing but strategies to pull you out of the trap of the known.

One glimpse of the unknown and you will be on the wing; then the mind can never trap you again. Once you have tasted the beauty of the unknown, the joy, the freedom, then it is impossible for the mind to have any attraction for you.

So don't be worried. Good, Moses.

This is Shunya's first visit.

> *Shunya:* I took sannyas in Spain, in Gitam ashram. I don't speak well, it's very difficult ... but I am happy to sit here.

Good! How long will you be staying here?

> *Shunya:* Here? I don't know — one month, two months.... my life!

Be here!

Anything you would like to say to me? he asks.

Shunya : Yes, my name is Shunya. Could you say something to me about my name?

Prem means love, shunya means utter emptiness — but it has no negative connotation in it. In no Western language is there a positive word for emptiness. 'Empty', in Western languages means empty of something; and shunya means *full* of emptiness. It is just as when you remove furniture from the room, all the furniture from the room : there are two ways to express it. Somebody can say it is just empty, and somebody can say it is full of roominess now. The second is the meaning of shunya : full of room, full of sky, full of space. And only in that kind of fullness does love arise. When one is utterly full of emptiness love is born, because in the fullness of emptiness one becomes a womb.

That's what sannyas is all about : to become a womb so that one can be pregnant with god and can give birth to god. Another name for god is love.

7

Come here ... come here! Here come Sangito, and fast asleep in his arms his two-and-a-half-year-old daughter, Simone; his wife, Daya; at her breast their son, five-months-old Llewelyn. English, this is their first visit, their first meeting.

When did you arrive? Osho smiles.

> *Sangito :* We arrived .... we arrived....

In the gazing, words escape him; A tear sits plumply on Daya's cheek.

> *Daya :* ... about a week ago.

Osho : Good. And now you have come forever?

They nod deeply.

> That's very good!

Llewelyn is to be given sannyas, and Osho bends his head to write his name.

Osho pauses in his writing, and turning to Mukta asks,

> The little one is a swami?

She nods affirmation and Osho calls the tiny swami to him.

> (to Daya) This will be his new name : Swami Prem Asa. Prem means love. Asa is Hebrew; it means healed by god. God heals, all healing is through god, god is the only healer : all those meanings are involved in it.
>
> The full name will mean : the god of love heals.

He turns to Sangito and smiles on the sleeping child lying in his arms.

> Bring her!

Her name is good. I will keep it : Ma Prem Simone. Prem means love. Simone is Hebrew; it means god has heard. The full name will mean : love that has been heard by god.

That's what prayer is. When your love is heard by god, the prayer has reached to the target : the arrow of the prayer has reached to the heart of the divine.

Sangito hangs his head and cries, and Osho turns to Daya and asks if she has something to say, then back to Sangito, still sobbing.

Just be here and be happy! Osho says, and calls them closer to be blessed.

You have come home : now settle. Good!

Emelea bends her head to receive her mala.

Osho indicates her sannyas name on the sheet of paper that he holds out to her.

This is your name : Ma Deva Amelea. Deva means...

Amelea inspects his writing and then says :

Amelea : E.m.

E.m?

Amelea : E-m-e-l-e-a.

This too is an 'e'? he asks, pointing to the first letter.

And what does it mean then?

Amelea : I don't know what the meaning is.

(chuckling) But I know what this means (much laughter), so you better change the spelling! At least one thing is certain : I know what it means!

Amelea : What does it mean?

It means the worker; it is Latin. Your full name will mean : divine work. Life is divine work. It is not for the mundane : it is an experiment for the sacred. That's why Jesus says 'Man cannot live by bread alone.'

The outer is only the periphery: the inner is the real work.

To know oneself is the goal of life, the very purpose of us being here. Life is an opportunity for self-knowing.

So change the spelling! Good, Amelea.

How long will you be here?

Amelea: I hope for one year.

That's very good!

Something you would like to say to me?

Amelea: No.

You have come to the right person!

Amelea: Yes!

Tsampa. He wants to know where she got the name.

Tsampa: From somebody in Vrindavan.

Somebody in Vrindavan? Mm mm (a pause). And has he told you what the meaning is?

Tsampa: Yes. It's a yellow flower, or it's the name of one of Krishna's gopis.

Good. Close your eyes!

Your name is good, I will keep it: Ma Deva Champa — divine champa. But the way you have been spelling it is not right. It makes it appear as if it is Tibetan! (he chuckles). C-h is the right way. Champa is one of the most beautiful flowers in India, one of the most fragrant. The fragrance has a certain quality in it: it is non-aggressive, it is very non-violent. It comes in such a way that you only *feel* that it is there. It is very indirectly there, its presence is almost synonymous with absence. And that is the beauty of it: it does not declare itself, it only whispers. That's the way of love and that's the way of god too.

That's the way of grace, that's the way of silence — you cannot hear its footsteps; suddenly it is there and suddenly it is gone. For a moment you only vaguely feel that it is there, and if you want to catch hold of it, it disappears. If you become very aware of it, it is elusive. It is there if you are receptive : it is there if you don't look it in the eye, if you allow it there, if you don't disturb, if you don't concentrate on it. Your very concentration, and it disappears. It is very shy, it is very feminine.

Hence the flower became very symbolic of worship, because it has the qualities of love. Love is shy. Even to say 'I love you' is so difficult. That's why women never take the initiative in love : they wait. They *can* wait, because to take the initiative will be a little aggressive. It is the man who takes the initiative. His love is a little gross, more earthly, more physical. His love is not so aesthetic; it tends more towards the sensual. The feminine love tends more towards the spiritual. And the more love tends towards the spiritual, the less and less direct it is, the more and more indirect, the more like the flavour, the fragrance, of champa.

And I say that this is the way love, god, grace, and all that is beautiful, comes. One has to be very sensitive to the indirect approaches of existence. If you trust only the direct, you end up with matter. That's why science ends up with matter : it is too direct, too male, too aggressive, too analytical. The essence of science is concentration, and the essence of religion is meditation — the difference is tremendously great. In the dictionary, both concentration and meditation mean the same, but only in dictionaries. In actual experience they are poles apart, diametrically opposite.

The concentrated mind is a tense mind, focused. The meditative mind is a non-tense mind, unfocused. The concentrated mind is a narrow mind; it goes on becoming narrower and narrower, it excludes more and more; then only can you concentrate. It includes less and less, and excludes more and more. Then only a single point is included, and all else, the whole existence, is excluded.

The meditative mind is all-inclusive. It is not narrow; it is wide, as wide as the sky. It is simply available. It is a kind of vulnerability, a receptivity, something like a feminine womb — waiting with great expectancy, but with no concentration. Then suddenly the indirect starts coming to you, the invisible starts approaching you; the subtle is heard, felt. One starts entering into the mysterious — call it god, the soul, nirvana, or whatever.

Science will never come to know the real; it will only know the factual. The factual is just like the hard shell, the outer shell, of reality. It is not the inner juice — that is available only to those who know how to be feminine. Hence sannyas makes everybody feminine.

Down the ages, those who have followed Krishna say that there is only one man, and that is the god, Krishna; everyone else is a woman. They are right, they are absolutely right, because that is the way of prayer and love — that it makes you feminine, it makes you more and more relaxed, available, in a state of let-go.

How long will you be here?

> *Deva Champa:* I don't know. My heart would like to stay, but my head is telling me I have to go back to Holland.

Follow the head first! Mm? be finished with the head, then come!

Anabhra replaces her. She'd written to Osho about the feeling to start a creative centre in Holland.

Many people are waiting for me to go back, she says, each word enunciated with significance.

Won't You Join the Dance?

Go and help them, Osho murmurs lightly.

But I must go differently, Anabhra says, with a touch of drama. I must go being able...

Her words are lost and Osho replies, You will be able to help many people; you can do much of my work there.

She talks about a name for the centre.

I called it — it called itself — the 'New Heart Centre' she says. Is that okay with you?

Mm mm, says Osho gazing at her, Then, I will have to get you a name for it. And would you like to make it a commune?

Yes, she would, she says, because so many people don't have anywhere to live.

I will give you a name and you start a commune, make a small ashram, mm?

She nods slowly and waits.

This will be the new name ... and she bends close to look : Premudaya. It means the rise of love, the rise of the heart, just like sunrise.

She wants to ask something now : What happened on the full moon night on Ibiza? (she'd written to him in the same letter about an incident that happened, the feelings that had overcome her while by the sea, the urge to simply walk and disappear into the water).

Everything was perfectly good. Don't think about these things, just leave them. Things will be happening : don't think about them, don't analyse them, don't make questions out of them.

Just leave them as they are. Enjoy and forget them and more will be happening. Everything is going perfectly well. I am aware of it. Just let it happen, and help people.

Hello, Murti. When are you leaving?

Anand Murti : I've been here nearly three months.

Mm, you have been here, but when are you leaving?

---

52   Won't You Join the Dance?

Anand Murti : Oh, I'm leaving the day after tomorrow, I'll be leaving Friday, Osho.

Tomorrow? Mm, your beard has grown beautifully! (laughter)

Anand Murti : Thank you!

Then with genuine admiration he adds :

Anand Murti : It'll never be as beautiful as yours!

Which makes Osho chuckle.

And when will you be coming back?

Anand Murti : As soon as I can. I hope soon.

Come back. Finally, be here.

Anand Murti : Well, that's been in my mind.

That is going to happen... just a little time.

Anand Murti : I hope your're right.

Anything to say to me?

Anand Murti : Well, Pratima (his wife) and I want to start our lives together again.

Mm mm. Very good.

Anand Murti : I think we could make a go of it.

Yes, it can be. It will be a totally different thing now — you both are so different now.

Anand Murti : Yes. I remember what you told me last time I was here, when I first came to darshan when I arrived.

Mm mm. Good!

Anand Murti : So, let's hope!

Won't You Join the Dance?   53

Start; and come back.

Anand Murti: Thank you, Osho.

Good, good, Murti!

Leela is back from England.

Something to say to me?

Prem Leela: Yes.

Mm mm.

Prem Leela: I came because I didn't know what sannyas meant any more and I had to come back to find out.

Mm mm.

Prem Leela: I'm not sure whether I know *now*.

Mm mm. This is a good sign.

This is really good, because sannyas is something that can never be known. It cannot be reduced to knowledge; it will remain something mysterious. The moment you know something it is already meaningless, because there is nothing more to explore in it. You have known it; all that can be done is that it can be thrown away. It is pointless to carry it.

Things which are really valuable — love, prayer, meditation, music, sannyas — are bound to always remain unknowable.

You will come to know many things, and still the essential core will remain unknown. But that's the beauty of all such mysterious experiences of life, that you can never catch hold of them; they are too big for that. The depth is such that you can go on and on, but you cannot fathom them out. In fact one day the searcher and the seeker disappear into the sought. A day comes when the seeker is no more found, the person who wanted to know has evaporated.

Then the mystery is total, absolute — and that's what enlightenment, realisation, salvation, liberation, is.

It is not that you have come to know truth, but that the knower has disappeared. The knower tries this way and that, the knower tries every possible way. He is frustrated, and fails in every attempt, and finally dies out of the frustration. When the knower dies, there is a kind of knowing; but because the knower is not there, you cannot call it knowledge. There is a kind of knowing, a very mysterious light — fulfilling, tremendously fulfilling, ecstatic, blissful — but the knower is not there, so it cannot be called knowledge.

So this is good, Leela. This is the beginning of sannyas!

8

Dutch Bram is first for sannyas.

Osho : This is your name : Swami Anand Bram. Anand means bliss, the ultimate state of consciousness where no content exists, not even a ripple of experience. Where all experiences have been dissolved, where only the experiencer is without any experience, that state is of bliss. There is no happiness, no unhappiness, because they are all experiences, they come from the outside. They are all disturbances. If you like the disturbance you call it happiness; if you dislike the disturbance you call it unhappiness.

That's why it is possible that happiness can become unhappiness any moment you start disliking it, and vice versa : unhappiness can become happiness the moment you start liking it. And likings change, so the same thing can give you great happiness and can drive you into deep despair. They are not different things; all that changes is your liking and disliking.

The state of bliss is not produced from the outside. The outside has completely disappeared; only you are, just pure consciousness, a mirror mirroring nothing. And that is the goal of all evolution.

Your name, bram, comes from Hebrew; it is the short form of Abraham. Abraham was chosen by god as the beginner of a new spiritual race. Abraham was a new beginning, a pioneer, a new breakthrough.

So is my idea of sannyas a new beginning, a breakthrough,

a new step in human evolution. Something is desperately needed. The way man has existed up to now is no more meaningful. We are finished with it, we have outgrown it; hence there is so much feeling of meaninglessness around the world. Why should one live? For what? Life seems to have lost all flavour, and the reason is that we have outgrown all the meanings for which we had lived up to now. The time has come to create new meaning, new goals, new futures, new utopias. The time has come to dream new dreams and hope new hopes. If we cannot do that then we are finished, then we have come against a cul-de-sac.

Abraham also was a by-product of a crisis such as we are facing today. The old religions, the old creeds, concepts, dogmas, had become irrelevant, and he became a new beginning. He culminated in Christ. Jews may understand it, may not understand it, but what began in Abraham reached its climax in Christ-consciousness, Abraham was fulfilled in Christ. But the gap between the seed and the fruit is so much that you may not recognise the fruit as a continuum of the seed. And that's what happened: the people who had loved Abraham could not recognise Jesus as the culmination, the crescendo, but he was the fulfilment. It was for people like Christ that Abraham was the beginning. It was for people like Christ that he opened the door.

There are very few pioneers in the world of spirituality, very few; they can be counted on the fingers of one hand. Even many great names are not pioneers. For example, Christ is not a pioneer but a culmination; the pioneer is Abraham. Buddha is a pioneer, a beginning. Mahavira is not a pioneer, he is just the ultimate flowering of a long long tradition of five thousand years; twenty-three masters preceded him.

Mohammed is also not a pioneer but, again, an offshoot of Abraham; just a branch of Abraham bloomed, flowers came. Christianity and Islam are both by-products of Judaism.

But it always happens : whenever a branch starts flowering, other branches start feeling jealous, angry. They cannot believe that they have not flowered and others have started flowering, that the spring has come to others before them. That creates anger, jealousy; that anger and jealousy murdered Jesus. If people had been a little more understanding, Jesus was not bringing anything new into the world; he was simply fulfilling all the old prophecies. He was a fulfilment of all the promises.

So I like the name Abraham.

Willem is next.

This is your name : Swami Anand Willem. Anand means bliss. Willem is Teutonic; it means resolution — a blissful resolution. Man becomes a soul only by absolute resolution, decisiveness.

Ordinarily people live in a kind of vagueness. Their life is so-so, lukewarm, neither this nor that; they are somehow managing. They are not a togetherness, they are not one piece; they are a crowd. They don't have a single mind, they are multi-psychic, they have many minds. There is no master inside. All the fragments are trying to possess the throne, but no fragment can become the master; at the most it can pretend for a moment to be the master, and the next moment it is thrown out. So one moment a person is one thing, another moment he is a totally different thing. Only on the surface do people maintain their identity, otherwise they have none.

If you look inside a person he is a flux, not an identity; a constantly changing scene with nothing as a centre, just a market-place, a multitude. That's what a man ordinarily is, and the reason is : lack of resolution, lack of decisiveness. The moment you start deciding.... It is hard, it is difficult to decide, it needs guts. To decide means to take risks, to decide means to choose — and whenever you choose, something has to be left. That's what choice is : if you choose to go to the left, then you have chosen to drop the direction that was going towards the right. That needs guts, because every resolution is a renunciation too.

For example, if you have chosen to become a sannyasin you have chosen to drop many things. If you have chosen to be a sannyasin you have chosen to be a universal man; now you will not be part of any ugly nationality. Formally you will be, but deep down you will know that you are simply a man, you belong to the whole mankind. You are neither Indian nor Dutch nor German nor English, deep down you are neither Christian nor Hindu nor Mohammedan. You are dropping many things by becoming a sannyasin : all the concepts, belief systems, dogmas. You are dropping the very idea of living through imitation, of living by following the past.

To be a sannyasin means a resolution to live one's own life according to one's own light. It is a resolution to be a light unto yourself. It is risky to be free, because it is always safe to throw the responsibility on others — that they have told you to do this, that you are not responsible. To be a sannyasin means that from this moment you will be responsible, that whatsoever you do, *you* will be doing it — that if good happens, it is yours; if something goes wrong, that is yours; that you will be doing your own thing, whatsoever the consequence; that you are willing to accept all the consequences, but you are not willing to lose your freedom.

Sannyas is a declaration of freedom, of individuality; it needs great resolution. But through resolution the soul is born, one attains to a soul. Sometimes small resolutions bring great integrity; and this is a great resolution.

Move into this new vision with a very determined step, with great trust in yourself. That's what I teach : trust yourself, trust your intelligence, trust your own heart, its feelings —and even if sometimes it looks crazy to follow those feelings, go with them. It is better to be crazy according to your own heart than to be sane according to others. That sanity is worthless. It will never bring you any joy, it will never bring you any benediction. All benedictions are for those who resolve to be themselves.

Annaliese is from Italy.

This is your name : Ma Anand Annalisa. Anand means blissful. Annalisa is Hebrew, it is made of two words. The first is anna; it is part of hannah, which means grace. The other part is lisa; that is part of Elizabeth. In Hebrew, el means god. Your full name, Annalisa, means : god's grace.

Life *is* god's grace, and so is death. Love is god's grace, and so is all that ever happens, good and bad too. The whole duality of existence is god's grace. One who understands this is not only grateful for all that is good but is also grateful for all that appears bad; that is real gratefulness. To be grateful only for the happy moments is nothing of gratefulness; that is simple greed, cunningness, but it has nothing to do with gratefulness.

Real gratefulness arises only when you are grateful even for unhappy moments, for all the pain and the suffering and the anguish that life brings. The moment one is capable of feeling grateful for both pain and pleasure, without any distinction, without any choice, simply feeling grateful for whatsoever is given…. Because if it is given by God, it must have a reason in it. We may like it, we may not like it, but it must be needed for your growth. And pain is needed as much as pleasure, darkness as much as light. Winter and summer are both needed for growth. Once this idea settles in the heart, then each moment of life is of gratitude.

Let this become your meditation and prayer : thank god

every moment — for laughter, for tears, for everything. Then you will see a silence arising in your heart that you have not known before. That is bliss.

Peter is before him.

This is your name : Swami Anand Peter. Anand means bliss, peter comes from the Greek, petros; it means rock. Your full name will mean : rock of bliss.

Everything else in life is in a constant change. Bliss is the rock of eternity : it is always the same, no change ever happens in it. It is the centre of the cyclone; all changes happen on the periphery.

The search for truth is the search for that rock which is timeless. One has to go within oneself until one finds that point, that unmoving point on which *all* movement depends. Life is like a moving wheel, but the wheel is moving around something unmoving. All movement needs a non-moving centre; the movement cannot exist without a non-moving centre.

Time exists as a wheel around the centre of eternity. Call it god, call it truth, call it bliss, the supreme self, or whatever you wish, but one thing about it is certain, that it has the quality of a rock — unchangingness, eternally unchanging. So it cannot be the body, because the body changes; and it cannot be the mind, because the mind changes; it cannot even be the heart, because the heart changes. We have to go deeper and deeper and deeper : we have to disidentify ourselves from the body, from the mind, from the heart. We have to go on disidentifying till we arrive at the point where only the witnessing self is left, where nothing more is there to deny, reject — just pure I-am-ness. Not 'I am the body', not 'I am the mind', but simply 'I am'.

When that I-am-ness is left, one has arrived. One has found the rock — the rock of eternity, the rock of timelessness;

the rock which is beyond all movement, all change, all death.

This is your name : Ma Prem Bonnie. Prem means love, bonnie is Latin, it has three meanings : sweet, good, beautiful. And those are the three qualities of love. Love is sweet, love is beautiful, love is good — not just good but the ultimate good, the summum bonum. Love fulfilled, all is fulfilled. Love realised, god is realised. Love missed, and the whole of life is a sheer wastage. One can go on trying to be good without being loving, but one cannot succeed; in the very nature of things it is impossible. One cannot be virtuous without being loving; one can only pretend, one can only be a hypocrite. One can have masks which will look good and beautiful, but behind the mask just the opposite will be the reality.

Without love, no one is ever beautiful. One can have a certain form of beauty, one can have a proportionate body — but if the soul is not proportionate, just the proportion of the body cannot make one beautiful. The body plays a very minor role, a very secondary role, like the shadow. Just because the shadow is looking beautiful, you will not call the person beautiful. The person may be ugly. He may be standing in a certain way, at a certain angle to the sun-rays, so the shadow is looking beautiful, but the beauty of the shadow is not necessarily his beauty. So is the case with the body : the body of matter is only a shadow. It *can* be beautiful, but if you are carrying an ugly soul within that beauty, it is utterly meaningless, a deception, an hallucination.

Love makes the soul beautiful. It gives the soul proportion, it gives the soul melody, it gives the soul the quality of grace, aliveness. It brings a certain poetry out of the soul. And once the soul is beautiful, the body automatically follows it. Even ugly bodies become beautiful with beautiful souls. Homely bodies become so luminous.

It is said about Jesus that he had a very ugly body. Christians don't talk about it much, but all the old sources say that he had a very ugly body. He had such an ugly face that it is said that the people who spat on him and threw stones on him while he was carrying his cross were not necessarily against him. His face was *so* ugly that it provoked people to spit on him — even strangers. And he was a very very small man, only four feet six inches, and a hunchback! All other sources say that, except Christian sources. There is every possibility....

Josephus's 'Capture of Jerusalem' contains the following description of Jesus : 'A man of dark skin, small stature, three cubits high (four feet six inches), hunchbacked, with a long face, long nose and meeting eyebrows, so that those who see him might be affrighted, with scanty hair and with an undeveloped beard.'

Tertullian also spoke of the 'ignominy of the face of Jesus' and said, 'No one would have mishandled, much less spat upon, Jesus, had not the face of the condemned provoked his tormentors to much brutality.'

But my feeling is that this ugly man became one of the most beautiful in the world. Those who came to see his love, those who came to feel his innermost core, they saw his real beauty. It was a miracle : two opposites meeting.

Buddha was a very beautiful man, so there was nothing of a miracle; his body was also beautiful. But Jesus is the meeting of the opposites : an ugly body with the most beautiful soul in the world. And because of the polarity, the tension between the two, he has a quality to his individuality which is lacking in Buddha. Buddha is just beautiful, simply beautiful. There is not the opposite in him; and without the opposite, the contrast is missing.

It is not accidental that Jesus has possessed many more people in the world than anybody else — because of the tension of the opposites. He has something very strange about him : the full range of beauty and ugliness. He is the whole rainbow, all the seven colours, from the lowest to the highest. He is a meeting point of the world and the divine, of matter and consciousness. In that way, Buddha is more like a solo fluteplayer, Christ is a great orchestra. His beauty comes not from the body but from the innermost core. It needs eyes to see it — and that's why he says again and again, 'Those who have eyes, see, and those who have ears, hear'. It was difficult to look into his deeper being. People can only see on the surface, hence while alive he could not attract many people.

Buddha attracted many more people while alive. It is almost impossible to think that somebody could insult Buddha the way Jesus was insulted by people; it is impossible to think of it. His very presence would have prevented them. On the surface he was beautiful; he was beautiful in the being too. But people can only see the surface.

With Jesus they could not see; only very few people who had eyes could see. But once he was dead, once he was crucified, he started rising into people's vision, he started haunting them. The cross became very significant. If he had not been crucified, people might have forgotten about that man, but the cross simply would not allow them to forget him.

Slowly slowly, the real body was forgotten and in the myth he became a beautiful man — tall, handsome, beautiful in every way. But in reality he was an ugly man, and yet one of the most beautiful : he was a paradox!

The beauty that happened to him happened through his love. He loved the world tremendously, he loved people tremendously. Nobody else has ever loved so deeply and so utterly and so unconditionally. Nobody has ever sacrificed himself so totally for his love.

You have a beautiful name. Remember those three qualities; they have to be grown. But they can grow only if you grow the central quality of love. Become more and more loving, become love, and you will find virtue arising, goodness happening, beauty following.

Prem Bonnie: But how?

Mm?

Prem Bonnie: How will I find it?

There is no question of how — just start being more loving. Love is already there in everybody's heart; it is not a question to be learned. Just as we breathe, we can love. It is natural, it is intrinsic. Just don't hinder it, that's all. All that has to be learned is how not to hinder it.

Prem Bonnie: It's difficult.

It *is* difficult, otherwise the whole world would have been beautiful. It is difficult, otherwise everybody would have loved immensely. It is certainly difficult, but that is the challenge, and the challenge has to be taken. The more difficult a thing is, the more adventurous it is.

That's what sannyas is all about: it will teach you slowly slowly how to remove the barriers and how to let the love energy flow. That's my whole function here. I cannot teach you how to love — nobody can — but I can teach you how to remove all the barriers, how to remove all the obstacles. That's all that is needed: remove the rocks and the spring starts flowing. It is already there, it is your very being; it does not have to be learned.

We just have to drop our attachments to the rocks. We have to see that they are rocks and our enemies, that we need not cling to them, that they are not protective, they are destructive. Once that is seen, those rocks can be thrown away. Those rocks are not clinging to us; we are clinging to those rocks. And there are all kinds of rocks, all kinds of stupid ideas, ideologies, which stop people from loving, which hinder people from growing into love — unnecessary fears, inhibitions, taboos. But this society has cultivated them because this society does not want people to be very loving; loving people are dangerous people. This society is not interested in real individuals; this society wants only slaves. And the best way to make a slave is to never allow his love to grow. He remains stunted, stifled, he remains an un-grown-up. And when you are an un-grown-up, you are bound to seek and search for somebody to cling to, to depend on, somebody who can order you. You will seek and search for your tyrants.

If you can love, you are free. Love brings freedom.

This is going to happen. Wait!

This will be your new name — the old one I have to change. Wolfgang means the walk of a wolf. Of course even the walk of a wolf has a certain beauty and grace in it, but all the same, it is the walk of a wolf! (laughter).

This will be your new name : Swami Prem Joshua. Prem means love. Joshua is Hebrew; it is the original name of Jesus. Joshua means : god is salvation, Jehovah is salvation. Salvation is in god and through god.

Man cannot become free through his own efforts. His own efforts will be very tiny, and the bondage is great. His own efforts will be very unconscious — from where will he bring consciousness to make conscious efforts? And whatsoever one goes on doing in unconsciousness brings more and more misery, brings more and more bondage, creates new prisons. Unconsciousness is darkness; if we go on groping in darkness we simply stumble here and there, we fall and we go astray.

The only possibility in this dark night of the soul is a ray of light from the beyond. And that's what prayer is all about.

Prayer means asking god for a ray of light, asking god to send some help, and if the help is asked for with one's totality, it certainly arrives. Jesus says, 'Knock and the doors shall be opened unto you, ask and it shall be given, seek and ye shall find.'

But what he means by seeking, asking, knocking, is not effort but prayer. Seek in prayer, ask in prayer, knock in prayer, and slowly slowly it gathers intensity, momentum, and a moment comes when your totality is prayerful. In that very instant, something from the beyond reaches you — a hand of help, some energy that is not yours, some light that you had never known before, some guidance. And to walk in that light is to get out of the prison, to get out of the dark night. That single ray is enough to take you to the source of light, to the very source.

Joshua is a tremendously significant word : god *is* salvation. And I am giving you this name because prayer will fit with your being very very deeply. More than meditation, prayer will fit you. Prayer will be your meditation; all meditations will simply help you to become more prayerful. So meditate, it will help; but finally the key will be prayer, so start praying too.

At night before you go to sleep, a fifteen-minute prayer, with tears in your eyes, with your hands raised toward the sky. If something comes to the heart you can say it, otherwise just silence will do. But go on remembering — and your name will remind you again and again — that god is salvation, so prayer is the door.

Good, Joshua.

Anand Asho, here for the first time, asks to know more about her name.

Anand means bliss, asho means hope. Life is not yet actual; it has to be actualised. It is only a hope, a potential, a possibility, but one can miss it. That is the danger, but that is the excitement also. With birth, only an opportunity is given — not real life, but only a possibility of attaining life. And because we have taken it for granted that we are alive, we go on missing it. Just by being born, one is not alive: another birth is needed, a deeper birth is needed. It has only given you the periphery; the centre is missing. It has only given you the body; the soul is missing.

That's what Jesus means when he says, 'Unless a man is born again, he will not enter into my kingdom of God.' But the hope can become actual, the potential can be realised. Religion is nothing but the art of realising the potential, and the master is only a midwife.

So you have to remember: bliss has still to happen, life has still to happen, god has still to happen. As we are born, we are empty; and we have to be full — not only full but overflowing. Only then is there contentment, only then is there significance, and a great joy and a great gratitude arise.

People cannot be grateful to god. For what should they be grateful? — because they are still only promises, hopes, dreams. The real is missing, so they cannot be grateful. Once you start having a few glimpses of the real, gratefulness follows of its own accord.

Let sannyas become the journey from the potential to the actual, from the promise to the fulfilment.

> *Prem Saddho:* Would you tell me what my name means?

What meaning was given to you?

> *Prem Saddho:* Trust, that's all it said: love, trust.

Prem means love; trust is a by-product of love, the fragrance of love. If you love, you automatically trust. You cannot trust without love. You can believe without love, but you cannot trust. Hence belief is impotent, it is superficial;

deep down you still doubt. Behind belief there is doubt; in fact the greater the doubt is, the bigger the belief needed to cover it. All believers are doubters, otherwise they would not be believers in the first place.

Belief is against doubt : trust is absence of doubt. It is not against doubt, it is simply absence of doubt.

That miracle happens only in love. When you love, you cannot find any doubt anywhere inside you : all is trust. And in that trust the miracle, the transcendence, the transformation.

To know what trust is to know the door to the temple of God.

Come-close time. Gyan Bhakti, ashram jeweller, had written to Osho about her low energy.

He calls Chetana to assist in Bhakti's energy dance, and when they are done, calls her back gently. She turns slowly round to face him; a tear plops off her face.

Everything is absolutely good. You need not worry, just leave everything to me. Sometimes low-energy moments come; that's part of growth, they have their work to do. Sometimes depression is bound to happen. One has to learn to be a witness of it. The energy is moving perfectly well. But it is a rhythm; you cannot remain high all the time, otherwise you will become exhausted, spent, burned out. You can absorb only so much of the height, then you will have to come back to the valley to rest.

Always think of those moments when you are not feeling very ecstatic as moments of rest, and when you have gathered energy enough you will be flying again. But energy is moving in a perfect rhythm, so there is no problem at all.

Good, Bhakti.

9

Our ashram team are recording darshan on video equipment tonight. In their spotlight is an actress from Sweden, Christina.

Osho : This is your name : Ma Prem Christina. Prem means love. Christina is Greek, it is from Christ. Christ is Greek for messiah, the one who has arrived; it is exactly the equivalent of the Buddha.

We *are* in the journey. Life is a pilgrimage, and only very few have arrived at the goal. These few are called the messiahs, the Buddhas, the Christs. It is the ultimate state of consciousness, bliss; the ultimate state of being, beyond which there is no goal — where one starts feeling at home, at ease, where tremendous contentment is felt and all desires disappear.

Desire is dis-ease. To desire means to be in discontent. When there is contentment there is no desire; when there is contentment there is fulfilment, one is simply joyous. That state of rejoicing is Christ; and love brings one to that goal. It is only through love that one arrives.

Start by loving more and more, for no other reason at all, just for the sheer joy of loving. And, slowly slowly, loving becomes your very flavour — not anything that you have to do, but a simple quality of your being. Even while asleep, one is loving. If nobody is there, still one is loving : one is love. Keep remembering; that it is a far-away distant star, but not impossible to achieve. It is our intrinsic potentiality to achieve it, we are meant to achieve it : it is our destiny.

She'll be here a few more weeks, Christina says. He gives her groups then:

Anything you would like to say to me?

Her lines forgotten, she hangs her head, her face love-flushed. And he has understood.

Good. No need to say anything. There are things which cannot be said but which still can be heard....

Judith is a psychologist from the States.

This is your name: Ma Deva Judith. Deva means divine or god. Judith is Hebrew, it means the praised one. Your full name will mean: god, the praised one. God is only when you are in the mood of praising existence. When you are in the mood of prayer, god exists; otherwise god is as non-existential as anything. God exists only in the vision of lovers.

It is futile to ask where god is, unless in your heart there is praise, gratitude, love, prayer. God is found only in the heart of one who is utterly in praise of existence because it is so incredibly beautiful, so utterly valuable. We have not earned it, we are not worthy of it. To be is a gift. Life is a gift, love is a gift, and all that is, is a sheer gift from god. All that we can do is praise him.

That very praising is enough, because that praise becomes prayer — prayer is nothing else. Prayer is the heart in tremendous rejoicing, thankfulness, saying the existence is good.

The moment you say that existence is good, god is: in that very assertion, god is. Hence god cannot be proved by any logical, rational approach; it is proved only by the loving heart.

How long will you be here?

Deva Judith: Until March the fourteenth.

Have you done any groups?

Deva Judith : No.

Would you like to do a few groups?

Deva Judith : No!

It's with a smile but the lady is quite adamant.

Just be here...

Deva Judith : Yes.

... and praise the Lord!

Deva Judith : Yes!

(chuckling) Good! Anything to say to me?

Deva Judith : Ohhh... I'm so grateful to be here!

(to Kai) This is your name : Ma Deva Kai. Deva means divine. Kai is Greek, it means rejoicing — divine rejoicing. Life is a song to be sung, a dance to be danced; and only those who can sing and dance and rejoice can know what life is.

Others only vegetate. Others live, but without any aliveness in them. They never know the ecstasy of being here, of being now; they never know exultation, they never reach to the peaks of being. It is only in utter rejoicing that one touches the optimum, the ultimate — and the moment one touches the optimum, the maximum, one has touched the divine.

People live at the minimum; their life is only so-so, lukewarm. That is not the right way to live. That is just a way of slow suicide — they only die.

Jesus says again and again to his disciples, 'Rejoice! Rejoice! I say unto you, rejoice! I say again, rejoice!' But it has not been heard; the disciples have not understood yet.

Christianity became very sad, serious; it lost the quality of playfulness. And the moment a religion loses the quality of playfulness it is dead, it is only a corpse. You can worship it, but it cannot deliver you, it cannot liberate you. In fact it becomes a bondage — a beautiful bondage of course, but the church becomes a prison.

If there is dancing and there is singing and there is joy and there is love, and life is respected not denied, not negated but affirmed, totally affirmed, with all that it contains — with all the pains and all the pleasures, with all the agonies and all the ecstasies — when life is praised in its totality, only then does rejoicing happen.

My sannyas is nothing but rejoicing; it is not renunciation but rejoicing.

This is your name : Ma Deva Serena. Deva means divine. Serena is Latin for serenity, tranquillity, stillness — divine serenity. It is not something to be cultivated. It is already there; we have only to uncover it. It is already at the very core of our being. Our innermost core is made of serenity; the stuff it is made of is serenity. We have only to reach to the core. We live on the periphery, and we go on round and round, never penetrating our innermost core. Hence we remain in a turmoil. Then a very false idea arises : people start asking 'How to be serene? How to be silent? How to be still?' Then methods are created — because whenever there is a demand, there is a supply.

When people start asking how to be serene, some cunning, clever guys are bound to supply the methods. They will say 'Repeat this mantra and you will become serene' or 'Do this method and you will become serene.' All those methods can only create a false serenity. That serenity, that false serenity, is against the turmoil of the mind; and all the methods are to repress the turmoil of the mind. It is a forced kind of serenity, imposed.

If you go on forcing the mind, the mind has to yield. If you go on sitting every day, repeating a certain stupid mantra, sooner or later you will *force* the mind to become quiet. But that serenity is false, because if you look a little deeper into it you will find all the turmoil moving as an undercurrent, just waiting for you to stop your stupid mantra so it can come back. The whole traffic remains; it simply goes underground, it is forced to go underground. This is not true serenity; I don't teach it.

There is no way to become serene, because we already are. There is no need for any method; all that is needed is a jump from the periphery to the centre. Real serenity is not against the turmoil of the mind; the turmoil remains and you become serene. Real serenity is the centre of the cyclone : the cyclone goes on and on, and the very core of it all is silent, utterly silent. It is our true nature. We have only to discover it, not to invent it, not to create it.

My approach is not of creating serenity, but of discovering it — because this is my realisation, that it is already there. One just has to look withinwards, one has to turn withinwards. And when one has come to know natural, spontaneous serenity, it remains with one for twenty-four hours, without any method to support it, without any artificial prop. It is simply there like breathing, it is simply there like your heartbeat. Then it is really a liberation. Otherwise the method becomes your bondage.

You become addicted to methods. Without the method you are at a loss, you don't know what to do now; without the method you are again in a turmoil. So you start clinging to the method. The method becomes so important — more important than serenity itself, because serenity seems to be just a by-product of the method. It is not; true serenity is not.

Remember it : you are not to cultivate it, it is already the case. Just look in as much as you can. Whenever you have time, just close your eyes and look in, and one day you will stumble upon it without any method. One always stumbles upon it. One should just go on groping in the inner darkness and one day, sooner or later, one stumbles upon it. One has found the source, the very spring of well-being. Then life has a totally different taste, a different quality — the quality of joy and the taste of grace. Then life is beautiful and each moment is a benediction.

When you are serene, the whole existence seems to be serene, because the existence only reflects you. Whatsoever you are, it reflects you. Whatsoever you are, it only goes on echoing you in a thousand and one ways.

Rose is a nurse from Australia.

Your name : Ma Anand Rose. Anand means bliss ... and a rose is a rose is a rose!

Life can become a rose of bliss — it *should*. There is no reason why it should not. It should have the fragrance of a rose, the freshness of a rose, the beauty of a rose, the joy of a rose. *It can*, it has all the potential, but the potential has to be transformed into the actual. The potential can die without becoming actual. That is the risk but also the excitement of experiencing, exploring, and the adventure also.

If it were an absolute certainty, there would be no joy in it. Because one can miss, to attain it brings such ecstasy. Because one can miss, not to miss makes one feel so tremendously joyous. But there is no reason why you should miss — the whole existence supports you in reaching the goal — unless you yourself stop the growth.

People are very afraid of growing, for a certain reason, because growth brings new problems, and they have to find solutions for those new problems. If you remain un-grown-up, your problems remain old and you know the solutions. It is cheaper, safer, more secure. You have a few problems and you already know the answers. But then there is no exultation; one simply lives a routine, dull and dead life.

People are afraid of growing, because the moment you grow, growth means going beyond the known, reaching to something unknown. And with every experience of the unknown, new problems are bound to arise; and new problems will demand new solutions — and that needs intelligence. Nobody wants to labour that much to be intelligent. People live in stupidity, in mediocrity, it is less risky, and much effort is not needed. People settle very early.

The average mental age of human beings on earth today is not more than twelve years. People settle too soon. One should not settle to the very last; in fact one should not ever settle — not even when one is dying should one settle.

One should be like a Socrates: even dying he is so tremendously excited. He is excited about *death!* His disciples cannot understand why he is so excited. They are crying, and he says: Stop crying! When I am gone you can cry; you will have all the time then. Right now don't cry. I am entering into a totally new experience. I have never known death. Life I have known, so I don't hanker for more life; I have known it already. I have lived long and I have lived in every possible way — good and bad, the way of the sinner and the way of the saint. I have lived all possibilities, I have exhausted all alternatives, so it is finished! Now I am excited about death, about what it is. I want to experience it, I want to go into it. Be quiet and be silent. And also meditate on my death: sooner or later you will die. Your master is dying — participate in his experience!

This is the way one should live and one should die — but this type of intelligence cannot die, this intelligence is bound to conquer death. How can death destroy such intelligence? Impossible! Existence cannot be so unfair. Death destroys only stupid minds. Death cannot destroy intelligence — in fact it sharpens it, it enhances it, it gives it more colour, more depth, more integrity.

The really intelligent person lives his life in totality and lives his death also in totality. And through totality is transcendence.

June is a singer from the States.

This is your name : Ma Prem June. Prem means love, June is Latin, it is from junius; it means young, youthful, fresh. Love is always young, it never becomes old. Its intrinsic quality is to be as fresh as dewdrops, as fresh as new lotus flowers.

The moment love starts becoming old, it is no more love. Love has disappeared; now you are only living in a memory, now it is nostalgia. But in fact it is no more there. If it is there, it is always young. And what do I mean by young? If love is there, you never think of the past; you never think of beautiful moments, love moments, of the past. One starts thinking of the past only when the present is pale compared to the past. When the present is no more so joyous, when the present is no more so alive, then one starts thinking of the past.

To think of the past is to become old. Only old people think of the past. Children think of the future, old people think of the past. The really young person lives in the moment, neither in the past nor in the future; he lives in the present. And if one can live in the present, one remains young. The body will grow old, but one remains young.

To keep that quality of freshness always around oneself is to have lived rightly. People gather too much dust, too much memory, and people live either in the past or in the future. And both are non-existential : the past is no more, the future is not yet. The only reality that is, is this moment. Reality is always this-ness, such-ness. It is now, it is here.

To live in the now and the here is to know the depth of life, the height of life. It is unimaginable, it is incomprehensible.

It is so mysterious that the more you know, the more mysterious it becomes. The more you know, the less you know it. And the person who lives in the present, of necessity lives in love; because life is so mysterious, how can you miss it? How can you manage not to love it? And vice versa : the person who loves lives in the present, because there is no other way for love to live. To love or to be in the present are the same, two sides of the same coin.

Serge nods amiably and listens. Osho adds Prem to his name and places him in the service of love.

Service can be without love too. Then it is superficial, then it is only a duty to be fulfilled; it is not a virtue. But in the past, religions have made much out of it. All over the world, the so-called saints have been teaching people to serve; they have been saying that service is the way to God. But just service with no love in it is not a way to God, and cannot ever be a way. It is just a motive for attaining some pleasures in the other life, it is nothing but greed extended to the other world. It has a profit motive, and then it is no more religious.

When you serve out of love it has beauty in it, because there is no motivation. You are not searching for any heaven as a reward; you are serving out of sheer joy. There is no other reward except itself, it is an end unto itself. Then your act is total. It is the means and it is the end too; the circle is perfect. And whenever an act is total, it frees you; it does not hang around you like a weight. You live it and then it disappears. You always remain unburdened by it; it never becomes a karma. And to make an act total means the act should arise out of your innermost core; it should not be an imposition from the outside.

That's what I mean when I say that service should well up in your heart out of love, for no other reason. Then it is *really* virtue, then it is paradise itself. One can live in paradise on this very earth if one knows how to act out of love.

The whole aspect of sannyas is action out of love, because action out of love is total action and total action brings freedom.

Your name is good : Swami Gopal Bharti.

Now try to go deep into meditation. Sannyas needs nothing, nothing external; its need is just internal, and that is that you should be deeply involved in meditation and all your energy should flow into it. It is only a matter of effort for a few days in the beginning. Once the rock is broken and the stream starts flowing, there is no difficulty. Once the stream starts flowing, then the stream itself will carry you to the ocean. Effort is needed only in the beginning. If you do it for the first four to six months with determination, without wavering and without relaxing your efforts, then meditation will happen by itself; you will not be required to do it.

How long are you going to stay here?

Gopal Bharti : As long as you ask me to stay.

Try all the meditation techniques here, and then regularly continue one of them that suits you.

Gopal Bharti : I do Vipassana.

Vipassana is good. Concentrate on Vipassana.

Gopal Bharti : When I sit in Vipassana, you appear in my thoughts, your picture appears before me. In the beginning it is your picture but then it seems to change.

Whatever it is, see it as a witness. Don't desire it to be there, nor desire it to go. Don't attach your desire to it; don't have any attachment to it at all.

You will have many such experiences that will be pleasurable, but don't cling to them, let go of them. You have to remember that a time should come when there will be no experiences; only witnessing will be there, only the witness. There should be no object to observe, just observing, plain mirroring. Be aware of it.

In the meantime, many things will happen during meditation. There will be pleasurable experiences, like the appearance of a fragrance which will thrill you, or an explosion of colours as if a rainbow has burst forth. You will also see that flowers are blooming and that spring has arrived; you will experience many sorts of light and sound and music. Sometimes you will feel so weightless that you can fly in the air.

Such experiences will be there when Vipassana deepens. You have to just be a witness to them all, without any identification, without any attachment. Just go on witnessing. You have to remember that you are a witness, just a witness. Do not identify yourself with any of the experiences. Always know, 'I am neither this nor that, I am just the observer before whom these experiences are taking place. I am not the observed but the observer. I am the witness.' This remembrance should always be there.

Slowly slowly, all the experiences will disappear. And the day when only the observer is there, the experience of experiences — the ultimate experience — happens. To call it an experience is not right, because no experience is left there. But that is the experience which we seek — call it samadhi, enlightenment or whatsoever you want.

Go on observing, and be aware of the observer.

Madhunad is leaving for the West.
Continue to meditate, Osho reminds him.

Remember, whenever you are in meditation, you are

close to me, I am close to you. So make it a point that at least once a day for one hour you will be with me. That's what meditation is all about — twenty-three hours for yourself, one hour for me (laughter). In the end you will find that those twenty-three hours that were for yourself are all lost, and only that one hour is saved!

Help my people there!

10

Osho : This is your new name : Ma Veet Sandeh. Veet means beyond, sandeh means doubt.

To go beyond doubt is the most fundamental step towards god. Doubt is a tremendously important method of enquiry into matter, but not into consciousness. It is utterly valid as far as matter is concerned, and utterly invalid as far as consciousness is concerned.

If you use trust in science, there will be no science at all. Doubt is a must; it is through doubt that science grows. Hence in the East, science could not grow — because of trust. But if you go on doubting and you forget how to trust, religion starts dying. That's how, in the West, religion is dead : god *is* dead. Once trust disappears, then you cannot see god anywhere. Only the eyes of trust, of tremendous love, are capable of seeing god, the divine, in existence.

For the outer journey, doubt is the way; it is perfectly right. I am not against doubt, but it has its limitations, just as trust has its limitations. For the inner journey trust is perfectly right, but for the outer it is utterly useless. To be a total man, one needs to be capable of both.

These are two instruments to be used; one need not get identified with either. The modern mind is identified with doubt. That identification has to be dropped, because initiation into sannyas is initiation into trust. It is the beginning of an inner journey — esoteric, a flight of the alone to the alone. It is going into exploration within the very core of your being; it is trying to confront yourself. It is not an objective enquiry, it is going into pure subjectivity. Doubt will not be needed, doubt will be a hindrance. Only trust can become the boat to the unknown.

Have you done any groups here?

Veet Sandeh : Yes.

What have you done?

Veet Sandeh : First the Centering group and then Massage.

And have you booked for anything else?

Veet Sandeh : No, because I will have a baby in two months.

How old is the pregnancy?

Veet Sandeh : Seven months.

Mm mm. Then you can take a few individual sessions after the camp — Shiatsu, Acupuncture — and book for one group, Zazen. If you enjoy it — because it is a very very silent meditation, one of the most deep-going meditations; it is just meditation, but you have to sit for hours — if you enjoy it, then you can do one more group, some time later on: Vipassana. If you enjoy Zazen, then Vipassana is on the same track — still further going, deeper-going. But if you feel any discomfort, then drop out of the group; there is no need to complete it, and don't do the others. Simply be here, enjoy singing, dancing, music.

Irene is from Switzerland.

This is your name : Ma Anand Irene. Anand means bliss. Irene is Greek, it means peace. In Greek mythology, Irene is the goddess of peace. Your full name will mean : blissful peace.

Remember, just peace is not enough, because it can become sadness very easily. It has to be blissful. Peace has two possibilities. It can be negative; when it is negative it is a kind of sadness. Yes, one is peaceful but there is no cheerfulness. One is peaceful but kind of dull and dead, one is peaceful but not alive. The peace is not a singing and dancing one; the peace is simply absence of turmoil. It is an absence, not a presence.

That's what has happened in the past to many religious people, they became involved too much in negative peace : avoid all situations of turmoil, activity, creativity, relationship; avoid the world, avoid people, avoid as much as you can so that you can be peaceful. Certainly they attained to a certain peace, but that peace was that of a cemetery, not of a garden where birds are singing and flowers are blooming and the winds are full of joy. There was no sunlight in that kind of peace. It was a dark night of the soul.

So I make it a point for every one of my sannyasins to always remember that one has not to fall into the trap of a negative kind of peace — which *has* its allurement. Peace, to be really true, has to be positive; not an absence but a presence, a well-being, a song ready to burst forth — alive, vibrating, pulsating. Then it has a totally different quality : it is life-affirmative, it is creative, it is active. It is not a kind of death; it is life abundant, it is ecstatic life.

And also remember that the negative kind of peace is easy to attain, because you have only to discard; you have only to negate, eliminate, you have only to escape. It does not need much intelligence to escape; any coward can do it. It needs only fear, that's all; nothing else is needed.

Hence, in the past, cowards became great saints. They were not intelligent people, but simply afraid of life. And out of fear they escaped — to the deserts, to the mountains. Wherever they could find a way to escape, they escaped from life, and in their monasteries they started a kind of living death; they vegetated.

I am utterly against *that* kind of peace. Remember, peace has to be full of sunlight. Peace has to be *in* the world; peace has to be earthly, sensuous. Peace has not to be just an abstraction in the mind. It has to be full of love, full of joy, full of hope. That is the meaning of your name.

How long will you be here, Irene?

> *Anand Irene:* This time I have been only since the first of February.

First February? And how long will you be here?

> *Anand Irene:* Only until the sixteenth of February.

Have you done any group here?

> *Anand Irene:* I did the Centering.

Good. Next time come for a longer period. You have something to say to me?

> *Anand Irene:* Maybe you would suggest another group for me for when I come back?

When will you be coming back?

> *Anand Irene:* I think in June.

In June? Then I will give you groups — because by that time so much water will have flowed down the Ganges, you will not be the same person! So I cannot suggest right now, mm? The medicine can be prescribed only in June when you come back.

> *Anand Irene:* Okay.

I will have to see the patient first!

She laughs with us.

This is your name: Swami Prem Matthias. Prem means love. Matthias is Hebrew, it means a gift of god — love, the gift of god. The greatest gift of god is love. It is a miracle that we are capable of love; and only those who go deep in love know what life is and know what god is. Love holds all the keys of all the secrets. But very few people go into love, although everybody thinks he is a lover. Everybody thinks that he loves, and loves too much. The father thinks he loves the children, the mother thinks she does; the husband thinks he loves the wife, the wife thinks she loves the husband, friends think they love each other. But look at the world : if so many people are so loving, the world will be a paradise — and it is not! It is the ugliest possible world that we have created. Love is utterly missing, love is not present anywhere. We only pretend to love, we don't love. We do something else in the name of love.

The father may be dominating the children, he may be using the children as part of his ambition. The wife may be dominating her husband, possessing him; she may be jealous, she may be clinging to him, afraid — if he leaves, what will happen to her? And all this she calls love. The husband may be very very possessive of the woman and may call it love, but love is utterly absent. How can jealousy and love be together? How can possessiveness and love be together? If you love a person you cannot possess him or her, because to possess a person is to humiliate him, to possess a person is to reduce him to a thing, to a commodity. When you possess a woman she is no more a woman, she is just a wife; you have reduced her to a commodity. You are exploiting her; you are using her for sexual purposes, for other purposes, but you are not in love.

The first thing to understand is that we are *not* in love; whatsoever we have been calling love is not love. To know the false as false is the beginning. To know the true as true, first one has to understand what is false; then one starts seeking and searching for the true.

Love is the greatest gift of god. And very rarely, once in a while, a Jesus, a Buddha, a Krishna — yes, these few people have known what love is.

Matthias is also the name of a disciple of Jesus who was chosen in place of Judas Iscariot to make the apostles twelve again. He must have been a man of tremendous insight, of love, because love is the message of Jesus. And all the eleven apostles voted for him — he must have been a rare man.

Remember : become love, and you become an apostle of god. To be a lover is to be an apostle of god.

How long will you be here?

Prem Matthias : As long as possible!

Good, good, Matthias!

Osho chuckles fondly — Anything to say? he asks. Matthias laughs; his open hands say it for him.

(to Stefan) This is your new name : Swami Shantideva. Shanti means peace, silence, stillness, serenity; and deva means love — god of peace, god of silence, god of stillness.

The mind is a constant turmoil, conflict, friction. It is a crowd, very noisy, of thoughts, desires, memories; one is utterly lost in the crowd. The noise is so much that one cannot hear one's own voice, one's own being. The still, small voice inside is suffocated because the mind shouts.

The mind has to be dropped slowly slowly, so that we can hear the still small voice within. That is god's voice, and that's from where we receive messages. It is from that source that the Vedas are born, the Koran and the Bible.

Each person is capable of giving birth to the Vedas, but the mind has to go; that price has to be paid, and it is worth paying. The mind has nothing of any significance; it brings only misery. Yes, it gives you great hopes, but it never fulfils them. It keeps you always expectant : something is going to happen, going to happen, going... but it never happens. It is always arriving, but it never arrives, and the whole of the life is lost.

The mind is really a perfect salesman. It goes on selling you things which are useless. You know that they are useless and many times you have decided 'Enough is enough, now I am not going to be deceived' — but again, when the opportunity arises, the mind deceives you. Many times you have decided not to be angry again, not to be greedy again, not to be this, not to be that — but when the opportunity arises, the mind again possesses you, drives you into the old rotten ways in which you have only suffered. But it is really clever at selling things. It says 'This time it is totally different. This is not the same thing, and this time something is going to happen — don't miss it.' This has happened a thousand and one times.

The most strange thing about man is that he seems to be almost incapable of learning from experience. If one learns from experience, then one thing is bound to happen sooner or later — and it will be sooner if one learns — that one will start dis-identifying oneself from the mind. One will not say 'My mind is me.' One will say 'This is the mind — I am separate.' One will create a distance between the noisy mind and oneself, one will use the mind but will not be used by the mind. Then one has come to the still small voice within, to the centre of the cyclone. To know it is to know all that is worth knowing. And that's what sannyas is all about — helping you to drop the mind so that you can attain to your being.

How long will you be here?

Shantideva: Until I arrive.

Good!

A bubble of laughter.
Hope is from the States.

This is your name : Ma Nirvan Hope. Nirvan means enlightenment, the state of ultimate realisation, the experience of one's innermost core, the actualisation of all the potential that one has carried all along, the seed turning into the flower. Hope is Anglo-Saxon; it has three meanings. One, the ordinary that is known — hope; the second, which is far more important — expectancy; and the third, which is even more important and which is not known, is cheerfulness.

Remember the third meaning : be cheerful because you are carrying the seed of ultimate flowering in you. Be cheerful because the kingdom of god is yours. Be cheerful because we are not accidental, because we are not meaningless, because we are the very crown of existence, we are the very salt of the earth.

Man is god's hope. Fulfil it! It can be fulfilled, and it can be fulfilled *very* easily. It is not difficult to attain to your ultimate nature — how can it be difficult to attain to your nature? To attain to one's nature must be a natural phenomenon. It must be just as fire is hot : no effort is made on the part of fire to remain hot, it is simply hot. Water goes downwards without any effort; it is its nature. Fire rises upwards without any effort.

So is the case with man : effort is not needed to become divine; we are already divine. All that is needed is to remove the hindrances, just the rocks that are blocking the path. My work here is nothing but removing the blocks so that you can be what you already are.

How long will you be here, Hope?

Nirvan Hope : I'll be here until the eleventh of March.

Have you done any groups?

Nirvan Hope : Not yet.

Would you like to do a few?

Nirvan Hope: Yes, I would.

The first group you can do is Intensive Enlightenment.

Nirvan Hope: Is that a residential group?

It is.

Nirvan Hope: I have a five-year-old son.

Five years old?

Nirvan Hope: And I don't know who would take care of him.

Find somebody.

Nirvan Hope: Okay.

Five years old is old enough. Modern children of five years old are far more mature...

Nirvan Hope: Yes.

... than they used to be in the past. And he will enjoy the freedom also!

Just let him be!

Susanne is from Germany.

This is your name : Ma Anand Susanne. Anand means bliss. Susanne is Hebrew; it means a lily. Your full name will mean: a blissful lily, a blissful flower, a blissful flowering, a flower of bliss.

Man lives in misery. That is his own doing; he is not meant to be miserable, he has earned it himself. It is not god's work, it is man's own inventiveness. God has meant man to be blissful, just as trees are blissful and birds are blissful and stars are blissful; but man has lost the right track. Rather than being more and more natural, spontaneous, he has become more and more artificial, arbitrary. And the more arbitrary you are, the more miserable you will be.

The greatest arbitrariness is the invention of the ego; it is the greatest lie there is. We are not separate from existence, but we believe that we are separate, and in that very belief the doors of hell are opened. We enter into hell-fire the moment we think we are separate.

Only a single moment is needed to enter into heaven too — just the realisation that 'I am not separate, I am not, I am one with existence' and bliss starts showering and one starts blooming. Then life has a totally different flavour: it has the flavour of divineness. Then god is not to be searched for anywhere else; one knows it in one's own heart — he is there! One feels him in one's breath, in one's heartbeat, in one's pulsating blood.

Then god *is*, without any proof. To be blissful is enough proof, to be blissful is the only proof. Then who cares about proofs? — bliss is enough. Hence in the East we have called god 'satchitanand'. Sat means truth, chit means consciousness, anand means bliss — three faces of god: one is truth, another is consciousness, and the third is bliss, the ultimate is the bliss.

So from this moment start dropping the patterns of misery, strategies of creating misery, techniques of creating misery — and the fundamental thing to drop is the ego.

Sannyas is a process of committing ego-suicide. And the day you succeed in killing your ego, you succeed in releasing your soul. You are liberated!

Gunther is from — guess where? — Germany!

I will have to change your name — your old name is dangerous. Gunther is Teutonic; it means war. German and war — it will be too dangerous! (much laughter).

This will be your new name: Swami Ananddeva. Anand means bliss, deva means god — god of bliss. That is our true nature, that is what we are to become. In the seed we already *are* that, hence the great Upanishadic saying 'Tat-tvam-asi':

that art thou. In the seed you are already that, but only in the seed. The potential is there; it can be actualised, but it can be missed also. If you miss it you will have to come back again and again; if you miss it you cannot be allowed to leave this earth. This earth is really a school, a mystery school: people who don't learn their lessons, people who don't do their homework, are sent back again and again unless they learn. The moment they learn, they disappear from the earth-plane, they rise to a higher plane, to a different world, to a different dimension.

Man is a student. It is good to learn all that life makes available, but one has to remember that sooner or later one has to go beyond it; and one has to prepare for that going. One has to remember continuously 'Whatsoever I am is not my total self; it is only a part of me. I have to seek and search for my total being.' Because only in knowing the total is freedom possible. Only in knowing oneself in utter nudity is one liberated.

To know oneself in totality is to be blissful. Not to know one's self, to remain ignorant of oneself, is to be in misery, is to be in darkness. Knowing and bliss are two aspects of the same coin, just as ignorance and suffering are two aspects of the same coin.

Your name is good: Swami Deepak Bharti.
What do you do at Rajkot?

Deepak: I am in service.

That's good. Have you started meditating?

Deepak: I am doing Nadabrahma.

Do you feel good? Then continue Nadabrahma and do it regularly. Even if you have to give up a meal, do it...

Deepak: I do so.

... but do not give up meditation. The more regular you are, the greater depth you will attain. And meditation is such a delicate thing that it takes months to grow but just a day or two to wither away. A delicate thing needs much regularity, continuity. Meditation is the highest; everything else is secondary. You will not miss much by missing a day's sleep. One can do without sleeping for five to seven days. It is okay if you miss a meal; man can survive without food for three months. You can go without drinking water for a day; you will not die.

But usually, people give much more importance to such petty things and think that for a day or two they can do without the things that are really significant. But let it be remembered that nothing will go wrong if you do not fulfil the petty things of your routine. You will not gain anything by doing them, neither will you be a loser by not doing them. But meditation is of the highest, and through it god is attained. If you do not meditate, you will not know what you were to gain and what you have missed; you will really not know what you have lost.

The greatest misfortune that can befall people is that they never come to know what they have missed. Apart from missing, people never come to know what they were to gain, they never become aware of it.

So always devote energy to meditation. I lay down no other conditions for my sannyasin; only meditation is enough. If meditation is attained everything is attained.

A weeks-old sannyasin, Hannah, is returning to Holland.

Something to say to me?

Prem Hannah: Yes.

Mm mm.

Prem Hannah: Before I came to Pune I had a very

difficult time and I was even thinking of committing suicide. Then suddenly I decided to come to you, to Pune. I feel very happy now, but I have to go back to my children; the fear is coming back.

Mm mm. And what actually creates the idea of suicide in you? Is there something particular, in particular?

Prem Hannah : Yes, I lost myself totally. I was very afraid of people and of situations which were difficult. To protect myself I closed myself.

Mm mm. And how many children do you have?

Prem Hannah : Two children.

And your husband? Are you living with him or not?

Prem Hannah : Yes, I am living with him.

And how is the relationship with your husband?

Prem Hannah : It was difficult but there were a few moments last month that were very close. I don't know what is going to happen.

Because the idea of suicide comes only if love is missing, otherwise it never comes. If love is there, then the idea simply never arises in one's mind. It is the absence of love that gives you the idea 'Why go on living? For what?' — because without love, life has no meaning, no significance. It is a drag, so why drag on? It is love that gives a dance to your feet and a song to your heart.

So suicide is never the problem in itself; it is a symptom. The problem is love. But it almost always happens that we become too absorbed in, obsessed with, the symptom. Don't be bothered about suicide, it is simply indicative that you are not loving as much as you should. And unless *you* love, you will not receive love. It is only by giving love that we get; there is no other way — the more we give, the more we get.

So pour your love into your husband, into your children, into friends; pour your love into trees, animals, birds, stones. Wherever you are, pour your love! Hug the tree; close your eyes and feel your love for the tree. Lie down on the rock; close your eyes and feel your love for the rock, shower the rock with your love.

Within two to three months you will be surprised that the whole idea of suicide has simply evaporated. It can be simply dropped, mm? But you are not to pay much attention to it directly; simply start moving into the direction of love, and it will disappear.

It is like darkness : if you fight with darkness you cannot destroy it. But just bring in a small candle, light the candle, and there is no darkness. Love functions like light; and if love is there, there is no death. What to say about suicide? — not even death exists for the lover. Love knows no death. Love is the only eternal element in existence. Everything else comes and goes : love remains. And for a woman it is more so; the woman lives on love, it is her nourishment.

I can feel, I can see, what is missing. Just go back and pour your love, even into strangers. Don't be too concerned towards whom you are being loving; just be loving, that is the point. Within two, three months, your whole energy will be transformed. I will see : it will be transformed.

When will you be coming back?

Prem Hannah : As soon as possible.

Come back soon!
Keep it (a box) with you...

Prem Hannah : Thank you.

... and whenever you need me and the idea of suicide

comes, put it on your heart : it will immediately disappear! (much laughter). Good, Hannah.

English — very much so — Devesh is back. He tends to go to and fro between England and Pune, dropping in occasionally on his country estate in France. It seems sannyas friends had been telling him he had to commit himself one way or the other, to Pune or the West. He has been at himself too for not being total in anything, and when he wrote about that to Osho, he wondered if he oughtn't drop sannyas.

The reply was to talk to Teertha (the Encounter group leader who does individual counselling too) and then to drop sannyas if he felt to.

Well, he hasn't yet, and Osho's voice seems particularly affectionate as he immediately tells Devesh to face Shiva with his arms towards him, to close his eyes and go with the flow. His arms are stuck out somewhat stiffly and don't budge. His forehead wrinkles concentratedly and there is a sense of effort, of holding, about him; but a sense too that something is happening anyway. Osho seems happy and pronounces everything perfectly good.

I have just one thing to say to you. It is time to learn one thing : drop the idea of being perfect. That is the sole cause of your misery. Nobody can be perfect, because the moment you are perfect you cannot be here. Perfection cannot exist on earth; on earth only imperfection can exist. Once the idea of being perfect settles in their hearts, it drives people crazy. They start asking for the impossible in everything, and because it cannot happen they are miserable. Their expectations are very high and they cannot be fulfilled; and when they are not fulfilled they think that life is slipping by, through their fingers. They become depressed; each day more depression will be coming, because each day more life will be disappearing.

To be a perfectionist is to be on the verge of neurosis. All perfectionists are neurotic, more or less; the difference is only of degrees.

That's what you have been trying : in everything you have to be perfect, you have to be total. You cannot allow any errors, you cannot allow any mistakes; and because you cannot allow mistakes and errors in yourself, you cannot allow them in others. And that becomes a barrier in love. You cannot love a person because your expectations are so much that nobody can fulfil them.

And forty years is time that you have wasted.

Now learn one thing : take life easily. Take it easy, with all its limitations, with all its imperfections. Enjoy it, and then the paradox happens : when one starts enjoying life with all its imperfections, it is almost perfect, but I say *almost*! (laughter). It is ninety-nine point nine percent perfect. That point one percent remains imperfect — that's the only way to exist here. But it happens only when you allow life as it is and you don't demand too much. There is simply no need to demand : you accept whatsoever happens.

If you look for a perfect woman you will never find one. If you look for a perfect religion you will never find it. If you look for anything perfect you will be simply miserable, that's all; you will find misery, more and more misery.

In the East in the old days there was a superstition that kings would not make their palaces perfect. They would keep one part of the palace imperfect to deceive god, mm? Because the palace was not yet perfect : So let it be, it can be allowed to exist. Mm? it is still in the process of being made. Once the palace was perfect it could collapse — that was the superstition, but it has a grain of truth in it : once anything is perfect, it collapses.

That's why Buddhas disappear from the world. Once a person becomes a Buddha, then this is the last time he is here; he will not be here again. This body just has to fulfil its momentum.

Relax, take things easily. God is not so hard. He is not such a hard taskmaster as you think. God is really compassion, love; existence is very compassionate.

That's why it allows all kinds of limitations, imperfections, and still it goes on showering all kinds of gifts.

Start enjoying. You have been trying to improve upon yourself too much. You have done forty-eight groups! (laughter). That must be the record.

Devesh makes noises of polite protest, his fingers scratching at the floor for nothing in particular.

Now it is enough! Yes, a few — fifteen, eighteen — is enough. Forty-eight is too much! Now forget all about groups and forget all about growth and growing — start living and enjoying.

That's what I wanted to say to you!

The gentleman in Devesh is abandoned; he can't allow Osho to escape so lightly. Still looking to the floor and flushed pink he murmurs:

Devesh : I haven't done forty-eight groups.

You *have* done forty-eight — you can't count tonight! (much laughter). I keep records!

Devesh : A fatal thirteen.

Mm? Thirteen?

Devesh : Yes!

You count again! (a pause). Maybe I am counting all the groups of all your lives! (much much laughter)

Devesh laughs at this totally incorrigible master!

11

Sannyasins of just a few weeks, Nico and Liesbeth bring forward their three-year-old daughter, Lotte; she's going to take sannyas too. Osho tells her to close her eyes — and to give her her due, she does try awfully hard, drawing her knees up and covering her eyes with her two small fists. Moments later there is a burst of laughter and I open my eyes to watch her peeking from between her hands at Osho. He looks up from his writing and chuckles, then calls her close to lasso her with a mala. Her name is good, he tells her parents; he has just added 'anand' to it.

Osho : Anand means bliss. Lotte is Teutonic; it means human being — a blissful human being.

Man is not man just because of his physical shape and form. It has to be earned; one has to *become* human. Man is born only as a potentiality to be man; it is not already the fact, it is still to happen. So all men are not human beings yet, only very few, very rarely. And to be human is far more difficult than to be a saint. To be a saint is really the least difficult thing in the world, because it is a choice. One can be a sinner — that is not difficult; or one can be a saint — that too is not difficult. The sinner has chosen the dark side of life, and the saint has chosen the light side of life, but both have chosen halves.

To be human means to be both together — light and darkness, summer and winter, love and hate, pain and pleasure. To be a man means to be a harmony between this polarity, this extreme tension between the opposites, and still to be non-tense. To be in this tension and still to be non-tense, that is the meaning of being a human being

Sinners certainly fall short, and saints too fall short. Both are inhuman; both are half, lopsided. To be human means to be total.

And that's my effort here : through sannyas, making you capable of being the polar opposites together, without any discord. And when one can be happy and unhappy too, and when one can allow both to happen, one is free, one is no more tethered, not in any bondage. It is difficult to allow yourself to be sad; but unless you allow yourself to be sad sometimes, your happiness will never have depth, it will be shallow. It is difficult to allow yourself to cry and weep; but if you don't allow that, your laughter will be false, pseudo.

A man can be a man only when tears and laughter are both allowed, given total freedom, and one is ready to move to any extreme. One does not become attached to any extreme, one remains available to the polar opposite. This availability, this vulnerability, is what I mean by being a human being.

So her name is beautiful!

Rosemarie from Germany now.

This will be your new name : Ma Prem Aloka. Prem means love, aloka means light — light that arises out of love. Love makes a person luminous; without love, one is darkness and nothing else. With love, a flame starts arising in the heart; with love, you are no more unlit. And to have the flame of love is the beginning of the death of the ego and the birth of the divine.

Love is the bridge between that which we are and that which we ought to be. Man is a seed, and much has to happen before one can feel fulfilled. Just remaining the way one is born is not going to give fulfilment. Something tremendously important is waiting to happen. Unless we allow it to happen, it is not going to happen. It cannot happen against us, it cannot happen in spite of us; it can only happen through us, it can happen only through our co-operation. We are responsible, whatsoever we are. If there is hell, we are responsible for it, and nobody else is responsible.

This responsibility is great, but it opens doors. If we are responsible for hell, then we are responsible for heaven too. So on the one hand the responsibility may look like a great burden, but on the other hand it is our only hope.

Man *has* to become love, because then and only then can he become light. And when one is light, one can see that which is, one can see the truth of existence. That seeing is liberation.

This is your name : Swami Anand Michael. Anand means bliss. Michael is Hebrew, it means one who is like god. In fact everybody is like god. The whole existence only reflects god, the whole existence functions as a mirror. God is the green of the trees, the red of the trees, the gold of the trees. God is in the stars, god is in the rocks. These are different reflections of the same truth — universal reflections, multidimensional reflections, but of a single entity.

It is as if you are looking in many mirrors, as if you are standing in a room with many mirrors : you are everywhere. Of course each mirror will reflect you in a little different way. The angle will be different, the glass may be different, certain mirrors may distort you a little bit, but still, even in those distortions, it is the same reality reflected.

Michael is a beautiful word, so I will keep it. Become more and more blissful by realising the fact that you are like god.

Down the ages, the priests have condemned man, they have poisoned the very source of our being. They have created guilt — that is their strategy to dominate. The guilty person is always ready to fall into anybody's trap. He is so shaky, so afraid, so self-condemnatory, that he is ready to bow down to anybody; he is just searching for and seeking somebody to dominate him. He knows that he is unworthy, so if he follows himself he is bound to go wrong; he has to follow somebody else.

That is the strategy of the priest : create guilt and people will follow you. But the moment a person starts feeling guilty he starts becoming sick, he is no more healthy. His energy has started shrinking, he is no more expanding. He is no more alive, he has started dying.

A man can live totally only when he accepts himself joyously, welcomes himself, knows his glory, splendour, feels himself as divine, as part of god, like god. And remember, these experiences, these feelings, are not egoistic at all. They become egoistic only if you think *you* are like god and nobody else is; then they are egoistic. Then you are free from the trap of the priest, but you are trapped by your own mind, which is a far more subtle bondage. But if you see that the same is reflected everywhere, you are as respectful to a tree as you are to yourself, then there is no question of any ego arising. You can declare 'I am god' and that declaration will not create any kind of bondage for you; it will be a liberation.

Pragan says in his soft and not unpleasant drawl that he's not sure when he'll be back (he works with sannyasin drug-addict-therapist Veeresh, in Holland).

> *Pragan :* I'm going to be involved in the Rajneesh Therapy Institute in the Hague. Whenever that, whenever I feel that's...

Find time — whenever it is possible. Mm? And help my people there.

You have something to say?

> *Pragan :* I want to stay, and at the same time I'm

scared of it. I'm not sure what I really want to do. I feel like I want to stay, but I know when I go back the whole thing starts all over again.

You have some responsibilities there?

Pragan: Not really. I have a commitment for six months as a consultant to two programmes, and then it's...

So it is good: go and finish things and all commitments and say goodbye to people and come. It is always good to say good-bye to people, mm? So in these six months, finish things. Don't make any more commitments. Now I am your commitment!

Upgeya is going back to the West too. He wants to return soon, but he wants his two children to come back with him.

Bring them!

Upgeya: My wife is not a sannyasin, she probably doesn't want to become a sannyasin.

But would she like to come? There is no need to make her a sannyasin — let her come first (much laughter)!

Upgeya: The problem is to make her come.

I will manage — you just try! With women I have my own ways (much laughter)!

Upgeya: There was something else. I had many crises of depression.

Where? When?

Upgeya: When I was in Italy I had a lot of depressive crisis.

Mm mm.

Won't You Join the Dance?

Upgeya : And I have a lot of fear of leaving.

Mm mm. This time it will not be the same. Something has changed in you. The fear comes because of the past, but I can see — the future is going to be totally different; it will not be a repetition of the past, unless you work hard to repeat it (laughter). Basically the grip of the past is already so loose on you that you can slip out of it easily.

Whenever you start feeling any depression coming, start enjoying it immediately.

Upgeya : I identify with the depression.

Don't have any fear about that. Enjoy it, identify with it; there is nothing to be worried about. Be *really* depressed — that's what I mean when I say enjoy it. Sing songs of depression (much laughter), dance very depressive dances (more laughter) — do whatsoever you can do for the depression. Be very artful about it, let it be a welcome guest, and immediately you will see its energy is changing. If you start enjoying depression, it is no more depression : you have transformed it, you have transcended it.

Sadness is sadness only if you don't enjoy it. It looks like a paradox — how to enjoy sadness? — but it is not; it can be easily enjoyed. And what is the point of missing it? When it is already there, enjoy it; at least enjoy it!

Come back soon! Keep it (a box) with you, and whenever you need me, just put it on your heart. Help my people in Italy.

Just tell your wife from me that she need not be so afraid of sannyas; she can come without being a sannyasin. And unless she asks thrice, I will not give her sannyas (laughter)! I have started working on her — you just go!

Harishado is also Westward-bound. He has just completed the Encounter group (it's here tonight), and says that much happened in it.

Harishado: I found out that I put my whole energy against changing.

Mm mm.

Harishado: Now I don't know. I have plans for the future and now I'm very unsure what I...

This is what everybody does: everybody puts great energy against change. That's the way of the mind, that's how the mechanism of the mind functions.

The mind is very orthodox; it clings to the known, to the familiar, it is very conventional. The mind is never revolutionary, cannot be. Even the Communist mind is as anti-revolutionary as the Catholic; there is no difference between the two. The mind as such is anti-revolutionary. It is against change, because not to change is safer, secure. You know where you are, you can be certain; even if you are miserable, you are certain about your misery. The mind is very much afraid of uncertainty, because in uncertainty it starts collapsing; it needs very certain props. Even though the uncertain is more blissful, the mind will choose the certain — even though it is miserable. A miserable certainty is far more important for the mind than an uncertain bliss.

So this is how everybody is functioning, this is the way of the mind. It does not want to change, it does not want any change anywhere, so that it can always move on certain and solid ground, so that it always knows the answers, so that its knowledge is worth something, so that its efficiency can function.

The moment you go beyond the known, you are no more efficient, your answers are no more valid, your knowledge is ignorance. You are a child again — and that goes against the ego.

But if you start exploring a little bit ... It will be with hesitation and fear in the beginning. It is natural, this fear and hesitation, but if you start exploring just a little bit — just go a few steps into the unknown and come back to the home base, but go on trying exploring — one day you will be gone forever. You will never come back to the home base — because once you start tasting the freedom of the unknown, the freedom of the uncertain, the innocence, the spontaneity that is bound to happen with the unknown and can only happen with the unknown, once the thrill has taken over, once you are possessed by the adventure, you will never come back.

But it takes a few explorations. Many times you will come back home, many times you may become too afraid. So there is nothing to be worried about; this is natural. Don't ask the impossible — this is simply the way of the mind. Just give a few experiences of the unknown to your being, then the being will never listen to the mind.

The being is always a revolutionary. We have only to give it a few tastes, just a few dewdrops — and once the taste is on your tongue, then the mind cannot have any sway over you.

12

*B*ruce has become Deva Anupam.

Osho : Deva means divine, anupam means uniqueness. It is a paradox — but existence itself is a paradox — that each individual is both universal and unique. It is very illogical, because if we are all one, then how can we all be unique? — we will be similar. But that is not the case. We are all one and yet each individual is unique. It is a paradox, it is illogical, but this is how it is. And existence has no obligation to follow our logic, it need not bend to our logical patterns. If anything has to change, it is our logic that has to change.

That's what happened in modern physics when for the first time they discovered electrons. A great problem arose, the greatest that science has ever faced : what to call it? — because it was behaving very illogically. It was behaving as a wave and also as a particle, simultaneously, which is absolutely absurd. It is not logically possible — either something is a particle or it is a wave; one thing cannot be both together and simultaneously. One thing may be both at different times, that's possible, but behaving in both ways at exactly the same moment destroys our whole geometry, mathematics, logic. But the physicists had to concede the electron. They had to shrug their shoulders but they had to accept the reality : it was so. And for the first time science came across a real paradox.

Mysticism has always faced it. It started accepting it very early in the growth of human consciousness. For at least five thousand years, man has accepted paradox in the world of mysticism. That's why we call it mysticism — because it is illogical. But for the first time science is becoming mystical. Anything becomes mystical whenever a paradox arises for which we cannot manage any logical explanation and which we have to accept as it is.

This is one of the greatest paradoxes, that each individual is universal, and yet individual. Each wave is part of the same ocean, yet each wave is unique; no other wave is like it, although all waves belong to the same ocean.

Richard is from Austria.

This is your name : Swami Prem Richard. Prem means love. Richard is Teutonic, it means rule or powerful ruler. Your full name will mean : love, the rule, the discipline. Love, if it becomes the discipline of your life, is the greatest transforming force. If it rules your life, then it becomes a totally different life. Love brings rebellion, revolution. Love brings insight into what reality is. Love brings light, clarity, things start becoming more and more transparent. Love bridges you with people and with existence; you are no more alone, all loneliness disappears.

The world is not strange, it is your home — and one can relax only if existence becomes one's home. If we remain outsiders we cannot relax. Outsiders are bound to remain tense, because they are in an alien country, in a foreign land.

Modern man is feeling it very deeply, that he is an outsider, and the reason is that love has disappeared from the world. Nothing else has changed, everything else is the same — the same trees and the same moon and the same sun and the same people. Only one thing has disappeared : love is no more there. Logic has taken possession of man; logic rules man, logic has become his discipline. That's why man is feeling so alien, uprooted, a stranger, an outsider. And when you live in the world as if you are an outsider, your whole life will be of great anxiety, tension, fear, paranoia.

It is bound to be so, unless love becomes your rule, your very life. Then suddenly a transformation, a metamorphosis, happens. Everything is the same and yet it is no more the same; you are bridged. It is your home. You have new eyes to see life and existence.

To be initiated into sannyas is to be initiated into love. Sannyas is a step out of logic, into love.

Helche weeps quiet tears to be near him.

This will be your new name : Ma Prem Divo. Prem mean love, divo means a small lamp — a small lamp of love. But that is enough to make one's whole life full of light! And the moment there is light we are no more groping, we are on solid ground. We know who we are, we know from where we have come, we know to where we are going, and suddenly life starts having significance and meaning.

Without love, man lives in darkness. He stumbles, gropes, falls, goes astray and is continuously trembling in fear, because he is not aware of who he is, of why he is. Even the most fundamental question 'Who am I?' remains unanswered. And if that fundamental question remains unanswered, everything else also remains unanswered. One is always indecisive, continuously thinking whether to do this or to do that. And whatsoever you do, you will repent, because whatsoever you choose out of darkness is going to be wrong; no choice can be right.

This is the miracle of light : you need not choose, you simply see where the way is. Without any choice you move in the direction of the right, because the light is there. And nothing else can bring the light except love.

Let your life revolve around the centre of love. Focus on it, pour more and more energy into it, and one day suddenly, the flame is lit. That is the moment of great rejoicing.

Pilar, Spanish wife of sannyasin Avigan, took three months to take the leap — but better late than never!

This is your name : Ma Prem Pilar. Prem means love. Pilar is Latin; it means to drift, just like driftwood, with no idea of any direction, like a cloud drifts without any will of its own, just wherever the winds take it. It is a state of let-go, utter let-go.

And that is one of the greatest secrets, if one can relax totally with existence and can say 'Let *thy* will be done. I have no more desires of my own, so now whatsoever happens is good; now wherever I reach that is the goal.' In this surrender, in this let-go, no frustration can ever happen, because frustration is a by-product of expectation. If you don't expect anything, nothing can frustrate you; then life has a calmness and a coolness in it.

Love is the art of let-go. Drift in love, drift in trust. Learn the secret of surrendering more and more to existence. If you can call this existence 'god', good — it becomes more personal, more intimate, a dialogue becomes possible. If you cannot call it 'god', no need to be worried about it. One can attain to truth without believing in any god. God is only a device — a device to create a communion between you and the whole, a device to create a dialogue — but it is not absolutely necessary. It is just an arbitrary device to help. It can be dropped : Buddha dropped it and yet attained, and many others have not used it and yet have reached.

The secret is not belief in god; the secret is in let-go. What matters is surrender. To *whom* you surrender — to god or to existence — doesn't matter. Surrender matters, surrendering matters.

Lisa is from Switzerland; she is a nurse.

This is your name : Ma Shanti Lisa. Shanti means silence,

peace, serenity. Lisa is Hebrew, it means divine. Divine peace — that will be the full meaning of your name.

Man is a tension, and only if man enters into the divine does he become capable of going beyond tensions. These tensions that human beings experience in life are not accidental; they are very much a part of human existence, part and parcel of it. Because man is half animal and half divine, hence the conflict, the tension. Half of man is being pulled backwards, and half wants to go ahead; it is a kind of tug-of-war. Half of man is pulled downwards by gravitation, and the other half wants to have wings and fly into the sky.

This is natural to the human existence. So by remaining human, nobody can go beyond tensions; at the most they can be managed in a little better way, or can be a little less. Those who can manage them in a better way are thought to be normal, sane people; those who cannot manage them are thought to be neurotic, mad. But the difference between the sane and the insane is only of degrees; there is no qualitative difference.

The real difference that makes the difference happens only when one transcends humanity. And that is the whole science of religion : how to go beyond this continuous conflict, how to transcend this polarity, how not to be identified with this or that, how to be neither this nor that, how to be just a witness.

In that very witnessing is transcendence, and in that witnessing, peace, silence, serenity, showers. One for the first time blooms.

(to Lanny) This is your new name : Swami Deva Agneya. Deva means divine, agneya means fire — divine fire. God *is* fire, and only those who are ready to be burned totally, who are ready to be consumed by the fire of god, only they can know him. Hence very few try.

Millions talk about god; talking about god is safe. Millions pay lip-service also; they go to the churches and the temples and the mosques, but it is all formal, a kind of social etiquette — something that helps to lubricate relationships with people, but nothing intense, nothing fiery, not really a commitment. They are not involved; their relationship with existence is superficial, lukewarm.

Sannyas means a commitment, getting involved — getting involved to the point of being consumed, getting involved to the point where it is a question of life and death. Only then, when it is a question of life and death, when all is at stake, does one reach to the maximum energy of one's being. At that moment, at that moment of one hundred degrees when one is at the optimum, is the transformation, the transmutation. The old simply disappears in the fire and the new is born : the resurrection. Then you have the body of a Buddha or the body of a Christ.

Jesus is gone in the fire : when Jesus is gone in the fire, Christ is born. Jesus goes into the fire and Christ comes out of it. The orange colour simply symbolises fire.

13

Mario, he's from Italy.

Osho : This is your name : Swami Anand Mario. Anand means bliss; mario can have two meanings, because it can either be derived from Latin or from Hebrew. In Latin it means god of Mars or god of war; in Hebrew it means rebellion. Choose the Hebrew meaning — god of war is ugly. If one wants to be a god, one should be a god of peace.

In fact it is a contradiction in terms; god cannot be a god of war. War belongs to the devil, peace belongs to god. War is evil, peace is the most virtuous thing in life. War is evil, peace is divine. So my choice is for the Hebrew meaning : be a blissful rebellion.

Rebellion can also be not out of bliss but out of misery. Then it is turned into something political. The moment a rebellion is out of misery, it is more a reaction than a rebellion : you act out of anger, you are aggressive, you are in a rage, you are destructive. And the true rebellion is creative, not destructive. The true rebellion is not a reaction against something but an effort to produce something, to create something, to beautify life a. little more.

Reaction is destructive but basically impotent. It destroys and then it knows nothing about what to do. That's why all political revolutions have failed. They destroyed much, they were very capable of destruction, because rage has that capacity. But once the revolution is finished, rage is gone, the leaders are at a loss : what to do now? Once the revolutionaries are in power they are simply at an utter loss — and not knowing what to do, they start repeating the same as that which they have rebelled against. That's how Joseph Stalin became the greatest czar.

Rebellion, to be true rebellion, has to be out of bliss. Then it is not against something but *for* something. Then it has a concept of how things should be, it has a vision; and because it is out of bliss, it creates bliss in the world.

Bliss is creative energy : it sings, it dances, it creates.

He is speaking to Eleanor, she is from Canada.

This is your name : Ma Deva Eleanor. Deva means divine. Eleanor is Greek, it means light. The full name will mean divine light.

We may find ourselves in darkness, but we are not darkness. In fact, to find oneself in darkness is proof enough that one is not darkness; to be aware of darkness means that we are separate from it. To be aware of anything means we are separate from it. Whatsoever we are aware of becomes an object and we are a witness to it.

It happens to every meditator that when he starts moving inwards he comes across a dark continent where everything is dark, utter darkness, darkness so deep and so dense that one has never felt it. The Christian mystics have called it the dark night of the soul. One can be very much frightened of it. One can rush back into the outer; there is some light on the outside. That's why very few people ever try to go in — and those who try, many of them sooner or later, escape. It seems to be dangerous to enter deeper into that darkness.

One of the English philosophers, David Hume, reading again and again in mystic treatises 'Go within and there is great light' tried it once. He was a sceptical mind, one of the greatest sceptics of human history. He tried closing his eyes for a few minutes, to see what these mystics were talking about. He could not find any light, it was all darkness. So he wrote in his diary 'It is all nonsense. I have tried, but there is only darkness inside and no light. All this talk about divine light is sheer nonsense.' But he missed the whole point. He could not understand the message of the mystics. It is so simple that one is surprised how such a great mind like David Hume could not see it; it is so obvious.

One thing is certain : whomsoever is looking into darkness is not darkness. The mystics were saying that *you* are light, not that you will find light. It needs a transfer of attention from the object to the subject, it needs a change of gestalt.

Once you start looking — not at what you are surrounded with, but at who you are — the light bursts forth. You will never experience light as an object, it will be felt as your inner subjectivity.

Remember it, because sannyas is nothing but going into meditation, going inwards, going in search of one's self, one's authentic self.

(to Bernd) This is your name : Swami Anand Bernd. Anand means bliss. Bernd is Teutonic, it is from bernard; it means brave, courageous — blissful courage. That's what is needed in the search for truth. Courage is needed — and not only courage, but a blissful courage is needed. Courage is a must. Religion is not for cowards, although cowards are the first to go to the churches and to the temples and to the mosques. They are the first to become religious, but their religion remains a formality. It never goes deep in them — it cannot; they never risk anything for it.

It is a social affair, it is nothing spiritual for them. It is a good sociality; just as they go to the Rotary Club and the Lions Club, they go to the church. It helps in their worldly affairs. If people know that they are church-goers it creates prestige, respectability — and you can exploit prestige and respectability. It is a good asset, economically, financially, socially, politically; you can exploit it. And that's what people are doing in the name of religion.

Only very few are really religious, because to be really religious means to be committed, involved — so much so that it becomes a question of life and death, so much so that truth is more important than life itself. If it is needed, one is ready to sacrifice one's life for it — not that it *is* needed, not that truth requires your life to be sacrificed. God is not a murderer; it is not that god expects you to kill yourself, to commit suicide, no : but unless you are ready to do even that, your life will remain lukewarm. It will not be really hot —and unless you are hot, one hundred degrees hot, you can't evaporate, you can't start moving upwards, you cannot whisper with the clouds, you cannot enter into the unknown, you can't have wings. Courage gives you wings.

But courage can be sad, courage can be out of despair, courage can be out of anger, courage can be nothing but a repression of fear. Then again you miss.

It has to be very very blissful. When it is blissful it has a spontaneity to it. When it is blissful nothing is repressed, because in repression bliss is impossible. When it is blissful there is no fear hiding behind it. When it is blissful it is not a desperate effort; it is an adventure. Lovingly, playfully, one goes into it. When it is blissful you are not a masochist just finding ways and excuses to torture yourself — because courage can be that too. It can be pathological : one can simply move into dangerous situations because one wants to torture oneself. It can be a strategy for self-torture; then you miss the point.

So I make it an absolute condition that courage can help only if it is rooted in bliss. Then it is not masochistic, it is not an effort to overcompensate for one's fears and paranoia. It is not just a suicidal attempt to go into danger, and it is not sad — because nobody can contact the divine with sadness in the heart. The divine can be contacted only when the heart is singing, is a singing, when the heart is in a state of dance, ecstasy.

Ecstatic courage : that is the most fundamental thing in the search for truth, in the search for ultimate liberation.

Judith is a psychologist from the States. He names her Deva Vipassana.

Deva means divine, vipassana means insight. Vipassana is Buddha's word for insight, for meditation, for going in, for turning in. Passana means to see, vipassana means to see in.

Man lives almost on the outside. The whole of life is lived on the outside, as if one has been given a palace but is not aware of it and lives only in the porch and thinks 'This is all.' Hence the misery : we cannot be contented with only the outside, because the outside has nothing compared to the inner. The real treasure is inside.

If we live on the outside we remain beggars, because we remain unaware of the treasure that we have, that we are. Once we turn in, life goes through a metamorphosis. Suddenly you are no more the same person, because now you are aware of things that you have, of which you were never aware. You have such an infinity within, such an unbounded sky of freedom, such an inexhaustible source of joy, such an eternity — how can you remain a beggar?

To move in is not against the outside. Once you have moved in, even your outside starts having new colours, because *you* have changed. So when you look outside, your eyes are different : the same trees look greener, the same flower looks rosier and the same stars are no more the same. The whole existence becomes luminous with the unknown, because you have touched it inside yourself. You meet the same people, but they are no more the same because now you know that they also have the same treasure; they are souls. First they used to be just bodies, first you used to see only their garments. Now you *see* them, now you can look into their eyes and now you can see that the same consciousness, the same bliss, the same truth, exists in them as it exists in you.

And it is not only so with people : it is so with animals, birds, trees; even rocks are no more dead. You can touch a rock and you can feel that it breathes, that it pulsates. You can touch the rock with love, and you can see and feel that it responds. You can touch it with anger and you can see that it shrinks back.

Once the inner is known, the outer is no more the same; a great insight has arisen. An insight into oneself is the first thing to happen, only then is insight about anything else possible.

Dipa is leaving for the States.

Something to say to me?

Prem Dipa : I feel I am just beginning to be here.

That's true!

Prem Dipa : I've been here two and a half months, but not until I told you I was going home did I begin to be here!

One has to wait for the right moment, and one never knows when it comes. It comes very unpredictably, it comes on its own; we cannot manage it. We cannot pull it, push it; we can only wait. But it has come, that's good. Now even if you are gone you will remain connected with me. The distance, the physical distance, will not matter.

This moment is the beginning of real sannyas. This is the communion, the first contact, the first penetration. Just continue to meditate and it will go on growing; it will not make any difference that you are far away, not at all. Sometimes it can even be helpful, because when you are far away and still you can feel close to me, you are far away and you can still feel here and whenever you close your eyes you are here, it can be a very deepening experience and very liberating — liberating because it will show that you need not depend on a particular space, on a particular situation; it can go on growing anywhere.

When will it be possible to come back?

> *Prem Dipa:* A couple of weeks ago I would say 'Never' but now I don't know.

Soon you will know!

> *Prem Dipa:* Thank you.

Keep it (a box) with you.

Her outstretched hands receive the gift.

> *Prem Dipa:* Oh!

Whenever you need me just put it on your heart. And help my people there!

> *Prem Dipa:* I feel there's a small leak in my heart.

I know!

Her first visit here, Prem Pathika asks to know more fully the meaning of her name.

Prem means love, pathika means a pilgrim — a pilgrim of love, a pilgrimage into love. And that is the ultimate journey; that's what takes you to the source and to the goal. It is only love that matters; everything else is immaterial. One can have all the money of the world and one will remain poor, because poverty is something inner and cannot be destroyed by the outer riches. One can have all the knowledge of the world and still one will be ignorant, because ignorance is within, and no knowledge from the outside can ever penetrate that darkness.

Some richness has to arise within you, some knowing has to happen within you. And the name of that richness, of that knowing, is love. We are carrying the potential but are afraid to express it. We are carrying all that is needed, but somehow the society has made it very frightened — so much so that relationship has almost collapsed in the world.

People don't know how to relate any more; people are really very much embarrassed in relationship, they feel very shaky. All that they do in relationship goes wrong, all that they do brings more and more misery. People have started moving away from other people. It seems far easier and safer to relate with a dog or a cat, to have a pet animal — less risky because the dog will not be too demanding, the dog will not be too binding, the dog will not be too possessive, the dog will not provoke your anxiety, your fear. The dog will not in any way become a mirror in which you will be reflected and in which you will have to see your own ugly face; it is far better.

And now things have become even worse : now in America they are selling pet rocks. Now, this is the last — you cannot go further downwards! In a beautiful box, just an ordinary rock that you can find by the side of the road anywhere — with instructions, because you will not even relate with the rock without instructions; everything has to be told.

A great how-to-ism prevails all over the earth : how to make love, how to do this, how to do that. So there are instructions with the rock, that the rock is very temperamental. Be very cautious! Don't shout at it — whisper! And they are selling like hotcakes (laughter)! Just an ordinary rock, and the price is ten dollars — one hundred rupees!

Now later on children are going to laugh : what happened

to man? They will never know what really happened : love disappeared. And there is a great need to love.

Now you can hold your rock to your heart and you can talk to it, and it will not talk back; that's the beauty of it. It will not interfere in your life. You can keep it in your pocket or in your box or you can leave it anywhere, and it will not shout at you and you will not need any divorce if some day you want to disconnect yourself from the rock.

Love has disappeared, and with love has disappeared god, with love has disappeared joy, and with love has disappeared *all* that is beautiful.

My teaching is only of love; that's my religion. And I call love the highest religion, the greatest truth.

Drop all fears, drop all inhibitions, drop all taboos, and love people — because this moment will never come back! If you love, this moment is saved; if you don't love, it is lost. Only those moments in which we have been in love are saved. By the time you are dying, you can count : only those moments are going with you which were shared in love, in which you loved and you were loved; only those moments are going with you. That has been your real life, all else was just utterly meaningless.

Your name has a message for you : become a pilgrim of love, because it is the pilgrimage to god!

Hasyo is a drama student from England. This is her first meeting this lifetime anyway! with her master.

Hasyo : Could I ask you about my name?

Prem means love, hasyo means laughter. Laughter has a tremendously spiritual value which has not been recognised down the ages. It is the natural built-in mechanism for relaxation. It relaxes you, and it relaxes you on all the levels of your being : body, mind, soul. When you are *really* laughing, the ego disappears, time stops, you are transported into another world; you are again a child, innocent.

Love, to be really liberating, has to have the quality of laughter in it. Once love becomes serious, it is a disease. Once love is no more fun, it is dangerous. Then it is like an octopus; it starts destroying the person you love. And when you destroy the person you love, naturally, out of sheer defence, the other starts destroying you. Lovers destroy each other, because they become too seriously involved in love, attached to it. They become possessive, they become jealous; then love is no more love. Love is love only when there is an under-current of laughter in it, when it is just a playfulness, when one is not serious about it.

If the quality of love and the quality of laughter join together, you have one of the most exhilarating experiences of life, the most relaxing experience of life. One relaxes into one's own being in those moments of love and laughter; one suddenly finds oneself centred, settled. That is enough if one can do it; then no other meditation is needed. In fact all other meditations only help you to attain love and laughter. If any meditation helps you to become unloving, beware of it. If any meditation helps you to become unlaughing, beware of it; it is something else, not meditation. It is some kind of pathology, it is some kind of neurosis.

So this is also a criterion to judge what meditation is worth going into. In fact, this should be the criterion of everything that you do : if it helps you grow into love and laughter it is good, it is virtuous; if it helps you to become more serious, less loving, then it is suicidal.

14

Mandira from the ashram bank and her two-weeks-old baby boy are first to be called before Osho tonight. The babe is very still and Buddha-silent. But when Osho malas him and makes to touch his tiny forehead, he moves away, and then again : a wary sannyasin this one! He receives the rather grand name of Prem Satish — god of love and truth.

Osho : These are the two most significant things in life. Truth has to be realised and love has to be lived. Truth happens in the innermost core; love is the flow outwards of the same energy. When you are full of truth, you can't help being loving; love starts overflowing, but the energy is that of truth. Without truth there is no love; all is just pretension.

With truth, *all* is love. Love follows truth. Truth happens in your inner space; and once it has happened, it starts relating with the outer space. That's love. Truth relating with existence is love, truth communing with existence is love. Truth is alone and *in* aloneness; love is a togetherness.

There are a few who try to be loving without truth; their love is false. There are others, a few, at the other extreme, who try to know the truth but who are afraid of love. Their truth remains stifled, just a seed; it never becomes a tree.

The ultimate synthesis only happens when love starts flowing from the experience of truth. When truth starts transforming itself into love, when one aloneness starts having a dialogue with another aloneness, when truth becomes communion, then it is love. Truth is the beginning, love is the fulfilment. Truth is the seed, love is the flowering.

This is your name : Swami Prem Fritjof. Prem means love; fritjof is from the Teutonic, it means peace — a peace that is full of love, a love that is full of peace. Both are possible without each other, but then something remains missing. Love *is* possible without peace, but then love tends more towards lust than towards prayer. Then it is down-going; then it is a fall, not a rise in consciousness.

If love is full of peace it starts soaring high, it grows wings. It becomes more and more free from matter, free from the body, free from the gross. It becomes more aesthetic, more musical; it attains more and more spiritual qualities.

At the lowest it is nothing but pure animality, at the lowest it is nothing but a biological urge. At the highest peak it is prayer — it is communion with god, it is meaning with the universal soul, it is dissolving into the ocean of the divine. But love can go high only if it contains peace in it. If the peace is missing, love becomes a fever, a dis-ease — tiring, exhausting — and creates a thousand and one miseries. It gives great hopes but never fulfils them — cannot fulfil them. Those hopes can be fulfilled only through peace.

Without peace, love is like fire : it burns, but it only burns — it cannot give you a resurrection. With peace, another dimension opens up : love becomes cool with peace, it is no more a hot fever. It is a silence — full of love, overflowing with love, but with no fever at all; there is no lust in it, no desire to get something, but a sheer joy of giving, of sharing.

Peace is also possible without love, but then it is dead; it is the peace that is found in the cemetery. It does not pulsate, it has no heart-beat, it does not breathe; it is without heart, it is mechanical. A peace which does not pulsate is of no use at all. Maybe it can protect you, it can become a defence, it can make your life more comfortable, convenient — because it will rub off all the corners of your life; you will be more round, there will be less friction with people, less fight with life. That much it can do, but slowly slowly it turns into your grave.

Both of these things have been tried. People who have tried love without peace are called worldly people; people who indulge, sinners. And there have been people who have tried peace without love — monks who have moved away from the world to the monasteries, to the deserts, to the mountains, to live alone so that there is no possibility of love. Because who knows? — in certain moments of temptation....

And love *is* tempting; it is something very intrinsic in you. It certainly fulfils something tremendously important in your being. So there is fear that if the other is there, a dialogue may start, the energy may start moving, and you may fall into the trap of love. Hence the monasteries, the mountains, the desert : escape, escape as far away from people as possible, be alone. That too has been tried, but monasteries become cemeteries.

People who escape from life become dull, stupid, lose all intelligence, sharpness of life, zest to live. All that they are doing in the monasteries is waiting for death, praying for death, asking god to deliver them from life — as if life is something wrong, as if life is not a gift but a punishment. Both these experiments have been done and both have failed.

My sannyas is a new experiment : love plus peace. Both have to be balanced — one has to be full of love and yet utterly peaceful, and one has to be full of peace, yet overflowing with love. Then life is a miracle. Then one feels grateful to god, then of one's own accord one starts bowing down to existence. Then a humbleness is born which is uncultivated.

To me that consciousness is a truly religious consciousness.

She is the sister of sannyasin Somen, and Osho keeps her name, just adding some bliss so she becomes Anand Ruth.

Anand means bliss. Ruth comes from Hebrew; it is a very significant word, with many significant meanings. The first is beauty, the second is compassion, the third is the capacity to see — and they are all joined together. It may not be so apparent how beauty, compassion and the capacity to see are related at all, but they *are* related.

Beauty does not mean the physical form: beauty means the quality of the inner energy, the inner music, the inner poetry. Whenever the inner poetry is there, it creates a physical beauty also, but the physical beauty is secondary. Physical beauty depends on many accidents — the accident of birth, the accident of a certain way of upbringing — it depends on so many things; it does not depend only on the inner.

For example, people who were born before the vaccine for polio was invented were unfortunate. Now if they are born they are fortunate, no problem. People who were born when there was no cure for, no prevention of, small-pox suffered much; they still suffer in poor countries. Their faces can become very ugly, their eyes can go blind.

Physical beauty is a very very arbitrary phenomenon: one day it is there, the next day it may not be there. It is accidental, it does not matter much. What matters is the inner beauty.

Ruth means inner beauty, the beauty of a soul. And the beauty of the soul is expressed as compassion. A beautiful person is, out of necessity, compassionate; he cannot be otherwise. He cannot be cruel; cruelty is a by-product of inner ugliness, compassion the shadow of inner beauty. And the person who has a beautiful soul and has compassion in his relationship with people, is bound to grow eyes that can see, that can see the truth, that can see that which is.

So, on the surface, in the dictionary, it may not be so apparent how these totally different meanings are attached to a single word, but deep down there is a relationship.

The ancient languages — Hebrew, Sanskrit, Arabic, Latin, Greek — were not just languages. Behind the words, great truths were put; only those who would be able to, would see them. So all the ancient languages have double meanings : one meaning that is apparent, and another meaning that is latent; one meaning that is for day-to-day use, another meaning that has some metaphysics in it, some philosophy in it, some vision of deeper things, of deeper mysteries. Hebrew particularly has that quality : each single word has some mystery in it. It is not only linguistic, it is not only grammar. Some keys are hidden — those who are perceptive enough will find those keys.

Ruth is a beautiful word. Contemplate on these three things : the inner beauty, the outer compassion, and between the two, the insight that is capable of seeing god happen.

This is your name : Swami Veet Robert. Veet means going beyond, transcending. Robert is Teutonic, it means fame. The full name will mean transcending the desire for fame, going beyond the desire for fame.

The desire to be famous is nothing but ego, and it is a very futile desire. It fulfils nothing. The whole world can know about you, still you will be the same — with the same problems, with the same miseries, with the same darkness.

Becoming world-famous is not going to bring any light to your being or any insight or any transformation. It may bring riches to you, but those riches will remain without, and your inner poverty will remain untouched by them. It may bring much attention, but even if you are standing with the whole world staring at you, nothing will be fulfilled by it. In fact, on the contrary, you will feel more empty than ever, more stupid than ever, more hollow than ever.

That happens to every person who becomes very famous — a great author, a great poet, a great politician, this and that. When a person becomes famous he simply sees the whole pointlessness of it all; but now he cannot go back either. He is stuck. He knows the futility but he cannot even confess, because if he says that it is all futile, that means he is saying that for his whole life he has been stupid — searching for it, seeking for it, struggling for it. It is better to keep quiet.

If all famous people *really* confess, the world will be a totally different world — but they cannot confess. They go on pretending *as if* they have attained, *as if* they have come. It is just 'as if'. They die in that 'as if': empty, hollow, utterly meaningless, is their life.

One of the greatest steps towards inner enlightenment is to drop the idea of being known to others. That is an ego-trip, and a sheer wastage of time, energy, opportunity — and an opportunity that is tremendously meaningful. If you can use it, if you can turn in, you can be utterly contented. Life has so much to give, but it gives only to those who turn inwards. And the person who is after fame never turns in, because his whole point is to catch the attention of others. He is really childish, still saying 'Daddy, Mummy, look at me, pay attention to me.' He is still searching for somebody to pat him, appreciate him. Deep down he feels he is nothing; he wants to be patted, appreciated, so that he can feel some worth. But even if the whole world pats you and the whole world appreciates you, you will remain the same. This is not the way to attain to worth.

Worth is attained only when one turns into one's own sources and suddenly finds the treasure, the inexhaustible treasure of god. Jesus calls it the kingdom of god, and he says again and again 'The kingdom of god is within you.'

So your name will mean: go beyond fame, go beyond the ego, go beyond all that nonsense that people hanker for. Be a nobody! And I am not saying ... sometimes nobodies also become famous. A Buddha becomes famous, a Christ becomes famous — but there was no desire, it was just accidental. There was no motivation, it was not the search.

When a nobody becomes famous it is totally different. It doesn't matter; whether a Buddha becomes known or remains unknown doesn't matter. He will be as blissful remaining anonymous, a nobody, as he will be if he becomes known all over the world. That is another thing.

Dropping the desire for fame does not mean that you will never become famous — you *may*, but then it will have a totally different quality. It will be a sheer accident, and you will remain the same: silent, at ease, fulfilled, contented.

Linda is American but she lives in Mexico where she is a teacher.

This is your name: Ma Prem Linda. Prem means love. Linda has two meanings: one is Latin, it means beautiful; another is Teutonic, it means a serpent — the symbol of wisdom.

Jesus says, 'Be ye as wise as serpents.' For centuries the serpent has been the symbol of wisdom, both in the East and in the West. Both the meanings are beautiful. The full name will mean: love that brings beauty, beauty that brings wisdom.

Love can bring many things into existence. Love is alchemy, pure alchemy; it transforms everything that it touches. Baser metal becomes gold, poison becomes nectar, ordinary life becomes extraordinary, and an ordinary person is transformed into a god or goddess. Love is magic, pure magic. It creates its own world; it is the only creative force in existence.

Love gives you beauty because it gives you grace. Love

gives you beauty because it gives you a feeling of worth, that you are needed — that you are not useless, that you are not just dirt, that you are respected, that somebody depends on you, that somebody will miss you; if you are not there, then somebody is going to cry for you. This is the ordinary love.

If love takes wings and becomes universal, then it gives you tremendous beauty. Then you know that this existence will not be the same without you. It gives you tremendous confidence, trust in yourself — and that trust brings beauty, that trust brings a settlement, a relaxation, a centering. You are no more desiring; all that is needed is already there.

Desire makes one ugly, beggarly. Love makes one desireless : one is suddenly an emperor. If love is there, the whole kingdom of god is there. In those moments of love and beauty, in those moments of the feeling of meaningfulness, wisdom arises. One knows, not through the mind but through the heart; one knows, not through logic but through love. Logic is a very indirect way of knowing : it goes round and round, about and about, and still it never comes to the point. It goes on and on; it is a vicious circle.

The heart penetrates into the reality directly, immediately, without any mediator. It simply faces reality as it is, without any screen of intellectuality, rationalisation.

Love is really the true way of knowing the truth. Logic is the untrue way of guessing the truth; it is never knowing.

She hasn't got a return ticket and there are no plans to leave, she says.
Just be here! he beams. Anything to say?
Just really grateful... very happy... and a lot of love!

(to Jennifer) This is your name : Ma Anand Jennifer. Anand means bliss. Jennifer is Celtic, it has three meanings : one is white lady, the second is fair lady, the third is white wave. I choose the third : a blissful white wave. That's actually what we are, waves in the ocean. Being a man or a woman is very superficial, it is just on the surface; deep down we are just white waves of an infinite ocean.

One can think oneself separate from the ocean, then misery arises. One can feel oneself one with the ocean, then peace comes. Bliss is really nothing that comes : bliss is the understanding of the truth. And misery is a misunderstanding : misery is living in a lie and thinking that it is true. Because it is not true and you believe it is true, you remain in a state of limbo, neither here nor there. You cannot make the lie true — and unless it is true it cannot be nourishing, nurturing; it cannot give you health because it cannot make you whole.

People are living on lies, a thousand and one lies. And the most fundamental lie, the foundation of all lies, is the ego — the idea that 'I am separate from existence.' The wave is not separate from the ocean, the wave is *part* of the ocean. To see it is to be transformed — because then all misery, anguish, simply disappears, is not found at all. One is surprised : 'Where have all those things gone? Where is my anxiety? I have not solved it — where has it gone? Where are the problems? I have not found the answers, but the problems have disappeared!'

There are no answers. If the problem is a lie, there cannot be any answer to it. If the problem is false, then there is no way to solve it. And the problem *is* false. Hence I don't teach how to solve your problems, I teach how to dissolve them. By seeing the truth they are dissolved, not solved.

And this is the truth : be a blissful wave, alert, aware that 'I am just part of the ocean : one moment I arise, another moment I disappear. My coming and my going does not make any difference. My birth is not a birth, my death is not a death, because before birth I was there in the ocean, after death I will be there in the ocean.'

Seeing the truth, one becomes disidentified with the part and becomes identified with the whole; and to be one with the whole is to live a vast, infinite life. We are unnecessarily living in small, dark tunnels, for no reason at all — the whole sky is ours!

Sudharm took sannyas in Ireland but hasn't got his piece of paper with his name on it yet.

So I will give it to you. This is your name : Swami Anand Sudharm. Anand means bliss, sudharm means true religion — bliss, the true religion.

For a long time, religion has been very sad, serious, sombre; and because of its seriousness and sadness, millions turned away from it. Even those who remained part of religion remained only formally so, because sadness is not the natural search of human consciousness, bliss is the natural search.

To propound sadness as a goal is pathological, but that is what has been done down the ages. It has been done for a particular reason; it was not just an accident, it was a cunning strategy of the priests. Early in the history of humanity they stumbled upon the fact that you can control only if people are sad; you can exploit only if people are sad. If they are blissful, it is impossible to control them; if they are blissful, it is impossible to reduce them to slaves. If they are blissful, it is impossible to force them to follow the authorities, the state and the church.

A blissful person is a rebellious person. And a blissful person need not go to the priest. For what? Why? When you are psychologically ill you go to the psychiatrist, the psychoanalyst; when you are not psychologically ill you don't go.

The priest came to know that people have to be made spiritually ill, only then can his profession prosper. The priest lives on people's spiritual poverty, spiritual illness, spiritual turmoil, anguish. Naturally he created a structure of ideology in which it is bound to happen that you will become sad, you will become afraid, you will become guilty, you will become so shaky that you will have to seek advice, that you will have to go to some expert. The priest was the expert; he had all the keys. In fact he was the *cause* of the disease, and he was pretending he was the cure.

My work here is to make you aware of all the damage that has been done by the priest down the ages, and not only to make you aware but to help you to heal those wounds. Hence, to me, true religion will mean bliss, will mean freedom, will mean individuality. It will not mean imitation, it will not mean following, it will not mean obedience; it will mean intelligence.

Of course if something appeals to your intelligence, follow it. But follow it because it appeals to your intelligence — not because it is dictated by the authorities, not because it is written in the scriptures, not because those who propound it have a long long tradition, credit, prestige, power. Follow a thing only if it strikes a chord in your heart; then you will be moving into the true direction of god. As one goes closer and closer to god, one becomes more and more blissful.

If one becomes more and more serious, then something is wrong; one has gone astray, one is not moving towards god. That is an absolute criterion : if you are coming closer to truth, your being will have more and more fullness of joy, well-being, overflowing love. You will be a singing, a dancing....

> *Nirvana :* Many times when I am doing Vipassana meditation on my own I get very drowsy and sleepy and have very low energy, physical and.... That's one thing, and another is that in many days in my life I feel very low energy. I cannot bring it out.

And how do you feel with active meditations?

Nirvana : I have been doing Dynamic every day for the last three weeks; and, for example, today I was very tired at the lecture.

Mm mm. No, no, but this was today. What was happening for three weeks?

Nirvana : I felt pretty good.

Pretty good?
My feeling is that at least for six to nine months you should do Dynamic meditation. Your energy seems to be low. The Dynamic meditation will help the energy to rise higher. Only then will Vipassana be helpful. Otherwise this happens : energy is low, Vipassana brings it even lower, because it is a very silent process. Then wherever energy is too low you will feel drowsy, sleepy, and you may start dreaming, and then the whole point is lost.

Vipassana can be done only when the energy is very high, so high that even if Vipassana brings it low, it cannot bring it so low that you start feeling drowsy. Otherwise in Buddhist monasteries that is almost the normal routine : out of one hundred monks, ninety-nine are drowsy, sleepy. That's why the Zen master has to move with a stick to hit their heads — they are all drowsy! In fact it is natural, mm? it is not their fault! They have to get up at three o'clock, early in the morning, and then start meditating; and it continues the whole day. Unless somebody really has very high energy, he will fall into sleep.

So my approach is : first bring the energy to such a high level that even when you do Vipassana.... It will go down a little : your heart-beat will be slower, your pulse will be slower, your blood circulation will slow down — everything slows down in Vipassana. You already look drowsy...

I glance at him; he doesn't respond.

... so in Vipassana you *will* fall asleep; it will not be of any use to you.

For nine months concentrate on Dynamic meditation, and after nine months start Vipassana.

When will you be coming back?

> *Nirvana :* I don't know, but I want to come soon.

Come back soon!

Prem Bharti and his partner Mangala are back from England after two and a half years.

How long will you be here? Osho asks Bharti.

I can't go away again, he replies, and Osho chuckles, Good, be here.

The rest of the interchange is brief, but Prem Bharti's face looks so full! Between each response to Osho he closes his eyes as if to slow down and savour better the precious moments....

Mangala is in chaos.

Mm mm. What is the chaos?

> *Prem Mangala :* My relationship with Bharti. A lot has been happening in the last two months. I have twins, two-year-olds, and it's been very hard for me : I've made it hard for myself somehow.

Mm mm.

> *Prem Mangala :* I find them very demanding on my energy. I feel I haven't been there for Bharti very much, I guess partly because of the children.

Don't be worried. Things will settle. Just be here for a few days. Just feel me more, mm? and things will settle. I don't see a real problem, mm? — just the ordinary problems that always arise in relationship. But those problems keep the relationship going on. If there are no problems, what will you do? (laughter). If there are no problems then you will be at a loss : what to do with your life?

Problems keep life interesting (laughter). One remains occupied and great things go on happening (Osho chuckling). Nothing is great, and nothing is happening!

Just wait a few days, listen to me carefully, and this will go.

Good!

15

Alok has come to say goodbye because he is returning to England with his two daughters, Shanti, five, and Madhu, one.

Something to say to me? Osho asks as Madhu gurgles noisily.

Just... thank you, Alok begins. I feel so blessed to be here. (And Madhu lets out a series of unceremonious splutterings.)

It's been beautiful to be in your presence, Alok continues, smiling at Osho (while Madhu clambers over him dribbling moistly). We've been celebrating at the time!

Good!

(then to Shanti) This is your box.

She takes it and our eyes turn to Madhu.

And you come here, otherwise you will miss the box.

Madhu stands and gawks, so Osho hands her box to Shanti and from her it is passed to Madhu, who promptly puts it in her mouth! The trio exit....

Petra and one-and-a-half-year-old Bruno from Germany take their place. Bruno squirms like a little fish all over his mother who is valiantly attempting to sit still and silent while she awaits her sannyas name. She sits splay-legged as Osho begins to talk, seemingly oblivious to Bruno who slithers over and under her arms, and several times nearly swipes her with his bottle of milk.

Osho : This will be your name : Ma Deva Petra. Deva means divine; petra is Greek, it means rock — divine rock. The temple of life has to be built on the rock of god. People build their houses either in the air or at the most on the sands. If one makes one's houses in the air, one is simply wasting time, energy, life. Or if one makes one's houses on the sands of time, then too death will come and all will be taken away.

Only god is the rock; and sannyas is an initiation into finding the rock on which the temple can be built. And it is not far away, it is within one's own being; we just have not looked for it. It needs only a little knocking inside, a little hammering inside. Good, Petra.

Come here! Your mala! Come on... come on! So good! Just look at me...

Bruno is abruptly quiet.

This is great — silent for such a long time!

We roar with laughter, so Bruno turns and surveys us.

Yes, everybody is impressed, really impressed; don't be worried!

His name will be Swami Deva Bruno. Deva means divine, bruno is Teutonic; it means of dark colour. In the East, particularly in India, god is painted with a dark complexion. The word 'krishna' means the black one. If you have seen the pictures of Krishna or the pictures of Rama you will be surprised: they are all dark — and there is a reason in it. Darkness has depth, whiteness is shallow. And darkness has something mysterious in it; whiteness is so clear-cut, mathematically comprehensible. Darkness is like the dark night, you cannot even see your own hand; everything is incomprehensible, mysterious. And god is a mystery. To represent that, in the East, god has been painted as having a dark complexion.

Bruno is a beautiful word: divine dark complexion.

Will Bruno allow you to do some groups? Osho asks, and Petra thinks she might be allowed during the day at least, so she's assigned the two new groups, Nartan and Flow.

This is your name : Swami Veet Richard. Veet means going beyond, transcending; richard is Teutonic, it means hard. The full name will mean : transcending hardness, going beyond hardness, becoming soft.

Hardness is part of struggle. We have learned hardness because we have been constantly fighting; and if one has to fight, one has to be hard. Man has been fighting with nature, with animals, with trees, with man — with *himself*. For centuries and centuries, life has been nothing but a struggle. Naturally, one has learned how to be hard, how to be like a stone wall, so that nothing can penetrate one; but this has created side effects of tremendous importance.

Because man has become too hard, he cannot love, he cannot allow love to happen. He cannot relax. He cannot go deep into meditation, he cannot go into his own being, because they need totally different qualities : they need softness.

Hardness is masculine, softness is feminine. If you want to go out into the world, into the world of ambitions, you have to be hard, very hard, otherwise you will be crushed. If you have to compete, you have to be aggressive and violent. Yes, it pays to be hard in the world of competition, ambition, but it is a hindrance in the inner world. If you are hard, you cannot take even a single step inside your being. If you are hard, your life loses all grace. It can't be a flower, it remains a stone. It can't have that velvety softness of a rose; it remains rough, it remains ugly.

Sannyas is the beginning of an inner journey. You will have to change the whole gestalt of your life : you will have to learn the ways of being soft. As much as possible, you will have to learn the ways of being vulnerable, open, available. You will have to learn the ways to bend, surrender.

Lao Tzu says : When great winds come, big trees fight, but they are uprooted, they are thrown on the ground. And the grass? — it simply bends, with no resistance. Once the wind is gone, the grass is back up — but the big tree cannot be back up; it is dead.

The secret of the grass is the secret of tao, the secret of religion : learn to relax, learn to surrender, learn to co-operate. In one word : learn to love!

What is the meaning of your name? Osho asks Tetsuya.
Nartan translates his reply :

Nartan : He says it means to be philosophical.

Good!

So you have fallen into wrong company now!

This is your name : Swami Veet Tetsuya. Veet means beyond; and tetsuya, you say, means to be philosophic. Your full name will mean : going beyond philosophy. That is the game that sannyas is — going beyond philosophy, going beyond thinking, going beyond guessing.

Man cannot think about the unknown. Whatsoever you think remains the known. You can chew it over again and again, but it is the same thing that you already know. You can make a few new combinations out of old toys; they may appear new but they are not.

There is no way to come to the new by thinking; thinking is totally irrelevant for the new. The new can be known only when thinking ceases. Truth can be encountered only when the mind is no more there. Truth needs no mediator, truth needs direct experiencing. One has to see to know, not think to know. One has to experience to know — and experience is a totally different dimension. You know love by being in love, not by studying love. If you study love, that is philosophy : if you fall in love, that is sannyas.

Sannyas is existential, not philosophical. And those who have ever known were not philosophers. Philosophers go on missing. They know much but their knowledge is all rubbish, because their knowledge goes about and about; they beat the bush around and around. They never reach the centre, they never reach that point which becomes a revelation.

The only way that your arrow can reach the target of truth is meditation, not thinking. And let me remind you : meditation is not another kind of thinking. It is not thinking about god, it is not thinking about truth; it is not thinking at *all*. It is a state of no-thought. One simply is, utterly empty of any thought, desire, dream. In those lucid moments, truth comes to you. In those open moments, mysteries start revealing themselves to you.

One has to learn to be still, to be silent; it is not a question of logical acumen. The greatest skill in the world is the skill of being silent, utterly silent.

In silence is the door to god, to truth, to nirvana. Anything to say to me?

Very straight-backed and very earnest, Tetsuya pauses then murmurs something to Nartan.

>   *Nartan :* He cannot say anything.

>   Good — good!

Tineke is from Holland.

>   Come here! What is the meaning of your name?

>   *Tinekee:* My name is Catherine; it comes from catharsis.

Mm mm! If it really comes from catharsis it is very good, but I suspect... (laughter).

(a pause) Close your eyes!

Then he calls her to him.

>   This will be your new name : Ma Prem Rechan. Prem means love, rechan means catharsis. Catharsis can be negative, it can be positive. If catharsis is negative, there is no end to it; one can go on catharting. That's why many cathartic

therapies can never be completed. For example, Primal therapy can never be completed. Even Arthur Janov is not post-Primal; nobody can be post-Primal.

If catharsis is negative, it is endless. And many Western therapies are caught up in negative catharsis: Encounter groups, Gestalt groups, Bio-energetics, Primal therapy, and many more. Yes, it unburdens you, but you are constantly creating energy. Man is a dynamo: the energy accumulates again, again you have to cathart. It does not change your basic life style. It does not change the fundamental of your life. It only helps you to release energy; it does not transform you.

Catharsis has to become positive, sooner or later. It is not only that you cathart anger, hatred, aggression; another step has to be taken which in the West has not yet been taken: you have to learn how to cathart love, compassion, joy.

If positive catharsis is learned, then there is an end to the negative catharsis, because the same energy starts moving into positive channels. Hate becomes love, anger becomes compassion, aggression becomes softness — just the opposite. Otherwise the negative path is endless and creates much hell. Once in a while, you will have a few glimpses of heaven. When the energy is released, the new energy takes a little time to arrive: between these two, you will have a little beautiful experience, but those beautiful moments will disappear sooner or later.

Unless we learn the art, the alchemy, of transforming all negative emotions into positive emotions, therapy remains incomplete. Therapy can be complete only with love, in love.

Carmelita from the Philippines comes forward

This is your name: Ma Prem Carmelita. Prem means love; carmelita is Hebrew, it means garden — a love garden. Love *is* a garden: much care has to be taken of it. It is not just weeds that grow on their own — if you want rose bushes and lotuses, then much care and attention is needed.

A garden has to be created. It is an art, and the greatest art about it is that it should not show that it has been created, that the hands of man should remain hidden, that the hands of man should only be instruments in the hands of God. They should not interfere; they should only bring the message of the divine. They should in no way hinder; they should only be silent, co-operative, empty vehicles.

A tree has to be helped, watered, taken care of, but allowed to be its own. It is not to be tampered with; it has to be allowed to grow in its own natural way. The most beautiful garden is that which looks like a forest. It is not a forest, it is a garden; it has been created with great tenderness. It is poetry composed of trees, but composed in such a way that the poet is invisible. If the poet is too visible, he has destroyed the whole thing. The garden has to be made but it should not be — at least not on the surface — man-made. It should be natural, not artificial.

There is a great story of a Zen master who was a great gardener; the emperor used to learn from him. The emperor was creating a big garden so that one day the master could be invited to see. If he approved, that meant that the king had learned the art — that was going to be the king's examination.

The master came. The king had really prepared hard; thousands of people were involved in the garden. Everything was so clean, so perfect, that the king was absolutely certain that the master would not be able to find any fault. But when the master came, the king became afraid, scared. The master wouldn't smile; he looked at the whole garden and he was very serious.

That was rare; he had never been seen so serious. Finally he said 'I don't see any dead leaves in the garden. Where are the dead leaves?' The king said 'We have thrown them out, just to keep everything clean.'

The master went out, brought back many dead leaves and threw them in the garden. The wind started taking those dead leaves all over the place ... and the rustling sounds of the dead leaves. The master smiled, and he said 'Now it looks like something divine! Without these leaves it was so dead, it had no sound. And how can a garden be without dead leaves? How can life be without death? They are partners together. If green leaves are there, then dead leaves are to be there on the ground. To remove them is artificial.'

Love is a garden. It has to be spontaneous, natural — and yet one has to be very artful. It is a paradox : to be artful and to be spontaneous.

In Zen they say that one should learn painting for at least twelve years and then throw away all the brushes and the paintings and forget all about it. For twelve years one should not touch the brush, should not paint. And then after twelve years one should start painting again. Now the art has been learned and forgotten; now one can paint naturally. The art will be there but it will not be visible; it will be something like a hidden current, something invisible.

Great art is always invisible; and love is the greatest of arts. No music, no poetry, no painting, can be compared to it.

Vihari is back from Japan. He has a question which Nartan translates.

Nartan : What does it mean to live?

Mm mm. It means nothing (laughter)! It has no meaning. Life has no purpose, it simply is. And that's the beauty of it and the profound depth of it — that it simply is. You can make anything out of it; it is just pure availability. It is an empty canvas : you can paint anything on it. You can paint a nightmare or a beautiful dream, you can create hell or you create heaven, but life gives you no directions. It simply gives you total freedom to do whatsoever you want.

Life *is* freedom, hence the great responsibility. If you miss, you cannot make somebody else feel guilty for it; you and only you will be responsible. And there is no intrinsic meaning in life, so you cannot find any readymade thing. Life is creation. You will find only that which you have created; first create and then you can find it.

This is the tremendous mystery of life. People ask 'Where is God?' and they have not created God yet; they cannot find him. People ask 'What is beauty?' First create it, and then you will know. First give birth to it, then you will know.

Life is simply available in all its multi-dimensionality. No meaning is imposed from above; you have to create meaning. Each one has to be a creator, a god in his own right. We live in the world we create, and we live the life we create. So whatsoever meaning you prefer, you can create. The ultimate is to be able to live without any meaning, not to hanker for meaning, not to be obsessed with purpose, not to think in terms of goals; that is the ultimate. Once a man is able to live life for no reason at all, he is a Buddha, he is enlightened.

Enlightenment means to live life without any hankering for meaning. Then whatsoever is, is good, and whatsoever is not, that too is good. Then each moment becomes so radiant, so luminous, so full of fragrance, but still there is no meaning.

Science searches for meaning and finds none. And because people are trained in science, everybody is feeling very disappointed. Art finds no meaning, but creates it — through poetry, music, painting. Religion also finds that there is no meaning, but it starts living the very meaninglessness of it. Art creates an illusion, it creates a beautiful illusion. Art is magic; at least it helps you feel that there is meaning. Science knows the truth, but is incapable of living it : it creates despair. Religion also knows that there is no meaning, but is courageous enough to live that meaninglessness of existence and finds great bliss and joy in it. These are the three approaches possible.

Science is the lowest approach, religion the highest. So if you ask the scientist he will also say that there is no meaning, but he will say it very sadly — he wanted there to be a meaning and it is not there. Ask the artist: he will say 'Don't be worried; meaning can be created.' Ask the mystic: he will say ecstatically 'There is no meaning — and because there is no meaning there is freedom, and because there is no meaning there is no bondage.'

If it is possible, become a mystic. If it is not possible, at least become an artist. Don't fall below that! If you fall below that, you are committing the original sin.

A definite grin hovers around Osho's face.

Would you like to do a few groups?

Vihari shakes his head.

What groups have you done before?

Nartan : Centering, Intensive, Anatta, Tantra, Tao.

And your shaking the head sideways, how have I to understand it — in the Japanese way, or the non-Japanese way?

The question has a history, and those of us who know it are already giggling. Last year when a Japanese sannyasin came to darshan with Prabuddha to translate, Osho had asked something like, You don't want to do groups? to which he'd nodded (because, unlike in English, in Japanese you respond with a nod to a negatively-phrased question), meaning, yes, he didn't want to.

Anyway, Osho was mightily amused when Prabuddha finally explained to us what was going on.

Japanese?

Nartan translates the question. Suddenly Vihari knows enough English to say quite decisively...

Vihari : No!

So we all laugh and Osho grins.

Non-Japanese (more laughter)? Mm? — because that is very puzzling, talking to a Japanese!

Nartan explains what Osho says, but the humour seems to have got lost in translation, for Vihari remains quite straight-faced. He wipes his forehead with his hand, then :

Nartan : He said he doesn't want to do groups.

That's perfectly good (laughter)! That's perfectly good — don't do them. But you could have done it in a Japanese way : you could have done this way (much laughter)!

And he nods up and down to our laughter, while Vihari beats a retreat from this madman.

16

*U*nmada is sitting somewhere in the group, no doubt following with her eyes the figure of her twin sister (and they look almost identical) as she wends her way towards Osho. Her name is Carin; Osho adds an 'a' to it, so it sounds a little more exotic!

Osho : This is your name : Ma Prem Carina. Prem means love, carina has two meanings; one is a star, a star of the constellation Orion — a love star.

Love is always a possibility, always a potential, and the potential is such that it cannot be actualised absolutely; it is inexhaustible. So it is always a far-away distant star; you are always arriving closer and closer, but you can never say 'I have arrived.' And that is the beauty, that one can never arrive, one only goes on arriving. The adventure remains an adventure, the pilgrimage remains a pilgrimage; it never ends.

Love is something that we can go on and on moving into deeper and deeper, but still it is unfathomable, it is immeasurable. We are very small; it is huge. We can only be possessed by it, we cannot possess it. Love is a whole universe; we are just a ripple in the ocean.

And the second meaning is the Italian meaning of the word 'carina' — and I am changing it from carin to carina. Carina is softer, has more beauty of sound, is more feminine. In Italian, carina means the little beloved one, the beloved.

Love is a double-edged sword : on the one hand it makes you a lover, on the other hand it makes you a beloved. It is not one-way traffic, it is not only that you give. The more you give, the more you get — in fact you get a thousandfold. What you give is small, what you get is tremendous.

Keep in your heart a single seed of love. Help it in every possible way, and drop all that can be a hindrance to it. Then there is no other need for anything else. Love is enough unto itself.

Something to say? he asks.
I'm so grateful she says quietly.
Magdalena now, she is a physician from Germany.

This is your name : Ma Deva Magdalena. Deva means god, magdalena is Hebrew; it means elevated, exalted — exalted by god.

In the very fact that we are, we are exalted by god. The very fact that we exist is enough proof that god has loved us. What more exaltation can there be than to be created by god? And life is not a single gift; it is a chain of gifts, gifts upon gifts. But man is so ungrateful and so blind that he cannot see what has been given to him. Rather than being thankful, he is continuously complaining. The complaining mind is the irreligious mind, and the grateful mind is the religious mind.

Religion does not consist of going to the church, to the temple, of following certain rituals, formalities. Religion consists only of one thing : an immense gratitude, gratitude that one is, because there is no reason *why* one should be — or is there?

It is a miracle that we are; we might not have been. It is a sheer miracle that existence has been showered on us, that being has been given to us. We are already exalted : to feel it is of tremendous importance. In that very feeling you start losing your anxiety — because if god has created you, he is taking care of you. Then let-go becomes possible, surrender becomes possible. Then you need not worry about yourself, you need not carry yourself on your own shoulders; you can relax, you can be, you can enjoy.

That's what my teaching is : feel exalted, feel tremendously gifted, and feel gratitude for all that has been given to you. The more grateful you become, the more will be given; and the more you have, the more you attract.

The law of outer richness is applicable to inner richness too. Money attracts money : if you are rich outwardly, more money will be flowing towards you. And so is the case with inner richness : the more rich you feel, the more richness will be pouring into you from all directions. If you feel poor, you will become more poor. Whatsoever you feel will be magnified, strengthened — because each time you feel something, you are strengthening that very thing; you are giving it energy, you are supporting it, you are co-operating with it. So why be poor? Why be a beggar? Be a god or a goddess.

It is not that only Jesus Christ is the son of God : everyone is!

What is the meaning of your name? he asks Nikki.

Nikki : I'd like to know. I don't know.

You don't know?

Nikki : No. Do you know?

My researchers have also failed!

Nikki : I heard that there is a meaning in Hindi for Nikki ... but I don't know.

Mm mm. My researchers have also not been able (much laughter) to find the meaning.

Close your eyes!

Then he calls her to him, places the mala over her head and looks at her. His finger is on her third eye, and in response her head immediately begins to bend backwards, her eyelids fluttering, her mouth dropping open slightly. Osho nods to Kirti, sitting directly behind her in the front row, to move closer to her lest she fall.

Good, Nikki! Perfectly good.

This is your name : Ma Prem Nikki. Prem means love, and this is just guesswork : Nikki possibly comes from a Greek word 'nicolette' which means victory. Your full name will mean victory through love; and that is the only true victory there is. Every other victory is ugly, every other victory is violent, barbarous. Every other victory is only superficial. You can silence people, but you cannot win their hearts by violence; and they will wait for a time when they can take revenge. There is no way to destroy the enemy by violence. It is only the miracle of love that the enemy evaporates, it is only through love that hearts are won.

But it is a very paradoxical process, the process of love : you have to surrender to become victorious. You have to allow yourself to be defeated to become victorious. It is very strange illogic, but of tremendous significance. Once one has learned the logic of love, the grammar of love, one has come to know the greatest key that can unlock all the doors of all the mysteries.

Surrender to win, disappear to be, die to be reborn into a life abundant.

Joyce is a systems analyst, and she is from the States.

This is your name : Ma Deva Joyce. Deva means divine, joyce is old French; it means joy or rejoicing. The full name will mean : a divine rejoicing. Rejoicing is better than joy, because joy means that something has ended, is finished, completed; the full stop has been put there.

Rejoicing is on-going, river like; it knows no stopping, the full stop never comes. And life is more like rejoicing than like joy, because the moment joy ends, you will fall into its polar opposite. You will become sad, you will be in despair, you will start longing for joy again. You will start remembering the beauties of joy, the nostalgia, and the despair that it is no more.

Rejoicing — that is closer to life; that's how life is and should be. One goes on flowing from one peak to another, and the flow is a continuum. It is possible only to make your life a continuous flow if sadness is also absorbed in your joy, otherwise not. If sadness is against joy, then joy will end and sadness will have its say, will have its time. Just as night follows day, joy will be followed by sadness.

Rejoicing is an art. It means that the dance continues. Whether it is day or night doesn't matter : one enjoys the day and the sun and the light; and when the night comes, one enjoys the darkness, the depth of it, the velvety touch of it. But the dance continues. In success, in failure, young, old, alone, together, in life, in death, rejoicing continues.

So my emphasis is more on rejoicing than on joy. Rejoicing is far more comprehensive : it contains the polar opposites in it, hence it has more totality. And whatsoever is total is divine, whatsoever is partial is no more divine.

Richard had written to Osho before darshan tonight, describing himself as a Deputy Attorney General working in San Diego. He said he felt to leave his job so he could be here longer; on the other hand he thought that perhaps his work would be a way for him to 'have some effect on the insanity which pervades the governments of the world.' And he rather wondered how orange would go down in court...

Orange-clad now, he is to be a tree. Forget the human body, Osho instructs him. It is raining, it is windy, and the tree is delighted....

He slowly sinks into his tree-ness, his arms moving backwards in a gentle swaying motion. Then he is moving closer to be mala-ed.

This will be your new name : Swami Anand Subudha. Anand means bliss, subudha means awakened — bliss awakened. Bliss is our intrinsic nature, but it is fast asleep.

It is in a state of unmanifestation, in a state of latency. It is like a seed which is waiting — waiting for the time, for the right opportunity, for the right soil, for the right climate, to die, to be reborn. The small seed contains so much that it is incalculable. Scientists say a single seed is enough to fill the whole earth with greenery — in fact not only the earth but the whole universe, all the earths and all the planets and all the stars. A single seed is capable of that miracle. It is not as small as it appears.

Appearances are deceiving; beware of appearances.

Sometimes things that look very big are really very small and things which look very small are really infinite. Who would have ever thought about atomic energy? Who would have ever thought that atoms which cannot be seen with one's eye would be able to destroy cities like Hiroshima and Nagasaki?

What to say about the seed of consciousness that exists in every being? It has infinite potentiality. God is simply another name for that infinite potentiality, nothing else. God is not somewhere out there, sitting waiting for you to discover it. God is hidden in you; it has to be grown, it has to be awakened, it has to be brought to manifestation. It is your future, it is your destiny.

Once this becomes a conscious effort, things are simple. Once it becomes a dedication — 'I have to attain to my full potential, I am not to waste my life in trivia; my basic concern, my ultimate concern, will remain my inner growth' — once this decision possesses you, things become very easy. Life takes a direction, energies start becoming channelised. And in that very channelisation of energies, in that very direction, life starts having a new flavour, a new quality, a new dance, a new meaning, a new poetry.

Sannyas means a conscious decision that nothing else matters than spiritual growth, that everything has to serve it, that everything is important *only* if it serves it, otherwise it is worthless. And that moment has come, the spring has arrived; now it is up to you to use the opportunity or to miss it.

How long will you be here, Subudha?

Subudha: About twelve more days.

Next time manage to come for a longer period; much has to be done.

Subudha: I plan to.

And if you feel like coming forever, this your home — come forever.

Subudha: Thank you. I feel at home here!

A Dutch couple — she a housewife, he a doctor — sit side by side awaiting their sannyas. Osho calls Edda to him first.

This is your name: Ma Deva Edda. Deva means divine. Edda is Anglo-Saxon, it has two meanings: one is happy, the other is rich. Both really mean the same thing. To be happy is to be rich; anything else is just pseudo-richness. Unless one is happy, one is poor; one may have all the riches of the world but one is poor. Drowned in riches, one remains poor, because poverty is something inner and no outer riches are able to fulfil that inner vacuum. They can't reach into your interiority. You can pile riches around yourself: others may think that you are rich, but you will know, surrounded by all your riches you will know even more acutely, that you are poor. In contrast with the riches, the poverty will be even more loud.

Real richness has nothing to do with outer riches. And remember, I am not against outer riches, I am not against anything. Outer riches are perfectly good; as far as they go they are perfectly good. Use them, but remember continuously that life becomes rich really only when there arises an inner well-being, an inner sense of joy, uncaused by anything from the outside. If it is caused from the outside, it will disappear : once the cause is gone, it will be gone.

We have to seek and search for something inside, which is not dependent on the outside. That brings freedom, independence, and that brings a joy that is yours forever. That is real richness.

You have a beautiful name!
How long will you be here?

Deva Edda : Till next Tuesday.

Leaving soon? Come back again for a longer period.

Loet is mala-ed.

This will be your new name : Swami Deva Bhaven. Deva means divine, bhaven means feeling. God is available not through thinking but through feeling. The door opens into reality not through the mind but through the heart.

The greatest problem that modern man is facing is that the mind is trained too much and the heart is completely neglected — not only neglected but condemned too. Feelings are not allowed, feelings are repressed.

The man of feelings is thought to be weak; the man of feeling is thought to be childish, immature. The man of feeling is thought to be not contemporary — primitive. There are so many condemnations of feeling and of the heart that naturally one becomes afraid of feelings. One starts learning how to cut off feelings and slowly slowly the heart is simply by-passed; one goes directly to the head. Slowly slowly the heart becomes nothing but an organ that pumps the blood, purifies the blood, and that's all.

In the history of man, for the first time the heart is reduced into something utterly physiological — it is not.

Hidden behind the physiology of the heart is the true heart, but that true heart is not part of the physical body, so science cannot discover it. You will have to learn about it from the poets, painters, musicians, sculptors. And finally the secret key is kept by the mystics. But once you know that there is an inner chamber of your being — absolutely uncontaminated by education, society, culture; utterly free from Christianity, Hinduism, Islam; completely unpolluted by all that has been happening to the modern man, still virgin — once you have contacted that source of your being, your life is lived on a different plane.

That plane is divine. To live in the mind is the human plane, to live below the mind is the animal plane. To live beyond the mind, in the heart, is the divine plane. And with the heart we are connected with the whole : that is our connection.

All the meditations that we are devising here are meant for a single purpose : to throw you from your head into the heart, somehow to pull you out of the mire of the head into the freedom of the heart, somehow to make you aware that you are not just the head. The head is a beautiful mechanism; use it, but don't be used by it. It has to serve your feelings. Once thinking serves feelings, everything is balanced.

A great tranquillity and a great joy arise in your being, and not from anything outside but something from your own inner sources. It wells up, it transforms you, and not only you — it makes you so luminous that whosoever comes in contact with you will have a little taste of something unknown.

After a false start with an interchange between them and Arup (she deals with the correspondence for Osho and happens to be at darshan tonight), then between themselves, then between them and Osho, it transpires that they'd written to Osho — somehow the letter got mislaid — about their seventeen-year-old son.

Is there some problem with him?

Deva Edda : Well, the problem is he was a very shy child and we pushed him and pushed him and pushed him and now he's closed to everybody.

He goes to school?

Deva Edda : He goes to school; he is passing his final examinations.

But there also, no friends?

Deva Edda : He has no... nobody.

Mmmm. It will be the best thing if you can send him here for a few weeks.

Deva Edda : Yes, we will send him.

He will simply relax here. It will be the best thing, because if you have been pushing him, then in your presence it will be very difficult for him to relax. Send him alone; Arup will take care. If you bring him with you, it will still be difficult. In fact whenever one member of a family has some problem, the whole family is involved in it. And you cannot change the problem within the context of the family, it is very difficult, because the moment he sees you, he will shrink back.

That's why many psychotherapists have come to recognise the fact that to treat a single individual you have to treat the whole family; and so family therapies are in vogue. But these are just amateur attempts. If you logically follow it, it means that if you treat the family you have to treat the neighbourhood (laughter), and then it becomes more and more unmanageable; if you treat the neighbourhood, then the whole town.

So the logical conclusion is : to change a single individual you have to change the whole universe. That cannot be done. But something else can be done, and that's my approach : for the time being, the individual can be taken out of the family and given a totally different kind of family. We have created here...

He indicates the orange semicircle about him.

...a totally different kind of family where it is impossible to remain closed, impossible : he will be dragged out of himself.

He would like to come out; it is just a habit that is preventing him. He has invested in it so much that now he must be frightened to come out of it. Just doing a few groups, meditations, living with new people who are all open, flowing, he will simply get the feel of it, he will catch it. Once he has caught it, once he has lived openly for a few days, then even in the old situation he will not fall back, because he has tasted something so beautiful that there is nothing that can pull him back.

It is like a person who has lived in prison for seventy years and then you take him out : first he will hesitate, he will be afraid, he will be frightened of the strange world. But once he has started moving in the strange world and has seen the stars and the moon and the sun and the trees and the people, and feels the joy, even if he goes back into his gaol he will never be the same person; he cannot forget the stars and the moon and the sun.

So my suggestion is : if *you* do something, you may make him more closed. It is not for you to do anything. Just send him here for a few weeks; for not less than six to eight weeks let him be here. After eight weeks you will find him totally different. Then just remember one thing : don't try the old things on him again. Help his new freedom. It is time that he gets out of it, because this is the time when things become utterly solid.

Eighteen years old is the peak of sexuality. At the fourteenth year is the beginning of the sexual being. After three and a half years, that is at seventeen and a half, nearabout eighteen, sexuality touches its peak. One is never so potential again; then things start declining. So this is the time, before he starts declining sexually. The more sexual energy is there, the more possibility of change, because sexual energy has something in it which helps rebellion. That's why at the age of thirteen, fourteen, children start rebelling, disobeying. It is part of the sexual energy, it is a biological built-in process, to revolt against the parents, against the family, against the structure — because sexually they are ready to have their own families. They want to be cut off from the old so that they can create the new.

But if more and more time passes, then it will become more and more difficult to help him to come out of his closedness. But he *can* come out. Thousands of people come here closed, and sooner or later — and it is more sooner than later — they come out.

Just send him; and when he is back there, you will have another problem, that he is too open.

Deva Edda : I hope so!

Good!

Sandy is last for sannyas.

This is your name : Ma Prem Sandy. Prem means love. Sandy is Greek, it comes from Alexander; it means a helper of mankind. The full name will mean : love, the helper of mankind. Only love helps. Love is therapeutic, love is the essential therapy. If you touch somebody with immense love, it is a healing force. Just to feel love for somebody is to nourish him; it is an invisible energy.

People who are not loved start shrinking. People who

don't love start feeling the meaninglessness of life. The people who love and are loved are the fortunate ones. They see the grandeur of life, the significance, the incredible ecstasy of it, and they live a healthy, holy, sacred life.

But everything should arise from love. One should not start serving people because it is virtuous, no; then it is no more virtue. One should not serve people because it is what the scriptures seek; then it will be phony. One should not serve people because that is the way one reaches to heaven; that will be an investment, business. Service should come out of love — for no other reason, for no other motive. Then in love all is found, all is fulfilled.

My teaching can be reduced to a single word : love.

Bodhimitra, an American minister of religion, is returning to his congregation in the West (having braved the Encounter group but not quite able to bring himself to do Tantra!).

He hopes to start a meditation centre within his church and asks Osho for a name for it.

Yes, I will give you a new name. You have to work for me there now.

This will be the new name : Utsava. Utsava means celebration, and that is the keynote. Religions have been teaching people to renounce : I teach people to rejoice. There is a renunciation that comes out of rejoicing, but there is no rejoicing that ever comes out of renunciation. Renunciation brings sadness, dullness. Renunciation is in the service of death; it is life-negative. It is against life, hence it is against god. Those who escape from life are condemning god in their escape; they are rejecting god's world. And if you reject god's world, deep down you have rejected god himself. If you reject his world, how can you be grateful? How can you be grateful for this great gift of existence that has been given to you?

You can only complain; you can have a grudge, but not gratitude. And your prayers will not have joy; your prayers will be dull, dusty. Your intelligence will not be sharp either, because it becomes sharp only when you face all the challenges of life. When you live in the world and yet you are not of it, then intelligence takes wing; it starts flying, soaring high.

My emphasis is live in the world, because it is god's world. Love the world, because by loving the world you are loving god. And yet remain above it, don't be lost in it. Celebrate, dance, sing.

So this is my message for your friends. Your group has to become more and more celebrating — and you will be surprised how celebration of its own accord becomes prayer. One need not do any other prayer.

A box for you : and whenever you need me, just put it on your heart and I will be there — don't be afraid!

Come back again!

17

Giglio is a student from Italy.

Osho : This is your name : Swami Anand Giglio. Anand means bliss; giglio is from Latin, it means a lily flower. A blissful flower — that's what man has to become. All the potential is there; it only has to be challenged, it only has to be remembered. It is a forgotten treasure. We have not lost it, it is still with us. It cannot be separated from us, because we *are* it. But just as the seed is asleep and knows nothing of the flower, so are we — seeds, utterly unaware of the possibility.

Unless a seed becomes a flower, it remains frustrated. The frustration is not very clear, it *cannot* be clear; it is not about something in particular, it is simply a general climate of frustration. Only when the seed has become the flower will it be able to know what the reason of frustration was.

Become a flower! And only when one is a flower can one be offered to god.

Peter comes forward. He is from Holland.

This will be your name : Swami Peter Premanando. Peter is from Greek, it means a rock. Premanando is Sanskrit, it means love and bliss. Become a rock for the temple of love and bliss. These are the only two things worth achieving, worth desiring, worth dreaming about; all else is just futile. And these two things are not really two, but two aspects of one experience, two facets of one phenomenon.

When meditation ripens, matures, one aspect is felt as

bliss; that is the inner aspect of it. One feels full of bliss — too full, infinitely full, inexhaustibly full. For the first time, fullness is tasted, what it is. And then one knows 'Up to now I have just been empty'.

The second aspect is felt because the fullness is too much; it has to be shared. To contain it becomes a pain, a very blissful pain; only very few are blessed with that pain. But it is too much and nobody can contain it; it has to overflow.

The moment your bliss starts overflowing, it becomes love. When it reaches to other people, it is understood as love. Bliss overflowing is love. Bliss is the inner aspect, love is the outer aspect of the same experience — the maturing of meditation, coming to the point where no thought exists and only consciousness is.

(to Carl) Come here. What is the meaning of your name? Have you invented it?

Carl: My parents gave me the name.

What is your full name?

Carl: Carl Swasey Gaskin.

What does it mean? Have you some idea?

Carl: The Carl Swasey is my grandfather's name.

It will be very difficult — Where will I find your grandfather now! (much laughter) Close your eyes: let me try your grandfather!

Good. Come close to me.

This will be your new name: Swami Anand Lazarus. Anand means bliss; lazarus is Hebrew, it means grace. Bliss is through the grace of god; it is not man's effort. We cannot cause it to happen, it can't be manufactured; there is no way to achieve it. The achievers go on missing it — just for the simple reason that they are trying to achieve it, they miss it.

Grace is not something that one can do, it is something that one can only allow. We have to be on the receiving end, utterly feminine, passive, womblike, ready to absorb. Man has to become just a welcome for the infinite to visit; and not only to visit, but to become a permanent guest in his being.

And the name Lazarus is also beautiful because of the story in the New Testament. Lazarus seems to be one of the most intimately related persons to Jesus, far more intimate than the official apostles. His trust must have been tremendous, because it is very difficult to hear and understand a man like Jesus even while you are alive, and he heard him when he was dead. When he had already been dead for three days he heard him — the moment Jesus came to the cave where his body was kept, and shouted 'Lazarus, come out! What are you doing there?' Nobody was ready to believe that anything was going to happen, the whole thing was so ridiculous. Everybody was waiting : 'This will be enough, this will be the end of this madman Jesus.' But Lazarus stood up, came out of the cave.

If love is total, then even death is not a barrier. Even in death, the voice of the master will reach. If one is just hearing with one's ears and not listening with one's heart then, even while alive, one goes on missing.

Lazarus coming out of death is also symbolic of each disciple who has really to go into the search, who has to die and come back again, who has to disappear as the old and to come as the new. There has to be a gap between the old and the new. That is the meaning of those three days : it is just symbolic, symbolic of three states of the mind — waking, dreaming, sleeping. Beyond these three is the fourth, which is not a state of the mind, which is the state of no-mind. Those three days simply represent three states. Lazarus had disappeared into the fourth. Only Jesus could have called him back, because in the fourth state the mind has simply disappeared. You can hear only that which comes from no-mind. Only a no-mind can communicate with another no-mind.

The story of Lazarus has been missed by the Christians. It is not just a miracle — then you make a very small thing out of something very significant. The whole emphasis of Christianity has been that Jesus did a great miracle, that he raised the dead. In fact the miracle is done not by Jesus but by Lazarus — that he heard his master even while he was dead, that he heard his master even when he had regressed beyond the mind, beyond recall. Even when no language communication was possible, something reached him, something non-verbal. Jesus' presence provoked him back to life.

And that is the function of the master. The disciple is dead, every disciple is dead, and the master has to call him forth : Lazarus, come out! What are you doing there?

And once you can come out from your death, which is called life in the world, then for the first time you are really alive.

How long will you be here?

Anand Lazarus : Three or four months.

That's good.
Anything to say to me?

Anand Lazarus : I feel alienated and separate a lot of the time.

How long have you been feeling like that?

Anand Lazarus : Off and on for my whole life.

Just wait, this will disappear; nothing to worry about. Just go through a few groups. It will disappear, because it is a very artificial, created thing.

To feel alienated means that you have created it; it is not the natural state. In the natural state we are one with existence; there is no question of alienation or separation. Just meditate, go through a few groups and go on reminding me; soon it will disappear. Good, Lazarus.

Miriam is a dental assistant from the States.

This is your name : Ma Prem Miriam. Prem means love. Miriam is Hebrew, it has two meanings : one is bitterness, another is rebellion. Both are significant in relationship to love.

Love is sweet, but it contains much bitterness too; it is not just pure sweetness. And the bitterness enhances its sweetness, it functions as a contrast. It is not opposite to sweetness but complementary. A love that has no bitterness in it will miss something. It will not have tone, it will not have salt, it will not have sharpness; it will be a little too syrupy. There is an intrinsic necessity for some bitterness in love; that gives it flavour, makes it richer.

Once we look at things in that way, then the whole of life has a different meaning. Then death is not against life, but complementary to it. Death defines life; without death, life will be very vague, cloudy, it won't have any definition. So is the case with every opposite : whatsoever appears opposite on the surface, is not really so in the depth; in the depth they are together, enhancing each other.

The second meaning is rebellion. Love is rebellion too. In fact only love is rebellion, because love can risk all, because love is never orthodox — it cannot be. It cannot be conventional, it cannot be conformist. Love is the beginning of individuality, of the assertion that 'I have to live my life in my own way, whatever the cost and whatsoever the consequence.' Love is a rebellion against the mob psychology, the crowd and its demands.

The crowd consists of the lowest. But it is very powerful, it is the majority, hence millions of people simply surrender to it. They start following the ways of the crowd, and crowd gives them respect, prestige, power. They will be known as saints, the crowd will worship them.

Just see : the pope is worshipped and Jesus is crucified. This seems so illogical. The pope must be something else : the pope must be against Jesus. If he was also part of the being of Jesus, he would be crucified; but he is worshipped and Jesus is crucified. They are opposites. Jesus is rebellion, pure rebellion, love, and the pope is just a conformist. The pope is a Christian, Jesus is not a Christian. The pope belongs to a church, Jesus belongs to no church. Jesus is alone — and to be alone is possible only when you are in tremendous love with existence. When god is with you, only then can you be alone.

Love is the way of rebellion. Hence all the societies of the world are against love, they all destroy love. They create false substitutes for love — marriage, this and that — but they don't allow love to function in its total naturalness. They make so many conditions on it that they kill it. Once love is killed, rebellion is killed.

My effort here with my sannyasins is to rekindle your love so that again there is that fire of rebellion.

A Swiss couple sit side by side awaiting their sannyas. Christine is a dance teacher; Osho malas her first and explains why he names her Veet Christine.

Veet means beyond. Christine is Greek, it means Christian. To be really religious, one has to go beyond being Christian, Hindu, Mohammedan; one has to go beyond all structures, creeds, dogmas. A Christian can never know Christ, a Buddhist can have no communion with the Buddha; the very ideology of Christianity prevents it, and the very expectation of the Buddhist becomes a barrier.

We have to go into reality by dropping all expectations, all ideologies. Ideologies are like garments, and truth has to be faced in utter nudity. We cannot go to truth hiding behind theology, philosophy, so many words, systems of thought. We have to encounter truth without any prejudice — and Christianity is a prejudice, Hinduism is a prejudice, any 'ism' is a prejudice. It means we have already decided what truth is. Without knowing, we have decided; this is arrogance. Without knowing, we have decided; that means we have fallen victim to mass hypnosis. Without knowing we have decided; it means we are not really enquiring after truth, hence we have settled for cheap beliefs. All beliefs are cheap. We can get beliefs just by being born in a particular home.

If you had been born in a Hindu home, you would have been a Hindu; if you had been brought up by a Mohammedan you would have been a Mohammedan. This is just conditioning by the parents and the society. The real seeker of truth has to renounce all conditioning; he has to come to a moment of unconditioning, of utter silence, purity. In that silence, truth descends.

So your name has a message for you: go beyond Christianity. And by Christianity I mean go beyond Hinduism, Buddhism, go beyond *all* isms. Don't trust in ideologies. Trust only in truth, not what is said *about* truth. Experience it, don't believe in it.

Richard is a doctor : his turn to be lassoed.

This will be your new name : Swami Veet Richard. Veet means beyond. Richard is Teutonic, it has three meanings — all wrong (laughter)! One means rule, domination, another means hard, and the third means a great ruler. You have to go beyond all these things.

There is no need to rule anybody. The very idea of ruling somebody is immoral; to dominate somebody is inhuman, to possess somebody is murderous. But that's how man has lived up to now. This has been the philosophy we have been brought up with; from our very childhood we have been spoon-fed on ugly ideas.

Down the ages it has been thought that one has to be hard, strong. Hardness has always been thought to be strong — it is not. Real strength is in flexibility, not in being hard. Real strength is in liquidity, not in being rocklike. Real strength is in the way water flows, not in the way rocks prevent it.

Become more and more liquid. Follow the watercourse way, don't be a hard rock, and you will have infinite possibilities opened for you. If one is hard, one remains closed. That is the only way to be hard — not even a window should be left open, everything should be completely closed. One should live a windowless existence, then only can one be hard. But that means that you are living in a grave. You are no more in communion with life and its joys; you don't allow the sun and the wind and the rain to reach you.

The third meaning — the great ruler — is even more ugly. The idea of becoming great is a projection of an inferiority complex. Anybody who wants to be great suffers from an inferiority complex; deep down he feels that he is nobody. He has to prove that he is somebody. But even if he becomes Alexander the Great it makes no difference: deep down, the same emptiness, the same hollowness, and the whole of life is wasted. Nothing ever is achieved that way.

No achievement ever proves to be an achievement. The real work is inwards — and the inward work has nothing to do with achievement: it is a spontaneous, natural blossoming of the soul. It is not an achievement, it is not a goal to be striven towards. It is something that is there if we relax. If we open up, if we are no more madly obsessed with ruling people, possessing people, dominating people, then suddenly the lotus in the heart starts opening its petals.

So, go beyond hardness, go beyond the idea of ruling, go beyond the idea of becoming great, and then the miracle : one becomes great. One simply becomes great, because one *is* great, everyone is great. And when there is no idea to rule anybody, one becomes a ruler. One's very presence becomes a discipline for others, one's very presence creates obedience in others — not that one wants others to obey one, but wherever one is, a great desire arises in people to obey.

Lao Tzu says that the real ruler is one who has no idea that he is a ruler. The real ruler is one whose presence itself creates obedience. We have known such rulers — a Buddha, a Jesus, a Zarathustra, a Lao Tzu : these are the real ones, the salt of the earth. Not Alexander the Great and Ivan the Terrible, not Tamerlane, Nadir Shah — these are not the real people. They are the most degraded human beings; they are inhuman, they don't know what humanity means. They have not even looked up into the sky full of stars. They are crawling in the mud, the dirty mud of the earth.

German Jutta doesn't know what her name means, so Osho tells her to close her eyes anyway. Then he calls her close and says that jutta can have either of two meanings.

One is old German, it means war. So many German names mean war that I am surprised (much laughter)! So forget about it — the German meaning is not right.

But there is a Latin meaning, it means just. That is beautiful. So your name will mean : just love. Love can also be unjust : whenever it is possessive, jealous, it is unjust. It is no more love; it becomes war, it turns poisonous.

Love to be just, love to be true, love to be really love, needs to be completely free from jealousy, possessiveness. Then it is the energy that makes you aware for the first time that you are not the body but the soul, that you are not born and you will never die, that you are eternal, that your real home is god. Love is the only key in our hands which opens the doors of god. But first we have to purify love. It is very much polluted, contaminated, by ugly things which pretend they are love.

Be watchful. If you can purify your love of jealousy and possessiveness, then nothing else is needed. That love will become the bridge between you and the divine. That love will be transformed of its own accord into prayer.

Ulrike is from Germany too.

This will be your new name : Ma Prem Parijat.

From time to time, newcomers submit questions to the morning talks about the significance of the new names Osho gives us. His replies vary, ranging from the meaningful to the simply amusing, to the outrageous. This morning when asked, he explained it thus : three wise men following a star came across a stable. The first entered and lay his offering at the feet of the cradle. The second did likewise, then the third. He was taller than his friends, and as he hit his head on a low-lying beam he exclaimed 'Jesus Christ!'

Oh, that's a lovely name! said Mary. I was going to call him Fred.

Prem means love, parijat is a beautiful flower. The full name will mean : a beautiful flower of love.

Man can flower only in the climate of love. Love is the basic nourishment for the soul. Just as the body cannot live without food and the mind cannot exist without oxygen, the soul cannot exist without love. There are millions of people on the earth, but very few have souls. What I mean is : their souls are still potential; they have not become actual yet, because they have not provided the right food for the soul to grow.

Hence the hankering for love. Everybody hankers for it, desires it, everybody wants to be loved — but the problem is that everybody only wants to be loved and nobody wants to love. And love comes only to those who love. The beginning has to be from your side : *you* have to take the

Won't You Join the Dance? 171

initiative, you have to start pouring love into people, into existence, and then the whole existence returns your love in many many ways, in a thousand and one ways. The existence is an echo point, whatsoever you give is echoed back : sing a song and millions of songs will shower on you.

Learn the secret of loving, so that you can have as much love as is needed for the soul to grow.

Robyn is a teacher; he's from England.

This is your name : Swami Anand Robin. Anand means bliss; robin is Teutonic, it means bright. Bliss is always bright, misery is dull. Bliss is always intelligent, misery is stupid. Bliss is always shining, radiant. Misery is dark, with no light in it — a long, long, dark night, with not even a single star; it is like moving in a dark tunnel. But people have decided to remain miserable because to be intelligent needs work. To be stupid, nothing is needed. To be in light needs search; to be in darkness no search is required.

And people are afraid of light — afraid because they may see things in themselves which they don't want to see, they may see things in others which they don't want to see. It may shatter their whole world. They have lived in darkness, in illusions, in dreams; and they have somehow managed, consoled themselves, and created beautiful ideologies that support their darkness and console them in their darkness. They are afraid of the light; if they come into the light, all that will be gone. Hence they are very much against people who make all efforts to bring them to the light : they crucify Jesus, they poison Socrates, they murder Mansoor. But to live in darkness is not to live at all; it is to miss life.

The only way to live is to live in utter intelligence, in the full light of intelligence, because only then are you sharpened, sharpened every day. Your soul becomes a sword. Your life starts having significance, meaning. You are not just accidental then; you are part of a significant universe — and an essential part, a significant part. It is not only that you need god, god also needs you. The day it is realised that god also needs you, a great explosion happens in consciousness : you are accepted, welcomed in existence, this is your home!

This is your name : Swami Deva Charles. Deva means divine; charles is Teutonic, it means man — divine man.

Man has a dual existence, because in man the earth and the sky meet, in man the mind and no-mind meet. On the outer, man is just material; in the inner, he is spiritual. That's why Jesus says many times "I am the son of man" and many times "I am the son of god." For Christian theologians, that has remained an insoluble problem. Why does he repeat such a contradiction? Either he is son of man or son of god. But he is really pointing at the mystery of man himself. Man is both : a part of him belongs to the earth, and a part to the beyond. And that's the beauty of man! That is his agony, but that is also his ecstasy too. He is not simple, he is complex; he is torn apart between two polarities.

Friedrich Nietzsche used to say that man is like a rope stretched between two infinities, a tightrope walker — just a single step and he will be gone forever.

The pull of the past is great, because it is the pull of the known, of the familiar. But the pull of the unknown is not less great, because it is the pull of the unknown, of adventure. And it is always a wavering, a trembling : where to go, what to choose, what to be? To be or not to be? Those who choose to go backwards miss the whole grandeur of manhood. The grandeur grows deeper and deeper as you forge ahead.

That's what sannyas is all about : risking the known for the unknown, the familiar for the unfamiliar, risking that which you have for that which you don't have — not only do you not have it, but it may not exist at all. Who knows? There is no guarantee.

But blessed are those who can take such a risk, who can gamble such a gamble. Their life becomes the life of insecurity — but anything that ever grows, only grows in insecurity. Anything that ever integrates, crystallises, crystallises only when impossible challenges are accepted — not only accepted, but welcomed.

How long will you be staying? Osho asks.

I came for one day, I'm staying two and a half months, and then after that... he replies.

Good! Be here. Anything to say?

Many things... but not herenow.

18

Osho : Look at me...

Victoria crouches close.

This is your name : Ma Antar Victoria. Antar is Sanskrit; it means the inner, and victoria is Latin; it means the victorious. The full name will mean : the inner victory, the victory over the inner. To win the other is not difficult, it is not really a great challenge. The real challenge arises from the inner : how to win oneself, how to be a master of one's own being.

It is easy to be a master of somebody else; that's why people have decided to be the master of somebody else. Somebody is a husband and he thinks he is a master; somebody is a wife and she also thinks deep down that she is the master, the parents think they are the masters of their children, and so on and so forth. All are escaping from one real phenomenon, and that is victory over oneself. Unless one is a master of oneself, all relationship remains phony. Because *you* are not, how can your relationship be true, authentic, real? It can only be superficial. When you are not then you function only through the mask, the personality, which is a cultivated thing. Unless the real inner explodes, overflows, one remains phony.

One never knows who one is, one never knows what treasures one is carrying within oneself. One never knows that one is a bearer of Christ-consciousness, of Buddhahood, that one has an inner kingdom. Compared to it all outer kingdoms are just stupid. Even to win a single inch of the inner territory is far more valuable than to become Alexander the Great, because all that is won on the outside will be taken by death — you will go empty-handed — but that which is won inside nobody can take, not even death.

Let this be the definition of real treasure : that which cannot be taken away by death is the real treasure, and the person is blessed who has it; he has something of eternity.

Terry has come from Australia; he's an actor.

This is your name : Swami Prem Terry. Prem means love, terry is Latin; it means soft, tender. Love can only be soft and tender; if it is not, then it is something else, not love. Many things pretend to be love, many things masquerade as love. Love is such a valuable thing that it is natural that many pretenders will be born. The false coins come into existence only because the real coin exists; they are copies. Love is utterly soft, delicate, tender, as soft as the lotus flower, vulnerable; it can be destroyed very easily.

It is difficult to destroy a rock; it is not difficult to destroy a rose. The rock seems to be stronger, the rose seems to be very tender, but still the rose has something which the rock has not got : the rose is far more alive than the rock and the rose has something of the beyond in it; that's its beauty. The rose has a poetry; that's its being. But always remember : whenever there is a clash between the lower and the higher, it is always the higher that suffers, never the lower. If you clash a rose with a rock, the rock will not suffer, only the rose will suffer.

In the inner world of human consciousness there are all kinds of things : rocks and roses, all kinds of things. Hate is there, like rock, great longing to be powerful is there like rock, anger is there like rock. Love is there like a rose flower, not even fully grown up, just like a bud, just on the way.

Anger can destroy it, hate can destroy it, jealousy can destroy it, possessiveness can destroy it — anything, and there are many things.

So only one who is really alert can be a lover — very alert to protect the tender, the soft, the delicate, the vulnerable.

It is not against others when you are full of hate; it is against you. It is not when you are boiling with anger that you are destructive to others — you may be, you may not be, but you are certainly destructive to yourself; it is not a question of perhaps.

One has to learn what is valuable in one's being and what is worthless. And one has also to learn to sacrifice the worthless for the valuable. Only then, slowly slowly are energies transformed, the alchemy happens. Then it is very surprising : even anger can become love, hate can become love, jealousy can be transmuted into love. All that is needed is : don't use these negative things for destruction. Even if they arise, watch, very silently, don't be moved by them. Let them be there — just be a detached observer — and slowly slowly they will subside. And when they subside, not by repression but by awareness, the transformation happens.

Awareness is the vehicle of transforming all that is lower into higher. Rocks can bloom like roses; and this is what I am trying to do here : to help you transform rocks into roses. It is possible, it is within your reach.

He adds Anand to Heinz' name so it now means 'let bliss become your home rule, let bliss become your inner discipline.'

Bliss is not a goal but a discipline. One just has to learn how to be blissful. We are born to be blissful, the quality is intrinsic in us; it is not something to be brought from the outside. It has to be drawn out; just as we draw water from a well, bliss has to be drawn out. That's exactly the meaning of the word 'education' : to draw out something that is already there. Bliss is an education.

Our so-called education is just doing the opposite. Rather than bringing out that which is intrinsic in the person, it goes on forcing something which is absolutely alien, something foreign, something that the whole being of the person resists, rejects, does not allow to be digested. That's why ninety-nine percent of all that one is taught in the schools, colleges, and in the universities, is immediately forgotten once one has passed the examinations. It was of no use, and it was *never* something harmonious with your being.

My own experience is this : that whenever something is in harmony with you you cannot forget it, it is impossible. And when something is not in harmony with you you cannot remember it, howsoever hard you try; at the most, for the time being you can remember it. That's why students only read the night before they are going to take an examination; and their examination is nothing but a kind of vomiting. They regurgitate whatsoever they have been somehow accumulating the whole night, managing, stuffing themselves with; their examination papers are nothing but vomit.

This is not education, education is a totally different phenomenon. It has to bring that which is hidden in you, it has to make it manifest, it has to help you to be yourself. Bliss is there, an inborn quality; it has to be helped.

Sannyas is an education, education in the true, literal sense of the word. And it can be learned. In fact it is difficult to learn the ways of misery because it goes so against your nature. It is very easy to learn the ways of being blissful.

Just a few small things to be remembered : one, emphasise the heart more than the head, and almost fifty percent of the work is done. Replace thinking by feeling. Think less, feel more, logic less, love more; and fifty percent of the work is done. And the second thing is : become more sensitive to life — its pains, pleasures, agonies, ecstasies. Don't create an armour around yourself to protect, remain vulnerable; and twenty-five percent more is done. And the third : never cling to the known, because the known is dead, and if you cling to the dead, *you* will become dead. Always seek and search for the unknown, become an adventurer. Listen to the call of the unknown, risk everything for it, and you will never be a loser; and the remaining twenty-five percent is done.

If these three simple things can be managed, bliss starts showering. One is drowned in it, one is drunk with it.

(to Hartmut) This is your name : Swami Anand Hartmut. Anand means bliss, hartmut is Teutonic; it means great courage. It is strange but this is how it is : to be blissful needs great courage. Misery can be afforded by any coward, it is cheap. It requires no sacrifice, it requires no learning; it requires nothing. It is just there, ready to be picked up. But bliss really needs great courage. And why is it so? It looks very illogical. It is so because misery has a few things in it which are very strengthening for the ego, nourishing for the ego.

The ego can exist only in the ocean of misery. Once misery disappears the ego dies; and who wants to die? We cling to our small egos, we cling hard. It is better to be miserable than not to be; that's our choice. And the first condition, the first requirement to be blissful is to drop the ego, to be in a state of egolessness, in fact to be in a state of non-being; only then does bliss happen. It needs courage because it requires total sacrifice. *You* have to disappear, then bliss happens, you have to make a space for bliss to happen. You have to create the context for bliss to happen, and the only context that is needed is egolessness.

And because we are taught continuously from the very beginning to the end that we are egos — strengthen your ego, become strong in your ego, otherwise how are you going to survive? be ambitious, be rich, be famous, leave a name in the world — it becomes easier and easier for us to cling to misery and more and more difficult even to have a little glimpse of bliss. Yes, that's why it needs great courage : it is going against all that has been taught to you. It is going against all the conditionings of the society. It is going against ambition, it is going against fame. It is disappearing into a kind of nobodyness, into a no-man's land. Only very few people have dared, but those who have dared were really born, they really lived, they really knew what life is all about. Their joy was infinite, their bliss was eternal, their benediction knew no bounds.

Nora bounces right up to Osho's feet.

This is your name : Ma Samadhi Nora. Samadhi is the ultimate state of consciousness. The mind disappears in it but awareness is total. Thoughts are absent but one is aware that there are no thoughts. It is as if the mirror is there reflecting nothing. Nora comes from Latin, it means honour; it comes from honoria. Your full name will mean : samadhi, the most honoured one. There is nothing else which is more valuable than samadhi. To know oneself as a pure consciousness is to know god.

These are the two possibilities of our being. If we are identified with the thoughts and the contents of the mind, we know the world but we become completely oblivious of god, we know the world but we don't know who we are. The other possibility is if thoughts are dissolved we don't know the world any more but we know ourselves, we know who we are; and in knowing it we know god himself because god is nothing but the pure consciousness of the whole universe. We are small drops of that pure consciousness. The difference between us and god is not of quality but only of quantity. To feel and to know oneself as part of god is to be honoured, is to feel worthy, is to feel immensely blessed.

All the meditations and all the groups that you will be going through here are ways and means of dropping the mind, of cleansing the slate of the mind, of making it a tabula rasa. Once that has happened you are standing on the door of the divine; the mind gone, god immediately enters.

This is your name : Swami Prem Reinhard. Prem means love, reinhard is Teutonic : it means pure heart. The full name will mean : pure heart of love. Love is the fragrance of a pure heart. One cannot practise love; the practised love will be just a plastic flower, untrue, pseudo, and of no significance at all. The danger is not only that it will deceive others; slowly slowly it can deceive you too.

When you deceive people, in the beginning you know that you are deceiving them, but when they start being deceived it becomes a feedback : you start believing in your own untruth. Because so many people are believing there must be something in it, otherwise how can so many intelligent people believe it? You can deceive one, you cannot deceive all. So slowly slowly deceiving others rebounds, and one is deceived oneself.

That's what is happening in the name of love : people are deceiving others and are being deceived by their own deceptions. People have completely forgotten that love is not something to be learned, not something to be cultivated, not something to be imposed on you; it is a natural consequence of a pure heart.

What do I mean by pure heart? I don't mean what it ordinarily means : a pure heart means one who thinks only good thoughts — of god and paradise and virtues and prayers and churches. By pure heart I don't mean *that*; all that is crap.

The pure heart is the heart of the innocent child who knows nothing of god, who knows nothing of the church, who knows nothing of prayer, but still who is innocent. Out of his innocence he is spontaneous. Because he has no ready-made answers he has to devise moment-to-moment; as the situation arises he has to respond. That's my meaning of a pure heart : to become a child again, so deeply a child that all knowledge is discarded and one moves in each moment responding to it, not from the past but from present awareness.

These are the two possibilities of encountering reality. One is reaction; reaction means from the past experience, knowledge and all that. Another is response; response means no past, no experience. Just this moment I am here, aware. The situation is there and I respond to the situation; out of my presentness, out of my presence, I respond.

The first act is of the cunning mind, the second act is of the pure heart; and out of this pure heart love simply arises like a fragrance.

Manda is returning to Holland but will be back very soon, she whispers, smiling shyly.

Then you are coming forever?

She nods.

Come forever — you are ready!

That's too much for her, and she collapses, and through her tears manages a choked, Thank you!

Fellow countryman Nisargam is leaving too.

At his last darshan he talked about his girlfriend and asked whether he should stay here or go to the West with her...

Hello, Nisargam. When are you leaving?

Deva Nisargam : In two days,

When will you be coming back?

Deva Nisargam : I don't know if I will come back or when.

That's good, mm?

Deva Nisargam : There's something I'd like to say.

Say it to me.

Deva Nisargam : I want to keep sannyas even though I don't like the mala and the reactions of people to it, and even though I trust the past more than you whenever there is some discrepancy. And I don't understand why....

Mm?

Deva Nisargam : I don't understand why I want to keep sannyas.

My feeling is that you should leave sannyas; that will bring you to your senses. You leave it! And if you don't like the mala....

Deva Nisargam : I don't like the reactions of people to it, that's all.

If you like the mala then you will like the reaction also. Then who cares? (a pause) If you *love* something, you are ready to suffer for it; the problem arises only if you don't love. And if your past is more important then I am the last person to take your past from you — live in it!

Deva Nisargam : About the *Path*... I wrote to you about a group called 'The Centre of The Living Force' that is another sort of ashram.

I discovered, I met them, about half a year ago. In half a year I trusted them totally; that is what I am saying.

So wherever your trust is be there. If your trust is not with me, then why waste my time and your time?

I want to weed out people.

He makes a sweeping away motion with his hand.

I am in a hurry, and I want only those who are really with me so I can work on them. I have something to communicate to people; once they are ready it can be communicated. People like you will not be ready, or it will take so long that by the time you are ready I will be gone.

So the best logical course is: you drop sannyas; and wherever your trust is, be totally there, maybe that's where you are to grow. And if some day you can be here with total trust, the doors are open; the doors are not closed for you.

This may be the right way. A few people are like that: they cannot catch hold of the ear directly; they go round about. You may be one of them. So before you go, leave sannyas. And there is no problem in leaving it. Sannyas is given happily and taken back *more* happily, because my boat is already too full, and I would like a few people to disappear.

Those who are half-hearted, their being with me is just useless: it is useless for the work, it is useless for you, because you remain divided.

And whenever you leave sannyas I am not angry, I am not in any way disappointed in you. Leave sannyas with all my blessings. My love remains the same; your being a sannyasin or not being a sannyasin makes no difference. But leaving sannyas will be helpful at this stage; you will be clear and at least you will not be divided. And whenever you feel that you can be totally here, totally with me, you are welcome; you can come.

So do it, Nisargam!

He says it with such tenderness that there is not a hint of rejection or displeasure in it, and Nisargam nods and smiles as if reassured.

  Deva Nisargam : Thank you.

Good.

Just arrived from France, Satdharma says he has a problem.

> *Lalita (translating):* He always feels very nervous and he would like to transform his energy, because he has two children and he gets very irritable with them.

And has this always been so?

Satdharma: Yes.

And does it remain — this nervousness — continuously or does it come only in certain situations?

Satdharma: In certain situations, not always.

Osho pauses, muses on the face before him, then calls Savita to be behind Satdharma and for the two of them to go into their energy. Savita seems to sink very quickly and very deeply inside and is quite still except for her right hand trembling with energy. Satdharma, as if triggered off by her, begins to shake too. When Osho calls him back, he opens his eyes and looks around at us so uncomprehendingly that we have to laugh.

Come back! It is nothing to be worried about. From your very childhood you have been repressing it, and now it has to be thrown out of your system. So whenever you feel nervous, just go into the room, close the door, and start shaking all over the body; shake as much as you can.

It is in the body everywhere, it has become a part of your physiology. By shaking it the energy will be thrown out. It will take at least three to six months, and then you will be free of it. Next time you come here remind me again. Some body work will be helpful, or if you can do something there like Rolfing, Postural Integration, Rebirthing, these three things will be of great help.

> *Satdharma:* I have already done Rolfing and Rebirthing.

Then start shaking; and really get into it, be possessed by it! Perspiration will come, allow it. It will be very relaxing, and it will clean your system of toxins. Good.

Nagara is here for the first time and in spite of the joke in the discourse about names, wants to know the meaning of hers.

Prem means love, nagara means a citizen — a citizen of love. Love has its own universe, and unless you are initiated into it you never become part of it. Love is a great initiation because it is the greatest art to learn how to die and how to be reborn again. In all the mystery schools of the world the initiation into love was one of the most secret processes, because love is the energy we are made of and love is the energy that is our life. Not to know what love is, is to miss the whole point of being here in the world.

The world is only a challenge to know and learn love. But a calamity has happened in the world, and the calamity is this, that everybody thinks they already know what love is; so nobody tries, nobody explores, nobody enquires. We are capable of love but we don't know yet what love is. We are born as potentialities but not as actualities.

My sannyas is simply nothing but an initiation into the world of love. In a way it is one of the most significant things; in another way it is the most simple too — simple because it is a natural growth of our being, difficult because the whole society is against it.

Our society is not based on love, it is based on competition, and competition is only a beautiful label for hate. Our society is rooted in ambition, and ambition is nothing but a cultured, cultivated kind of violent struggle.

To be a lover one will have to drop the ambitious mind, the competitive mind, the jealous mind, the possessive mind; in short, one will have to drop the mind itself in toto. Then another kind of life starts, the life of the heart, through the heart and for the heart.

That is the meaning of your name : become part of the universe of love, and by becoming part of the universe of love you become part of God, because God is love, because love is God.

19

Osho : This is your name : Ma Prem Ida. Prem mens love; ida is Teutonic, it means happy — happy love. Love can be born either out of blissfulness or out of misery. When love is out of misery it creates more misery; it takes you deeper and deeper into hell. When love is out of blissfulness it gives you wings; you start soaring high. The difference is very significant, and should be understood. And the difference is so subtle that unless one looks very deeply into it, one is not going to detect it; both the loves look alike.

A man falls in love because he cannot be alone : then it is out of misery. He is not really in love with the other, he simply hates his own company; it is negative. It is not going to give you fulfilment; it will create a bondage, a dependence. This love will become possessive, is bound to become possessive. This love will be a kind of exploitation, and all kinds of exploitations are destructive — and love is more so, because it destroys the freedom of the other, it destroys the consciousness of the other, it destroys the very soul of the other. And when you destroy the other, the other starts destroying you; it can never be one-way.

Real love arises not out of loneliness, not out of misery; real love arises out of tremendous happiness. When you are alone, if you are blissful then you have the right beginning for love. If you are alone and you have no need of the other, then only can you move in the right direction towards a creative love. When you don't need the other you can share.

So either love is a need — then it is wrong; or it is just a fragrance of your being that you would like to share with all the winds — then it has tremendous beauty, then it is liberation.

This is your name : Swami Anand Yvan. Anand means blissful, yvan is a Russian form of the Hebrew john. In Hebrew, john means Jehovah has been graceful, god is gracious, life is the grace of god. Your full name will mean : a blissful, gracious gift from god.

One should start from this vision, this should be the first step into sannyas : a tremendous acceptance, a great love for yourself — because god has loved you! His love is absolutely certain, otherwise he would not have created you in the first place. And it is not only that once he has created you then he is finished with you; he still goes on breathing in you, he is your heart-beat, he pulsates in your blood, he is your very life. So it is not that the gift is finished at a certain point; the gift goes on coming, god goes on showering.

If *this* can be the beginning of sannyas, then you have the right frame of mind to transform your energies, you have the positive attitude. The negative is destructive, the positive creative. To think of oneself as just an accident .... That's what science goes on saying to people, that everything is accidental, that there is no purpose in life, that there is no meaning in life, that you are not really needed; if you are, or if you are not, it doesn't matter. Science has humiliated man, destroyed his confidence in himself, destroyed the very possibility of his inner growth — because the positive frame has disappeared.

If you think of yourself as just an accident of circumstances, how can you be happy? How can you be blissful? How can you feel the benediction of existence? Then it is impossible.

Begin with the positive, and God is very close by! Begin with the negative, and God is still close by, but your eyes are closed to him.

He changes Christina's name to Deva Albina.

Deva means divine; albina is Latin, it means whiteness.

The full name will mean divine whiteness. The colour white is the purest colour, because in fact it is not colour at all; it is colourless colour, hence it has become the symbol of purity. It has nothing foreign in it. All other colours are imposed on white; white is the natural state, colours are conditionings.

For example, a child is born, he is white. Then he becomes a Christian or a Hindu or a Mohammedan — those are colours. That's why I am changing your name, Christina; those are colours, imposed by the society.

White is also the symbol of renunciation. Physics says that there are seven colours; white and black are not included in them. Black represents greed, because whatsoever rays fall on black, it absorbs them; it does not leave any ray. It is very greedy, hence greed all over the world is painted as black. Death is painted as black, devils are painted as black.

White is just the opposite : whatsoever colour rays fall on the white, it returns them all, it absorbs nothing. It simply turns them back to their original source; it remains unaffected.

Remember, this quality has to be learned : one has to become unaffected by all that happens in life — good, bad, beautiful, ugly, success, failure. There are millions of things happening, but one has to remain a white colour, leaving them, renouncing them, not clinging to them, remaining always in a state of unclinging non-attachment. Then one starts feeling a tremendous whiteness inside, a great purity, a great light — and that light is divine. That is the first glimpse of god.

This is your name : Ma Linda Devamo. Linda is Latin, it means beautiful; devamo is Sanskrit, it means divine — divine beauty. All beauty is divine. Wherever you see beauty, think of god. Wherever you come across beauty, bow down to god. It may be in the sunset, it may be in the song of a bird, it may be in the fragrance of a flower, in a human face, in a child giggling, in the sound of running water. Wherever it is, without any conditions, feel the presence of god, because beauty is his temple. All other temples are man-made — and god is not found there; god is found in his own temple that he himself has created. And the name of that temple is beauty.

Love beauty, respect beauty, revere it, and slowly slowly your life will become full of prayer, because beauty is everywhere. If one has to be prayerful only in church, then one can go once in a while; but if one has to pray each time beauty is felt, then it becomes a continuous affair, a continuum. And when prayer is a continuum, it transforms. It only transforms when it becomes an undercurrent.

Michael is a civil engineer, he is from Germany.

This is your new name : Swami Michael Vedam. Michael is Hebrew, it means one who is like god. Vedam is Sanskrit; it means wisdom, the ultimate wisdom. It is wisdom that makes a man like god. It is wisdom that helps a man to transcend humanity and enter into the world of the divine. But wisdom is not knowledge, wisdom is not information. Wisdom has nothing to do with the head; it is a totally different phenomenon. It is a growth in the heart, it is the growth of love.

Love brings insight, love brings a different kind of knowing in its wake; love makes one perceptive of things which cannot be seen with the ordinary eyes. Love makes the impossible possible, because it helps you to see that which cannot be seen and helps you to hear that which cannot be heard.

Wisdom is a miracle, knowledge is ordinary. Any stupid person can gather as much knowledge as he wants. All that is needed for knowledge is a good memory mechanism. Now that can be done by computers very easily, so there is nothing special about it. If computers can do it, then the mind is just a biocomputer, the mind can do it.

There is only one thing the computer cannot do: the computer cannot become a Buddha, the computer cannot be enlightened, the computer cannot be wise. You can feed knowledge into the computer and whatsoever you have fed, it is always ready to answer you, but it can never be more than what you have fed into it.

Wisdom is a transformation. It is not a question of being fed with more and more information; rather, it is the beginning of a light in the heart. It does not come from the outside, it explodes within. Meditation is the spark that triggers the process. Once the heart is wise, one is like god, one is divine.

Both of them potters, Alan and Ann are from England.

This is your name: Swami Deva Alan. Deva means divine, alan is Celtic: it means harmony — divine harmony. And that is the most important thing to imbibe. Life can be a discord, life can also be in deep accord. If it is a discord you will miss all that is beautiful, all that is true, all that is divine. You will miss god, because god is not a person but the feeling of being in utter harmony. When your life functions like an orchestra, you feel god. God is a feeling, not a person somewhere that you have to encounter and say hello to.

God is not a person but a presence felt in deep harmony.

But if the harmony is not there, which is generally the case — that life is a conflict, a crowd, a marketplace, noise and noise and noise, much ado about nothing — then you cannot hear that still, small voice, then you cannot hear the presence; you are too full of your own noise.

Sannyas is an initiation into harmony, an effort to drop

the mind, an effort to disperse the crowd, an effort to say to the mind 'Be quiet' and slowly slowly learning the art of how to put it on and off. That is the secret of all meditation. Once you know how to put it on and off, you have become a master of your own being. When you need it, you can turn the ignition on, use it; when you don't need it, you can turn it off and immediately you fall into harmony.

That harmony is deathless, eternal; it is not of the body, it is of the soul. Knowing it, one knows that god is; knowing it, one knows that the soul is; knowing it, one knows that everything else is trivia, the real treasure is somewhere within.

How long will you be here?

> *Deva Alan:* About another week.

Have you done any groups here?

> *Deva Alan:* Not groups. I'd done some meditations in England, weekend ones.

Good. What date will you be leaving?

> *Deva Alan:* I think it's the twenty-fifth.

Then come again for a longer period; much has to be done.

> *Deva Alan:* It's quite an experience coming to India — a shock!

Mm! Something you would like to say to me?

> *Deva Alan:* I think just that coming here... we were both so very surprised that we decided to come, in fact. It suddenly happened, and we had about ten weeks to wait.
>
> I don't like travelling, I find it a hassle, and we had ten weeks of hassle getting it fixed up. Bombay was

such a shock that we nearly turned around and flew straight back home again.

Mm mm!

Deva Alan : But it's all been good. It's all led us here, and I feel that really my whole life has been pointing me here, I haven't decided anything consciously; it's been like a series of happy accidents.

Mm, that's how it happens (much laughter)! When it happens as a series of happy accidents, it has a beauty of its own; then it is simply a gift from god.

Come back, Alan!

(to Ann) Come close to me!

This is your name : Ma Deva Ann. Deva means divine; ann is part of hannah, it is Hebrew. It can mean many things : it can mean grace, mercy, and prayer, but I would like to emphasise the meaning 'prayer' — because whenever there is prayer, grace comes on its own, like a shadow; and whenever there is prayer, life becomes mercy, compassion. So prayer is the central thing; everything else moves around it.

Your full name will mean : divine prayer.

Prayer can also be of two types. One, that which is done by you. That cannot be of very great depth, because it will remain something of the mind. There is a totally different kind of prayer that is not done by you but only *allowed* by you. Then it has depth. Then it comes from such deep sources of your being that it will appear in the beginning as if it is coming from somewhere outside, because we are not aware of our own deeper layers.

When for the first time real prayer arises, it feels as if God has spoken to you. In fact your own unconscious has spoken to you, but because it is so separate and because we are unacquainted with it, it appears as if it is coming from some other source. Slowly slowly, as prayer starts settling, you become more and more aware that it is your own depth talking to your superficial mind.

Prayer has to be allowed, not done. How to allow prayer? Just sit silently, close the door, fall utterly quiet. Say to God 'Possess me and do whatsoever you want to do with me. These are moments for you, this is your space: I am available, I am simply available. If you want to dance through me, dance; if you want to sing through me, sing; if you simply want to sit silently in me, then sit silently. I am at your disposal.'

That's all that one has to do. Then wait, and you will be surprised: many things will start happening. Sometimes you will see your own hands moving in gestures, your body swaying; or maybe you stand up and you start dancing. Or you start singing a song which has nothing to do with religion, nothing to do with scripture, nothing especially Christian or Hindu or Mohammedan. Maybe it is just a song that you used to sing in your childhood, just a song heard somewhere or just a tune that you start humming. Or you may start saying gibberish which means nothing, baby talk, what Christians know as glossolalia — just meaningless sounds, but of tremendous beauty and in an inner harmony. The meaning is not clear, yet it is felt that there is great meaning.

So each day at least for forty minutes, be in this space, and miracles will start happening to you. And we are entitled to all those miracles!

How long are you here — the same time?

Deva Ann: Yes, a week.

Something you would like to say to me?

Deva Ann: Just that I've loved it here.

Good, come back again, and be here for a longer period.

Deva Ann : I think I will, yes!

Peregrine was here a couple of months ago, and has found his way back again.

This is your name : Swami Anand Peregrine. Anand means bliss, peregrine is Latin; it means a wanderer, a traveller, a pilgrim. The full name will mean : a blissful wanderer. Life has infinite beauty if you are not searching for a goal, if you are just a wanderer enjoying the very act of wandering, not going somewhere in particular, not going in a particular direction. Whenever one starts moving in a particular direction, tension arises, because you have to choose, and all choice brings conflict. Who knows whether this direction is right, or the other that you are not choosing? There are so many directions, so many paths — who knows which one is going to lead you to the goal? There is no guarantee. The direction, the path, that you have chosen may end in a cul-de-sac; then your whole life will be a wastage.

To choose is to remain in misery, to choose is to become anxious. To choose means that you have stopped living in the present and you have already started living in the result, in the goal, in the future : that's what misery consists of.

Be a wanderer, just like a dry, dead leaf in the wind, so wherever the wind goes, the leaf goes. It has no private goal of its own. It does not say 'Where are you taking me? I want to go to the right; I want to go to the south, and the wind is blowing north.' The leaf simply goes with the wind wherever it is going. The utter joy of relaxation and the tremendous beauty of let-go : that is the meaning of being a wanderer. God comes to wanderers!

That's why I have chosen the meaning of wanderer, not the meaning of traveller; because the traveller has a direction, a goal, a destination. That's why I have not chosen the other meaning of pilgrim; that is even more dangerous than the traveller. One has a religious goal; one is going to Mecca or to Jerusalem, then one is a pilgrim.

Life is not going anywhere; life is simply here! It has never gone anywhere. It is the sheer joy of just being herenow. It is an eternal dance, for no purpose, it is a playfulness. Only the wanderers know what it is.

Become a blissful wanderer. You need not go to god : if you can become a blissful wanderer, god is going to come to you!

How long will you be here?

Anand Peregrine : I don't know.

Be here as long as possible, or as long as the wind allows! Have you done any groups here?

Anand Peregrine : No.

Would you like to do a few?

Anand Peregrine : I don't know.

I know — do a few!

Peregrine grins wryly and allows his mind to be seduced by his heart.

Assigned groups, and on his way, Peregrine makes space for Grazia.

This is your name : Ma Anand Grazia. Anand means blissful, grazia is Latin. In Latin, grazia can have four meanings. One is grace, which is the literal meaning of grazia. Another is joy, the third is beauty — which are all part of grace. Grace brings joy, joy brings beauty. These three are mythological graces. But my preference is for the fourth meaning which is not so prevalent; that fourth meaning is thankfulness, gratitude.

To me, to be thankful to god is the whole of religion, to be thankful for all — good and bad, pain and pleasure, joy and suffering, for all that life implies — to be thankful unconditionally, to just be thankful. In that very thankfulness, grace starts descending, one becomes joyous.

If one can be thankful for everything, good and bad, how can one ever be miserable? And if one is thankful continuously for everything, that very thankfulness gives you an inner beauty.

Learn to be grateful — and there is so much to be grateful for, *so* much. We cannot be grateful enough.

Our third engineer for sannyas tonight, John is a New Zealander.

This is your name: Swami John Sanando. John is Hebrew; it means god is gracious. It is also the name of one of the apostles of Jesus, the most beloved disciple of Jesus; so slowly slowly the meaning of john has become: the most loved disciple.

To be a disciple is one of the greatest arts. It needs many things. It needs the courage to trust. It needs guts to be in love — and it is a love which is non-sensuous, a love which is not physical. It needs the capacity to surrender, which is almost impossible for millions of people, because we are brought up as egos. Our whole training has been to create a strong ego: our whole training is against being a disciple.

The miracle of disciplehood has disappeared from the world. But if one can be a disciple, things which look almost impossible immediately start becoming possible, because there is nothing which love, trust and surrender, cannot make possible.

And sanando means blissful. That is the outcome of being a true disciple. Blissfulness comes of its own accord; one need not seek and search for it.

Dharma Yogi has a bus in which he carries sannyasins from different parts of the globe to Pune and then away again. He is never around for very long, not long enough to do a group or to work, so it feels like a sharing, an exposing of himself, a wanting to make a connection, when he tells Osho he has a problem.

Dharma Yogi: It's a three-year-old problem already. It's what you said before, about being together out of necessity. I've got a problem with myself; that's the actual problem about it all. I go off to other women all the time, and my partner takes it very heavily and out of this arises the big problem. So I don't know what to do about this.

I basically think I just go away because there is too much tension there and a sexual thing always comes out of it then, even if I don't want it all the time, but I feel forced... oh, I don't know why; it's just a force there.

Mm mm (a pause). This is one of the most eternal problems; it has nothing to do with you in particular. It is really natural to be interested in many women, nothing is wrong in it. But down the ages the woman has learned a totally different attitude; she has been *forced* to learn it. The situation was such because she had to look after the child, she had to look to her comfort, her security, because when she was pregnant she could not work. So for centuries and centuries she has been afraid that if her man starts moving with other women then where is her security?

And god has really been heavy on women. If *I* am to decide, then one pregnancy will be the woman's and another will be... (laughter). Then things would have settled; it is such a simple thing, but... (with a chuckle) I have no say about it (much laughter)! The woman has to suffer all the pregnancies, so she demands some compensation. If she is suffering for you and *your* child, then at least this much she would like as a contract, that you will not start moving with other women.

Although now we are living in the post-pill era, the old habit persists; it will take a little time to go. Now there is really no need for the woman to be afraid, but the fear has gone deep into the guts. It is not a one or two days' habit; for thousands of years the woman has remained afraid, trembling. She knows perfectly well that if the man is interested in her, he is bound to be interested in other women too; about that she is certain.

If she can be certain that you are no more interested in any woman, that means that she is also included in it. Then she will leave you at ease; but then too there is a problem, because she misses you — you are no more interested in her. If you are not interested in any woman, she is included, and then she misses the companionship, the friendship, the love. If you are interested in her, out of the corner of her eyes she remains suspicious; if you are interested in *her* body why can't you be interested in other beautiful bodies? And there are so many beautiful women, she knows; she has nothing special. So she has to arrange it in such a way that no other woman is available to you, so that you have to fall upon her again and again, so that you become dependent.

And naturally, you never think of her. Everybody is so selfish. She thinks of herself, hence she becomes jealous and creates so much trouble for you that the small enjoyment you can have with another woman is so little compared to it that you decide it is better not to create the trouble, mm? That is simple logic; she makes the trouble so heavy that you sacrifice your pleasures; or slowly slowly, seeing that it creates trouble, you start becoming uninterested in the whole thing. But then you become uninterested in the woman, your own woman, and then she also suffers.

The only way out ... and now it is possible, in fact this age is fortunate in many ways — now it is possible : the woman need not be so afraid because all those old insecurities are gone. She is as educated as man, she can work, she has all the facilities that the man has. She need not be continuously pregnant, she need not go on bearing children again and again, year in and year out, torturing herself and wearing herself out. There is no need; now she can decide whether to have a child or not. But the old habit will take time : I think twenty-five years more, particularly in the West, and twenty-five centuries more in the East (laughter)!

Just talk to her. Make it absolutely plain that you become interested.... And in fact it is not disruptive to marriage. No, not at all; in fact it is helpful. If once in a while you can go with some other woman just for a change, your wife is really benefited. When you come back to her again she is new, and seeing many women again and again, finally you come to see the point that there is not much difference either! So why bother and why destroy your intimacy? Why create a hell around yourself?

Talk to her, and if it is too difficult to be with her then drop this idea of being with one woman; just be free. Then move with this woman and that, and do whatsoever you want to do. But then too you will miss something; you will miss intimacy. Sexual relationship is one thing, intimacy is totally different; and intimacy is more nourishing than sexual relationships.

Man is a complex being, and one has to be very very understanding to solve one's problems. There are no ready-made answers to them.

20

*O*din hides, nestling into his mother's side while a sannyas name is found for him. This is your name, begins Osho.

Osho : Swami Prem Odin. Prem means love, Odin means god of poetry — god of love and poetry. Good, Odin. Keep it with you.

Odin takes the piece of paper and shows to his mum his certificate. Assigned some groups, she asks to know the meaning of her name.

Anand means bliss, viresha means courageous. Bliss is only for those who are courageous. It needs tremendous courage to drop misery because we have invested in misery for so long. Our ego subsists on misery, our whole life is rooted and based in misery, so to drop it means to die as you have known yourself. To drop it means to destroy the identity that you have always thought you are. Hence courage is needed. It is dying to the old, only then can the new be born.

Bliss *is* possible; that is not a problem at all. The only problem is how to gather courage to drop misery — and that's what I teach here. Bliss cannot be taught, but how to drop misery *can* be taught. And once misery is not there, bliss is.

Good, Viresha, good.

Cecilia is from Switzerland.

How do you pronounce your name — Cecilia (with a soft 'c')?

Cecilia : Yes.

The Italians pronounce it 'Cecilia' (with a hard 'c'). (A

chuckle) I was worried (laughter)! Close your eyes.

This is your name : Ma Veet Cecilia. Veet means beyond; cecilia is Latin, it means blind. Your full name will mean : going beyond blindness. To live in the mind is to be blind. To think of oneself as the body is to be blind. To live only in an extrovert way is to be blind. Turn in, and for the first time one starts feeling that one has eyes; only by seeing the within do the eyes open up.

Watch your mind, observe its ways, become detached, see that you are not it, you are the witness of it, and you attain to eyes. In the same way, slowly slowly, go on watching your body : one day it was small, the body of a child; some other day it became young, some other day it will become old. It is constantly changing, but something in you remains eternally the same : the consciousness. I am the child, the child will not be there forever; I am young, the youth will not be there forever — but that quality of I-am-ness persists. It persists even when one dies; it has no birth, no death. To know that eternal quality of one's consciousness is to have eyes, is to become a seer.

Good, Cecilia.

From Germany, Edgar is a student. Osho adds Prem to his name and explains what it means.

Prem means love; edgar is Anglo-Saxon, it has four meanings. One is fortunate spear, the second is lucky spear, the third is a warrior. All these three meanings are German, and I don't choose any of them. The fourth meaning is rich; that is non-German. I choose the fourth meaning. Your full name will mean : the richness of love.

In reality, only the lover is rich, nobody else. Only the lover *can* be rich, and nobody else; all other riches are substitutes for love. Because people *cannot* love, are afraid of love, are not courageous enough to love, are not intelligent enough to go on that adventure, they start loving stupid things: somebody loves a house, somebody loves money, somebody loves power politics. These are escapes, escapes from real love; these are pseudo substitutes for love. But the mind is a coward, and it always finds something cheap, something in which there is no risk involved.

The heart has the courage to go into the unknown. The heart loves — and the more the heart loves, the more rich you become. The inner poverty simply disappears, the inner darkness is found no more. The hollowness that people feel, the emptiness that people feel, is suddenly gone; one is full, overfull, overflowing.

Love makes a man an emperor; without love, everybody is a beggar. So love more, love unconditionally, love each and all. Let love become your very lifestyle, let love be your sannyas!

Just look at me, he invites Wilfred.

This will be your name: Swami Deva Wilfred. Deva means divine. Wilfred is Teutonic; it means one who is determined to attain peace, one who has resolved to attain peace, a resolution for peace. The full name will mean: a divine resolution for peace.

That's what sannyas is all about: a resolution to change one's life — not just to modify it, but to change it, root and all; not just to reform it, to whitewash it here and there, to renovate it, no, but to demolish it totally and to create a new life: a life of love, silence, God.

Man ordinarily lives in a madhouse, and unless one makes a total decision to come out of it, it is almost impossible to come out. The totality of resolution creates integrity, makes you one-pointed, turns your consciousness into an arrow. And that arrow is capable of coming out of the imprisonment.

Good, Wilfred!

(to Sandra) This will be your name : Ma Prem Sandra. Prem means love, sandra is Greek, it is part of Alexandra; the meaning is : helper of mankind. Only love can be of any help, and without love, all help becomes harmful. The world is suffering very much from so-called good people, the do-gooders. They are the most mischievous people in the world; and because they do good, nobody can prevent them. But their basic motive is egoistic. Their basic motive is to gain more and more power, to oblige people; that is the simplest way to become powerful over them. The moment you help somebody you are becoming higher, holier, saintly, generous, and all that crap! You are reducing the other to a dependent; in fact you are enjoying his humiliation.

Without love all kinds of service, help, are dangerous. Love has to be the fundamental thing; only then, whatsoever you do will be good. But always watch whether love is there or not. Good is a fragrance of love. Without love, the good is only pseudo, pretension. Humanity has suffered from pretenders for so long that it is time to get rid of all of them.

Good, Sandra.

How long will you be here?

Prem Sandra : Three or four months, maybe longer.

Very good.

Elisabeth is an air hostess and is from America. I have to change your name, he explains....

Elisabeth is beautiful, but we have so many Elisabeths here!

This will be your new name : Ma Deva Adelina. Deva means divine; adelina is Teutonic, it means serpent — divine serpent. In the East the serpent is the symbol of the energy that is unmanifest in you. It is as if a serpent that is sitting coiled up inside, needs uncoiling. Hence kundalini is called the serpent power. It is accumulated exactly at the sex centre, hence the serpent also became a symbol of sexuality.

If it goes lower, it becomes sex; if the serpent starts moving upwards, it becomes samadhi — it is the same energy.

The whole thing depends on how we use it. If it remains under the influence of gravitation and is pulled downwards, and if we don't know how to take it upwards, then life is wasted. Life simply remains in the hands of some unconscious biological force. Then we are victims of nature; we play a role that nature gives to us and then we disappear. This has been going on and on for many lives.

But the serpent can rise upwards. And that is the miracle of meditation : it releases the serpent from the confinement of gravitation, it makes available to it a space to move upwards. And the higher it moves, the more and more peace and tranquillity and silence and bliss start happening. When it reaches to the highest peak, the seventh chakra, then one blooms, then the ultimate manifests, flowers. Call it God, nirvana, enlightenment, or whatsoever you wish, but the whole game is with the serpent energy.

To turn it upwards is not really difficult; we just have not tried, that's all. It can move as easily upwards as it can downwards. One thing is certain about it, that it *has* to move. If you don't allow it to move upwards, if you don't create the context for it to move upwards, it will move downwards. It is *movement,* hence it is called the serpent.

And because it needs no legs to move, that's also one of the reasons why it is called the serpent. The serpent can move on a wall, it can move upwards on a tree, with no legs. It is a miracle to see it moving on a tree!

Zen people say that to talk about enlightenment is like putting legs on a serpent — the talk is not needed at all. In fact if you put legs on the serpent, you will make it very very difficult to move. It does not need legs, it moves as pure energy. In the East the serpent power has been respected for centuries; in the West too the serpent has been always thought of as a symbol of wisdom.

The Old Testament says 'Be ye as wise as the serpents.' Good, Adelina.

Peter is from Canada where he works as a biochemist. Osho indicates his new name to him, with an explanation...

We have many Peters. Jesus needed only one, and I have so many (laughter)! So I will make a little change : Swami Anand Petros. That is the original of Peter, the Greek original, petros. Anand means bliss, petros means a rock. The rock symbolises the eternal; it symbolises the non-temporal, the unchanging, the abiding. If we watch existence deeply, it is bound to be noticed that there are two things happening everywhere : the periphery goes on continuously changing — it is a flux; but at the deepest core of it all there is a centre, the centre of the cyclone, which remains eternally the same. That is petros, and to find it is to find God. To find it is to find something eternal which can become the base of the temple of your life. Otherwise people are making their lives on sand : by the time they have made them, everything will start disappearing.

To be too concerned with the fluxlike life is a wastage. You are playing with foam. It looks beautiful, sometimes so silvery in the moonlight, but when you catch hold of it...

A hand grasps the air...

...you don't have anything in your hands —

...and opens to discover itself empty.

...just plain ordinary salt water. So is life on the periphery. Each periphery has a centre, but to know the centre of other peripheries, the first requirement is to know the centre of your own circumference. The body is your outer circumference; then there is the mind — a little inner; then there is the heart — a little more inner; and then there is the being — a little more inner. Then there is the non-being, the ultimate centre : petros. To find it is to find bliss, is to find benediction.

Ronald is from Holland; he's a healer. Osho places the mala around his neck.

This is your name : Swami Veet Ronald. Veet means beyond; ronald is Teutonic, it means mighty power. The mind is in search of great power. If the mind is looking for more money, it is not really for more money but for more power — because money brings power. If the mind is searching to become famous, that again is a power trip. The mind suffers from a great inferiority complex, hence it wants to overcompensate. But this is understood, that in the world people hanker for money, for power, for prestige, respectability, because these searches are very gross.

When a person starts turning spiritual, the search remains almost the same; it only becomes more subtle. Again it is the same game played on another plane. Now spiritual power, psychic power — powers that are brought by telepathy, clairvoyance, the power to levitate, the power to disappear, the power to read others' thoughts, and so on and so forth — psychic powers or ultimately spiritual powers… to be in heaven with all the joys and all the pleasures available there, to be special even in heaven. But it is the same trip. So the worldly and the other-worldly are not different, they are the same people. Maybe they are standing back to back, but nothing has changed.

My vision of sannyas is to drop this whole power trip. Seeing its futility, seeing that it is a kind of pathology, seeing that it arises out of an inferiority complex, it starts disappearing of its own accord. And then what is left? A very ordinary human being. That ordinary human being, that nobody, is a Buddha.

To be a nobody, to be as if you are not, to be as if you are of no account, to be in a state of fana — that's the word Sufis use — alive and yet dead, to have no special claim, just to live the ordinary life, silently, consciously, moment-to-moment, you create the space in which god is possible. In that very ordinary space, god becomes possible. In that very ordinary state, extraordinary things start happening. So, to me, to be ordinary is to be the most extraordinary phenomenon. To ask, to desire, to be extraordinary, is very ordinary, because everybody else is doing it.

That is the meaning of your name : go beyond all power and the desire for power, howsoever disguised it is, howsoever camouflaged in spiritual words, go beyond all power trips. Then suddenly, chopping wood, carrying water from the well, is more than one can ask for. Then each moment is a miracle, a surprise.

Seiji is to start a centre in the centre of Japan. He's already received the name 'Satgyan' for it, but would like Osho to say something to him.

(a pause) Mm mm. Satgyan means right-wisdom. One can gather wisdom from others, then it is wrong. When it wells up within your own being, then it is right. Truth borrowed becomes a lie. You cannot depend on others' truth; only the truth that has happened to you can liberate you. Jesus says : Truth liberates. It is certainly true, but Jesus' truth liberates only Jesus, nobody else. In fact others who think that they will be liberated by Jesus' truth, become imprisoned in a lie.

So in the name of religion there are many prisons on the earth. And when a person becomes very tired of one prison, he changes the prison; he goes to another prison, hoping that the other will not be a prison but will be a freedom. But these hopes are always just hopes; they are never fulfilled.

Make our centre a place where information is not to be

imparted, but where people are helped to go inwards. Don't make them knowledgeable : make them wise.

When will you be coming back?

Prabuddha (translating) : In October.

Good. Keep it (a box) with you, and whenever you need me just put it on your heart. Start the centre — and many many people are going to come. You start the centre and I send the people (laughter)!

Bhavana is back from California with her partner, Prabhat.

Come here! How long will you be here now?

Bhavana : I don't know.

She just finishes the sentence, then collapses into crying.

Then just be here, there is no need to go anywhere. Something to say to me?

She gulps and smiles and then confesses...

Bhavana : I'm a little scared... to jump!

You are not scared!

She laughs with us.

Bhavana : Okay!

You are just happy, too happy. And sometimes it is difficult to say 'I am so happy' so people say some other thing. To be happy has become so embarrassing in the world!

What about you?

Prabhat : I'm happy too (laughter).

You will be staying?

Prabhat : Three months, maybe more.

Good!

21

*T*his afternoon I caught fragments of the rumour that was later confirmed as being so, that each evening now, a certain sannyasin (a different one for each night of the week) will come to darshan to assist as a vehicle for his energy.

It feels like the beginning of a new phase, a stepping-up, an intensifying of his working on us — all of which he has been indicating to us so frequently lately in the morning talk and at darshan. So, more than ever it feels as if the verbal communication that happens in darshan is just part of the preliminaries, a bridge that is still necessary, perhaps particularly for newcomers, to help us establish contact with Osho.

Ferrel is sitting in front of him, awaiting her sannyas. She doesn't know the meaning of her name, and he finds her a totally new one.

Osho : This will be your new name : Ma Prem Almiro. Prem means love; almiro is Arabic, it means exalted. Love is the most exalted state of being. It is just next to God : one step more and God is reached. Love is the last thing; beyond that is the infinite, the eternal. Love is our boundary; if we remain on this side, we remain in the world. If we cross the boundary of love, we enter into another kind of existence, a totally different dimension. This side is ego, that side, no-ego; and love is the fence between the two. Love has to be transcended, but all transcendence is through living. One cannot repress it, one cannot by-pass it; it can be surpassed only by deeply living it.

Love is the way beyond love.

This is your name : Ma Deva Maria. Deva means divine. Maria is Hebrew, a form of Mary, but the meaning of it is tremendously significant : it means rebellion. And a man like Jesus can be born only out of rebellion. Only rebellion can give birth to Buddhahood. And rebellion is always virgin because it remains unpolluted by the past. Rebellion is always pure because it is not a reaction. Rebellion is not reacting against something; it is simply a declaration to live one's life according to one's own light. And that was the sin of Jesus for which he was punished. The society does not allow rebellious people to exist; the society needs slaves, obedient people, conformists.

It is very unfortunate that we have not yet been able to create a society where rebellion is respected. The day rebellion is respected, taught, we will have a totally new humanity — a humanity which will be divine, a humanity which will be very close to god.

Good, Maria.

Maria's partner takes her place; he is Josep!
What is the meaning of your name? Is it a form of Joseph?

Josep : Yes.

Then it is simple! Close your eyes!

He calls him close to show him his name with Anand added to it.

Anand means bliss, josep is a form of Joseph. In Hebrew, joseph means : god increases, god goes on giving, god is a giver. Your full name will mean : god is the giver of bliss. All that is needed on our part is to receive it, to welcome it — but we don't even do that; we keep our eyes closed. We are very miserly about receiving.

You have heard about the misers who are miserly in giving, but the real misers are those who are misers in taking. In fact, because you cannot take, you cannot give. The ordinary worldly miserliness arises out of the first miserliness. The moment you are ready to receive god's gifts, you have so much you cannot contain it within yourself. It will start overflowing from you, it will start reaching people.

So open up, become more and more receptive. Become a womb and you have become a sannyasin.

Jane is next. She is Australian but lives in New Zealand where she works as a therapist.

This is your name : Ma Prem Jane. Prem means love; jane is Hebrew, it means god's gracious gift. The full name will mean : love, god's gracious gift. Love is a happening; you cannot do it. If you do it, it will be only acting. You cannot manufacture it. If you manufacture it, as millions of people are doing, you will have only a plastic kind of love; it will not be a real flower. It will not have roots in your being. It will not give you any fragrance, any fulfilment; and when it will not give any fulfilment to you, it will not give any fulfilment to anybody else either. Hence the absurd situation : everybody is loving everybody else, and yet there is no love. The world stinks of hate; it doesn't show any sign of love. It shows all kinds of destruction but no creative fragrance of love, and the reason is that we have been told, we have been hypnotised, that we can *do* love. It is not a doing : it is always a gift.

We can bow down in prayer, and love comes from the beyond. We can only be on the receiving end. It is something which has never been done and will never be done; and unless one trusts in existence, one remains without love.

Trust, surrender to existence, feel in tune with the world, and slowly slowly you will see a new quality arising in you that you had never known before : a love growing. And as love grows, fulfilment arises; as love grows, one starts feeling contented. And when the spring comes, when the time is ripe and love blooms, one has arrived home.

Her partner, John, replaces her.

This is your new name : Swami Premananda. Prem means love, ananda means bliss. Premananda means bliss that arises out of love. In fact that is the only kind of bliss there is; all other kinds are bogus — painted smiles, pseudo faces, acting masks. The true bliss arises only out of a loving heart; and we have forgotten the ways of the heart. We are hung up in the head, and the head knows nothing of love. It knows the word 'love', but the word 'love' is not love.

And the head cannot experience love. It cannot experience anything; as far as experience is concerned the head is utterly impotent. It can talk about it, it can philosophise about it, it can speculate about it, but all remains wordy, verbal. If one looks deep down into it, there is no substance in it.

Sannyas means a shift from the head to the heart, which is our original home. Each child is born with the heart; the head is a social imposition. We drag the child from the heart towards the head, because the head pays. In the marketplace it is needed; and the more you have of it, the more success you will have. The man of the heart is going to remain a failure in the world; people will think of him as a fool. They even thought of Jesus as a fool, of Francis as a fool.

So the society starts pulling the child out of the heart towards the head. It is such a manipulation, and the child is so helpless that he cannot protect himself; he has no ways to protect himself. He is a dependent person; her cannot survive without the parents, so whatsoever they say, he has to follow. Reluctantly, in spite of himself, slowly slowly, he forgets the language of the heart and learns the arithmetic, the calculation, the logic, of the head. And then he lives his whole life in that desert land of the head. The heart is an oasis.

Sannyas is the beginning of another childhood; it is a rebirth. It is bringing you back home. And once it starts happening it is so easy, because it is natural, spontaneous. It is intrinsic to our being to be in the heart. To be in the head is a tension, a constant anxiety, because it is against nature. It is going upstream; it is a struggle and a dissipation of energy. When you go towards the heart you start moving with the river, you no more push the river. Then life becomes a tremendously beautiful experience, a relaxation, a let-go.

Maureen is mala-ed.

This is your name : Ma Prem Maureen. Prem means love. Maureen is Latin; it has two meanings, and both meanings are tremendously significant : one is dark, and the other is great. Love has both the qualities. It is certainly the greatest experience, incomparable, unique; and it is also a very dark experience, dark in the sense that it has depth. Light is shallow, darkness has depth. Light is public, darkness has privacy. Light is known, darkness remains not only unknown but unknowable. Light is explainable, darkness very elusive, mysterious.

Love is a great darkness, a great mystery, a great indefinable experience; something unfathomable and something utterly private, intimate; something so close to the heart that it cannot be talked about — inexplicable, indefinable.

Very few people are aware of the beauties of darkness, very few, because of an unnecessary association with darkness — the association of fear. And because of that association, darkness has become a symbol of all that is fearsome : death is dark, sin is dark, the devil is dark and hell is full of darkness. These are just projections, they have nothing to do with darkness; and these projections are made by people who have no experience of darkness. Otherwise darkness is really relaxing, very calm, it has a music of its own. It has a special touch, it is very velvety... and the infinity of it. Light is always finite, it comes and goes. Light always needs a cause for it to exist; once the cause is exhausted, light disappears. But darkness always is, uncaused; it needs no fuel.

All the religions of the world say 'God is light' : it is just to help people not to be afraid of god. But the truth is that god is more like darkness than like light — the eternity of darkness and the unfathomable mystery of it.

Science has been able to understand what light is, but about darkness everything still remains in the dark. Science has been able to measure light. If you collect the rays that fall on five square miles, they have a certain weight, one tenth of a kilo. Light is measured, its mystery is known, it can be used, you can put it on and off. Light has been reduced to a slave.

Darkness still remains beyond our grasp. It is better now to think of god as darkness than as light.

Hanny is Dutch, and her name comes from Johanna, she replies in answer to Osho's question.

Johanna? That will do! he grins.

This is your name : Ma Prem Hanny. Prem means love, hanny means grace, mercy, prayer. All the three meanings are beautiful, and all the three meanings arise out of love. The loving person cannot be anything *but* graceful; it is natural. The unloving person cannot be but ungraceful. The very idea of love deep down in your heart makes you luminous; a certain grace starts surrounding you — a beauty that is not of this world, a fragrance that comes from the beyond. It is something from god, and is available only to those who allow love to happen in their hearts.

The person who is loving, graceful, is bound to have compassion, mercy. And there is a great difference between sympathy and mercy. Sympathy is only in specific situations : somebody is miserable and you are sympathetic. Mercy is simply the way you live. It is not a question of specific situations — that you are compassionate to the beggar because he is hungry, and merciful to the blind because he is blind. These things are good, but mercy is something more : it is simply your very lifestyle; whether somebody needs it or not is irrelevant. It is not a response to somebody's need, but an overflowing of your own heart. It is not a reaction created by the outside, but a sharing of your joy — because you have so much, you would like to share it.

And the third is the ultimate expression of love : prayer. When one loves one person it feels so good, but it brings misery too. You love one against so many, hence the misery of love. If you start loving more and more people, less and less misery arises out of love; and the day your love becomes universal, it becomes prayer. Then there is no misery, then love is sheer joy. Then love is rejoicing, a celebration. And when somebody is able to celebrate love on that plane of universality, god is happy; one has entered into the garden of Eden again.

Satlok is going back to Australia. She hasn't had Osho talk to her at length, and says now she'd like him to talk about her name.
What meaning was given to you?
True land of love, she replies.

We don't live in one world; there are as many worlds as there are minds, and each mind creates its own world. We live in the world *we* create. There are people who are living in hell — they may be your neighbours, they may be sitting just by your side. There are people who are living in heaven — they may again be your neighbours, or sitting by your side. The world is not something outside us : it is our inner creation.

Truth happens only whenever a heart is overflowing with love. When the heart knows nothing except love, when the heart is madly in love, in that madness the greatest of sanity becomes possible. Love opens the eyes for the truth.

Love more, love intensely, and love without asking anything in return. Let that be your meditation, and you will be surprised : as love grows, life becomes truer, authentic, sincere. And with sincerity, authenticity, truth, bliss starts showering from all directions. It rains — it rains cats and dogs! It comes like a flood. It is so much that it is uncontainable; it simply takes you off the ground. A totally different dimension of life opens up. That's what religion is all about, and that's what the search of sannyas is.

Parinamo is returning to Norway.

Something to say to me?

Parinamo : I wonder if you could say a little about creativity. I feel like being more creative, but I don't get really into it.

Mm?

Parinamo : I feel like being more creative in music and writing, but I don't get really into it. Is there anything I can do to get more into it?

(a pause) Have you been playing music before?

Parinamo : Yes.

But you don't get into it?

Parinamo : Yes, but I feel that there is some kind of hindrance. I can get into it and then suddenly I'm out again, when I play and am improvising.

And what happens in writing?

Parinamo : The same thing.

The same?

Parinamo: I can feel much inspiration, but when I sit down suddenly I'm just empty.

Mm mm (a pause). My feeling is that you have a great desire to be famous, and that creativity is only a means towards it. That is causing the trouble.

Forget about becoming famous, then there is no problem. Then when you feel like playing music, play; when you feel like writing, write. If you don't feel like writing, don't write — even if in the middle of the sentence the inspiration disappears, so what? Stop, then and there.

The problem arises because you would like to make it a beautiful piece to be appreciated, you would like to become a great musician or an author. Somewhere deep down there is ambition — and ambition is very very dangerous for creativity. If one can be creative without having any ambition, then creativity flows so easily, so spontaneously. But still I am not saying that by dropping ambition you will become a great musician. I am not saying that, otherwise one can drop even ambition, hoping that by dropping ambition one will become a great musician — but that is the same thing from the back door.

Creativity somehow became entangled with fame. That's why so *very* few people in the world are creative; they all want to do great things. Every painter wants to become a Picasso — and when he cannot, the inspiration disappears. Every poet would like to become a Byron or a Shelley — and when he thinks 'These lines that I am writing are just worthless, these are not going to make me a Byron' the inspiration disappears.

If you are not after fame, then the question does not arise. You are not writing these lines for somebody else; you are writing for the sheer joy of writing. There is no end, no goal-orientation; the writing in itself is its own end. And if you are playing on the guitar, you are playing because you are enjoying it. The moment there is no enjoyment, stop. Why go on prolonging it? What is the point? But the ambitious person cannot stop there. The ambitious person has to go on polishing, he has to go on practising; if he wants to become famous it is an arduous path.

So my feeling is that you call it the desire for creativity, but deep down search : somewhere unconscious, coiled up, is a desire to become famous, to be somebody special. Then there *will* be trouble. All cannot become great poets, all cannot become great musicians — and it is good that all cannot, otherwise the world would be such a mad place. It is already! If everybody is a musician, just think : everybody practising eight hours, ten hours! People will simply go mad, they will start committing suicide.

Disconnect the idea of the ego from creativity, and then there is no problem. Then whatsoever you feel ... then even cleaning the floor is creative, cooking food is creative, watering the garden is creative. Then sometimes just sitting silently doing nothing is creative.

Creativity has nothing to do with anything in particular. It is a graceful state, a joyful state, and in that joyful state whatsoever you do is good. And the end is in itself; it is not a means to anything else.

Just observe it : if you can drop the ego, there is no problem. If you cannot drop the ego, then the problem will persist, then it is better that you drop your creativity, otherwise you will be in trouble, in great tension.

When will you be back?

Parinamo : In Autumn.

Good. Keep it (a box) with you. Help my people there!

As Mukta has a throat infection, Arup is sitting in her place on Osho's right, so from there she calls out the next sannyasin, Deva Gita — who happens to be her mother!

Gita was here for a few weeks with her sons and husband, and went back to Holland with them just for a fortnight. She's back again for a long time.

Hello, Gita. How has the trip been?

Deva Gita: The trip has been excellent. It all went well, very well.

Good — that's very good.

Deva Gita: Yes. But coming back has been really a nightmare.

Mm mm.

Deva Gita: Being here the first two weeks, I think I had expectations, but suddenly.... I wanted to speak to you about emotionality: it jumps upon me and then somewhere the mind gets in and guilt comes in and headaches and, well, you know, I cannot get out. It's lasted two weeks. Only this morning after lecture I thought 'I'm going mad, I'm absolutely going mad — even here!'

There is a ripple of affectionate amusement.

Deva Gita: So I cried and I thought 'Well, then I go mad; that's how it happens.' And then the gestalt turned, and that was all.

You look perfectly okay.

Deva Gita: Yes, I am now, but it's frightening, Osno, very frightening.

No, sometimes the unconscious throws out things. Through just going there and coming back and coming now to stay for long, the unconscious may have got stirred up, and that stirring may have brought something. But it is good that it was released. Remember, next time it happens, rather than repressing it, rather than consoling yourself, rather than

---

220   *Won't You Join the Dance?*

rationalising, close the doors, have a good cry. Roll down on the floor, cry, cry your heart out, and within fifteen to thirty minutes you will be out of it.

> *Deva Gita:* But I have so many tears, I can go on crying days and days and then I start again.

You just try it.

> *Deva Gita:* Yes, I'll do that.

Crying will be tremendously helpful. And start working now.

> *Deva Gita:* Yes, I started.

Good, Gita!

22

Yuri is our first for sannyas. He's from America and is a polarity therapist. Osho retains his original name—which has a beautiful meaning: a farmer. He adds Anand to it so he becomes a farmer of bliss!

Osho : Gautam the Buddha used to say again and again : I am the farmer, I sow the seeds of bliss. There is a way of inner farming, of creating a garden of the inner. Many never become aware of it; they are the unfortunate ones. Otherwise it is just so close — just a one-hundred-and-eighty-degree turn and it is in front of you. But we go on keeping our backs to it. The desiring mind goes on running after outer things. Only when one is finished with desiring, is totally frustrated with desiring, has come to know that desiring leads nowhere, that the whole effort is futile, then one turns inwards — and a new beginning, a new birth. Then one can sow seeds of bliss and one can reap the crop of God.

Good, Yuri.

How long will you be here?

Anand Yuri : A long time.

Be here!
Anything to say to me?

He has already booked up for two groups; just to keep him out of mischief, Osho assigns him three more, then asks :

Anything to say to me?

Anand Yuri : Just that my heart feels...

The tail of the sentence is lost to me; his hand is on his chest.

Just be here and enjoy!

Miriam is from Holland. She's a sculptor, so the meaning Osho chooses for her name seems particularly pertinent.

Miriam has many meanings, but one meaning that I would like to emphasise is : a desire to become a mother. It is intrinsic in every human being to mother something, to create something. Don't take it literally, because a man can also become a mother, just as a woman can become a mother.

Picasso is a mother; he mothered so many paintings. Anyone who creates is a mother; motherhood is a by-product of creativity. Certainly Miriam was the incarnation of all motherhood : Jesus was born to her. Each person has to become such a mother, so that the quality of Christ-consciousness becomes possible in their lives. It is our potential; we have only to develop it. And unless a person becomes the mother of Christ-consciousness, he has not lived at all.

This story is also beautiful, that Christ had only a mother, not a father; it is of very psychological significance. I am not concerned at all with Christian theology and all their nonsensical interpretations. I am not concerned with its historicity either; those are irrelevant things. My concern is psychological.

The father is an unnatural phenomenon. It is artificial, arbitrary, it is social; the mother is natural. Fathers have not always been in existence. At the most fathers have existed for five thousand years; before that the institution was non-existential. There was a matriarchy, the mother was all; and all the children were known not by the name of their father but by the name of their mother. Nobody used to ask anybody 'Who is your father?' or 'Whose son are you? — that would have been absolutely meaningless. The question was asked 'Who is your mother?'

You will be surprised to know that the word 'uncle' is older than 'father', because people used to live in groups, communes, so all the people who were of the age of the father — who was not known, who was anonymous — were called uncles. Out of all the uncles somebody was the father, but nobody knew exactly who the father was. So uncle is a more ancient word than father. Father came only with private property. And there is every possibility that the day private property disappears, private ownership disappears, the father may disappear again. In fact he is on the way out.

It is beautiful that Jesus is born only out of a mother; the father is not taken into account at all.

Whenever somebody creates something he does not become the father, he becomes the mother — because all creativity is feminine. Destructiveness is male, creativity is female. It is not a coincidence that Germans call their land the fatherland. No other country calls its land the fatherland; all other countries are motherlands. There is something in it — some fighting quality, some inclination to war, some tendency to destroy.

So create a great desire to give birth to Christ-consciousness.

This is your name : Swami Anand Eli. Anand means bliss. Eli is Hebrew; it means the highest, the god. Your full name will mean : bliss, the highest, the god. Bliss is another name for god. God is not a person, but the experience of bliss. You cannot see god, you cannot encounter him, because he is not the other. He is not there to be confronted. He is your innermost core, he is your hidden treasure. You are the bud, he is the flowering, he is your highest expression. You are a song unsung; he is the same song sung.

The difference between you and god is only that of manifestation and non-manifestation. There is no other difference, no qualitative difference. You are on the way to becoming god, or we can say that god is on the way to discovering himself.

This has to be allowed to sink as deeply into the heart as possible. We have been taught for so long that god is there far away, a thou, that it has become almost natural for us to think of him as the other. Even a man like Martin Buber used to think that the highest form of prayer is a dialogue between I and thou.

The highest form of prayer is not a dialogue at *all*. That is the lowest form of prayer, because at the highest peak there is no I, no thou. How can there be a dialogue? There is just silence, utter absolute silence — communion of course, but not communication.

The pretty tinkle of her anklets heralds Elizabeth's arrival. She's a nurse and is from New Zealand.

This is your new name : Ma Deva Adora. Deva means divine; adora is Greek, it means a gift. The full name will mean a divine gift.

Meditate on the fact that God has been very gracious. There was no reason at all for us to exist. The existence could have been perfectly well without us; still, we are. We have not earned it, we have not earned the right to be alive. We have not earned the right to see the beautiful sunset and the night sky full of stars and the colours of a rainbow. We are unworthy of this beautiful existence — yet we are, yet we have been given all for which we had not even asked. It is a gift. And the giver is so shy that he does not come in front of us; he hides. We only see the gifts, we never see the giver. Once you start feeling the hand behind the gifts, prayer arises. And that's what sannyas is : the search for the invisible in the visible, the search for the beyond in the herenow, the groping for the ultimate in the immediate. Good, Adora.

Won't You Join the Dance?

This will be your new name: Swami Deva Cosmo. Deva means divine; cosmo is Greek, it means the universe — divine universe. Existence is not just that which appears to the eyes, it is much more. Existence is not only the surface of it; it has a hidden centre of life in it. Existence is meaningful: that is the literal meaning of cosmo. It is not a chaos, it is a cosmos. It is not accidental, there is a hidden current of purpose running in it which keeps it together. It is very orderly, hence science is possible.

If it were a chaos, there would have been no science; and because it is a cosmos, religion is also possible. If it were a chaos, then no Buddha would have been of any help to anybody. If there were no order in existence — if one day two plus two are four, and another day two plus two are five, and one day love leads you to god, and another day love leads you to hell — there would be no possibility to help anybody, there would be no possibility of guidance.

Science is possible because existence is very orderly; it follows a few laws very consistently. And religion is possible because in the interior world of consciousness it is also very orderly. Meditations can be developed, yoga can be found, tao, tantra — all these things become possible because we have been able to find out a few fundamental laws. Maybe they have to fit with each individual a little bit this way and that, but the foundation remains the same, the essential core remains the same.

How long will you be here?

Deva Cosmo: I don't know.

Have you done any groups?

Deva Cosmo: No.

Would you like to?

Deva Cosmo: Actually not.

No? Have you done any before coming here?

Deva Cosmo : No.

Then it is better to have a new experience. Do at least two or three groups and then decide : if you don't want to, then it's okay, but never decide without experiencing something.

He suggests three groups, then says that if he wants to do more then he can ask.

This will be your new name : Ma Prem Alva. Prem means love; alva is Latin, it means white. White is a symbol of purity, innocence. Love is white because love is innocent. Love is always innocent. The moment that love becomes clever, calculating, it is no more love; nothing destroys love more than calculation. Love can live only in deep trust. It needs intelligence but not cleverness, and intelligence is a totally different phenomenon. Cleverness is part of the mediocre mind. The stupid mind is trying to be clever — he has to, because he has no intelligence and he has to substitute for intelligence. And sometimes we over-substitute.

The really intelligent mind is unassuming, anonymous, a nobody. He trusts his intelligence; he knows that whenever need arises he will be able to respond to the situation in the correct way, so there is no need to think about it, to plan it, to calculate about it.

Love and intelligence are two aspects of the same energy. Become love, become innocent, become intelligent : these are my teachings. And once you are loving, innocent, intelligent, then there is no need of any other character to be imposed on you. You will be able to find your path towards God.

I don't give you a map and I don't give you a direction; I simply give you a lamp of light so that you can find your direction, your way. And it is tremendously beautiful when one finds one's own way; its ecstasy is different.

A friend of Karate instructor, Satchidananda, Peter sits in what looks like a Karate posture, his hands upturned on his knees, very straight-backed. Within minutes, his hands have begun to tremble with energy and a little smile appears and turns up the corners of his mouth.

This will be your new name : Swami Satbodhi. Sat means true, bodhi means enlightenment — true enlightenment. There is a possibility of untrue enlightenment. The ego can play the last trick : the ego can start pretending 'I am enlightened'. And it is so subtle that it is almost impossible for others to detect it, because you can talk like enlightened people very easily. Scriptures are available, you can cram them; you can repeat the Upanishads, the Bible, the Koran. You can analyse in such a subtle way, with such philosophical acumen, that it can be easily proved to others that you have attained. You can live a life according to people's expectations of how an enlightened person should live. If they expect that you should live naked, you can live naked. If they expect that you should kiss lepers, you can kiss lepers. If they expect that you should serve the poor and the ill, you can serve the poor and the ill. It is easy to manage.

That is the last trick that the ego can play upon oneself. One has to be very very aware at that moment, otherwise one slips back to the original place, one again falls to the same ground from where one was trying and trying hard to rise.

How to decide whether it is true enlightenment or untrue? The only decisive factor is : the absence of I. In true enlightenment, the idea of I simply disappears, it is not found. There is nobody to claim 'I am enlightened', there is simply nobody to claim anything. It is a pure nothingness, full of light, full of joy — very spacious, it can contain the whole sky, but the 'I' is found nowhere, not even a trace of it. Then it is satbodhi, then it is true enlightenment.

How long will you be here, Satbodhi?

Satbodhi : Until about April 15th.

Good!

He has already done the intensive Enlightenment group; now he's got three more groups.

And next time come for a longer period. Something to say to me?

Satbodhi : You make us all so happy. I wish I could always make you laugh!

You will — you will!

This is his first visit from Holland, and Gyani tells Osho that he's done some groups with Veeresh...

Gyani : ...who sends you his love.

Good. Next time come for a longer period, so you can do a few groups here.

Gyani : Can you tell me something about my name?

Anand means bliss, gyani means wise, wisdom. Bliss makes one wise, and wisdom makes one blissful. They go together, they are two wings; neither can exist without the other. Either become blissful and you will become wise, or become wise and you will become blissful. The path of wisdom is the path of meditation, and the path of blissfulness is the path of love : these are the only two paths in the world.

Either follow love and go madly into it — you will be blissful, and sooner or later, suddenly one day, wisdom arrives without even informing you; suddenly it knocks on your door. Or follow the path of meditation : become more and more aware, alert, watchful, and wisdom starts happening — because awareness is another name for wisdom. Then one day the same miracle happens : love knocks on the door, suddenly, from nowhere, from out of the blue. But whenever one reaches the peak, the other arrives automatically; they are inseparable.

This is Mahadeva's first visit too. He's a psychotherapist from the States.

How long will you be here?

Mahadeva: Two more weeks.

Good, Mahadeva. Something to say to me?

Mahadeva: Just that I thought the lecture this morning was fantastic. I enjoyed it very much. I'd like to come back and see you before I go, in two weeks.

Come back and see me, mm?

Mahadeva: Then I'll have more to talk about.

Mm mm. Come back, and next time come for a longer period.

Mahadeva: Yes, it was not... I didn't expect ... (he laughs) I didn't expect what I found here.

Good that you have come!

Mahadeva: Thank you.

Nanda's mother, Vimala, is returning to England, and has asked for an energy darshan before she leaves.

Osho has her face me, and Chetana and Vivek stand behind her, all three with their arms in the air.

All three of you start feeling the energy moving upwards — feel pulled upwards.

All feel together as if one energy. Just take it up. Don't be afraid. Feel pulled up.

If sounds start arising, allow it.

Now feel the energy going back down, just as if the whole energy is going down, as if you are disappearing into the earth.

Vimala opens her eyes and slowly turns around to face him as Osho calls the three back to earth.

Perfectly good, Vimala.

Things are perfectly good. Keep it (a box) with you and whenever you need me, just do the same experiment: sit silently, first start feeling energy going up. Raise your hands and feel pulled, and keep a tension being pulled, for at least five to seven minutes. Then relax, and then feel you are disappearing into the earth; even if you fall onto the earth, fall, and then rest for four or five minutes. This will give you tremendous transformation.

When will you be back?

Vimala: Very soon.

Good. Come back forever!

Kamma from the screen-printing department now: Savita is positioned behind her, and behind her is Vivek. They are to feel the energy rising up, and then bring it down again.

Completely forget yourselves; just become energies, all together, all four of you. Let it become a dance together.

Just stop all movement. Be perfectly still. Be utterly like statues.

They freeze instantly; then very slowly, to Osho's instructions, come back into themselves, and one by one return to their places.

Now it is Amrit's turn, and he sits facing Vivek, Savita behind him, and Chetana to help as well. They're all to feel as if they are not bodies but energy.

Just do one thing: the energy is at the sex centre, so all of you pull the sex centre up and then relax it, pull it up and relax it, seven times, not more than that.

If any sounds start coming, feel orgasmic, feel sex energy moving upwards.

Feel ecstatic. Let the energy become pure bliss. Be in a dance.

23

Roger is before him; he's from England.

Osho : This is your name : Swami Prem Roger. Prem means love; roger is Teutonic, it means spear. Love *is* like a spear : the moment it penetrates the heart it is the greatest agony possible, but beyond the agony is the ecstasy. Love is pain, pure pain, but out of the fire of pure pain, bliss is born. The pain is the price we pay for the bliss. Once the bliss is attained, then one knows that what one gave was nothing. But unless it is attained, it is too much to bear, it is unbearable, and many times one wants to escape.

People are very much afraid of love for the simple reason that you have to pass through pain, agony, fire. The way to heaven goes through hell, and those who avoid the pain part will never attain to the ecstatic flowering.

Lorraine is American. She's a farmer.

This is your name : Ma Anand Lorraine. Anand means bliss, lorraine is a symbol of victory, the laurel. The full name will mean : bliss, the symbol of victory. One can have as much money as possible, and it is not a symbol of victory; it may be just the opposite, that the man has wasted his whole life in collecting junk. One can even conquer the whole world, can become Alexander the Great, and yet when one dies, both the hands are empty. One cannot take this kind of victory with oneself. Only one thing can be taken beyond death, and that is blissfulness. It has nothing to do with the outer; it has something to do with your inner energy, the flowering of your inner energy.

Once it has happened, there is no death. No time is going to make any difference to it, it has eternity in it. And that is the only victory there is; all other victories are covers to hide our defeats and failures. And the beauty of bliss is this, that you need not depend on *anybody;* no outer cause is needed at all — as you are, you are enough to be blissful. It is only a question of starting to live it; it is not a question of attaining, achieving.

One cannot believe that it is only a question of living it — because one has lived in misery for so long, how can one suddenly become blissful? But try and see the miracle happening. Tomorrow morning get up blissfully, with a decision that today you are going to remain blissful, whatsoever happens you are going to remain blissful. Persist, and remind yourself again and again; old habits will be there, coming back, knocking on the doors, but go on smiling deep down with your heart, and you will be surprised : it is possible. And if it is possible one day, it is possible every day. Slowly slowly it deepens; slowly slowly it becomes such a natural phenomenon that you need not even remember; you are simply blissful.

That is what sannyas is all about : living life blissfully without any effort, without cultivating it; living bliss spontaneously, uncultivated, unpractised, effortlessly. Lao Tzu calls it wu-wei, action without action.

Miracles can be done without any doing, and this is the first miracle. If this happens, then everything else becomes possible. Then god becomes possible, then paradise becomes possible, then nothing is impossible.

Orna is from Israel.

What is the meaning of your name?

Orna : Light.

And from what language does it come?

Orna : It is Hebrew.

Hebrew? Mm mm. Close your eyes.

This is your name : Ma Anand Orna. Anand means bliss; your full name will mean blissful light. Light in itself is delight. If we can be full of light within, our life becomes a tremendous, unbelievable delight. Bliss is an expression of inner light. It is light overflowing in you, reaching to others; it is a fragrance of your flower, riding on the winds. And just the opposite is the state of misery : it is a by-product of inner darkness. People are living in inner darkness, because people are living without self-knowledge.

Socrates says a life unexamined is not worth living. He is right; a life which has no awareness to examine itself, to look at itself, can't be worth living. At the most one can drag. That's what millions are doing and have been doing, down the ages — carrying mountains of burdens for no reason at all. One day they die because of those burdens, are crushed under those burdens, never knowing a single moment of joy. They could have lived their whole life as joy — just one thing went wrong : from the very beginning they were taught to know everything *except* themselves. That is where the original flaw is.

Sannyas has to be a beginning of self-knowledge. Everything else is secondary. If you don't know anything else, it doesn't matter much, but let a great decision be born in you that 'I will know myself', that 'I will know who I am'. In that moment of knowing, suddenly the inner being becomes enkindled, knowing becomes light, light starts overflowing. And that overflowing light is delight, is bliss.

Hywel is from Wales and teaches in Italy. Osho retains his name, adding the prefix of Anand.

Anand means bliss. Hywel means eminent, famous, special, extraordinary, the quality of uniqueness. Bliss makes everybody unique, misery is anonymous. Bliss makes one an individual. That's why to be blissful is dangerous, because you become so eminent, so different from others, and people don't like that. They don't like anybody to have any difference to them; they become afraid, they feel offended.

How dare you? They are so miserable and so anonymous and you are becoming so extraordinary and unique? They are so dark and you are becoming so light? They are living in hell and you are dancing in joy? Just out of sheer cowardice, millions of people who could have been blissful have never dared to be blissful. The crowd does not like that, the crowd wants to be part of the crowd. The crowd wants you to be a sheep, not a lion — and bliss is a roar, a lion's roar.

Gather courage to be blissful, risk everything to be blissful. Even life can be risked for bliss, because without bliss life has no meaning. Even to live blissfully for a single moment is better than to prolong a hundred years in misery.

(to Leo) This is your name: Swami Prem Leo. Prem means love, leo is Latin for lion. There are two possibilities for the human psychology: one is the psychology of the sheep. It is rooted in fear. That's how crowds live — in a sheepish way, always searching for a tyrant, a shepherd, always in need of being dominated, always hankering to be commanded. They feel good only when there is a leader to lead them. If there is no leader, they start freaking out — freedom is unbearable. That is one kind of psychology; the majority of human beings live in that world. But if you live in fear, you don't live at all; you go on missing the opportunity.

The other psychology is the psychology of the lion. It is rooted in love; it is individualistic, it is not collectivistic. It does not depend on somebody, it tries to live its own life. It risks going into the unknown without any map. It is not ready to remain confined to the familiar, to the comfortable, to the convenient. It is the psychology of the wanderer, the explorer, but its basic root is in love : one loves existence so much that one wants to explore it. We want to explore somebody only when we love them. You love a woman; you want to explore her body. You love a rose; you want to explore its touch. All exploration is out of love.

The lion is an explorer and the lion walks alone. He is not afraid, fear is not his way of thinking. And once one is free of fear, life has a totally different taste : it is utterly beautiful, it is immensely precious. But it depends on what kind of psychology you choose.

To be a sannyasin is to be a lion, and to be a sannyasin is to choose the psychology of love, the psychology of exploration, the psychology of the wanderer. It is accepting the challenge of the unknown. It is getting ready to risk all for that which is not known yet and for which there can be no guarantee.

This will be your new name : Swami Deva Sagaro. Deva means divine, sagaro means the ocean — the divine ocean. We have all become identified with the waves, and because of this identification we have lost contact with the ocean. This is our misery, this is our only problem : the identity with the waves, the identity with the part. Once we become obsessed with the part too much, the whole disappears from our vision. All that is needed is a change of gestalt. All that is needed is to uncling from the part, disidentify yourself from the wave, and suddenly the ocean is heard, roaring all over. And suddenly that which had been forgotten is remembered, that which has been lost is regained. One is again whole and holy.

Never think in terms of the part; always think in terms of wholes. This whole existence is a single unity, it is one individuality. That's exactly the meaning of the word 'God' —

that existence is one individuality, undivided, that we are members of each other; that you are in me, that I am in you, that is the only way to be. The mountains and the stars and the trees are in you and you are in the mountains and the stars and the trees. That is the only way to be! We participate in each other's being, we criss-cross each other. There is no way to be separate; the very idea of separation is the root cause of our being in hell. The moment the illusion of separation disappears, one is back in paradise.

Veda has been translating Osho's words into Italian, then recently he did a spell of work in the kitchen. So I'm rather surprised to see that he is leaving, and wonder what the story behind his decision is.

He seems unsure about what he is doing.

>*Anand Veda:* I'm always fighting, a victim of my mind. Just today I was seeing everything inside; everything is upside down. I'm just afraid that it will happen again, that the reaction is part of my system.

Everything will go, don't be worried; it just takes time. It is so many lives of rubbish that we are carrying, it is so deep, that you go on digging, and layer upon layer comes up. Sooner or later it is finished; it is not infinite, that much is certain. And our capacity to dig is infinite — so rejoice!

>*Veda:* I thought it was the opposite...

No, it is not.

>*Veda:* ...that the number of the layers is infinite.

No, it is not so, otherwise there would never have been a Buddha. The darkness is great, but it is nothing compared to light. This is what trust means: the misery is great, but hope is greater than the misery. Then there is no fear.

It is never unbearable. People say that pain is unbearable — it never is. You can bear it, your capacity to bear pain is infinite. And if you start witnessing it, then suddenly a distance is created. The pain is there and all nonsense is there, but you are no more affected by it, you are no more a part of it. You are just a pure witness, a watcher on the hills, and everything else is just there, dark, far away in the valley, none of your business really.

This distance is liberating; but when it comes, nobody knows. It comes, that much is certain; but as to when, nothing can be said.

So one has to wait, one has to be patient and one has to go on working.

When will you be back?

Veda : I left everything here to decide.

So whatsoever happens, just relax into it.

Veda : So you suggest that I really go back to Italy?

It will be good this time if you go for a few months. It will be helpful, mm? it will do something good; and then come back.

Help my people there — they need you there!

Raman is going back to Japan.

Good! Something to say to me?

Raman : Please say something to me.

Mm mm. I will be with you! So whenever you need me, just close your room, close your eyes, dance for fifteen minutes. Then just sit as you are sitting in front of me, ask any question and it will be answered through your own heart. But that fifteen minutes' mad dance is a must — it has to be before, only then will you be in tune with me.

Keep it (a box) with you.

When will you be coming back?

Raman: November or December.

Good! Help my people there.

Nanda has just come back from Australia.

Anything to say to me?

Nanda: Since I arrived last Saturday I've had a lot of pressure in my head from the inside pressing outwards. It's all over my face, and my hands go slightly rigid. What is it?

Mm mm.

Nanda: What's causing it?

It has never been there before?

Nanda: Yes, sometimes.

It has happened before too?

Nanda: Mm, but it is very intense here.

This time it is very intense?

Nanda: Mm.

Everything becomes intense here! Don't be worried, it will be gone. It will be gone and it will be gone forever, it will never come again. So don't try to repress it. Let it have as much intensity as possible, so it is finished once and forever. If you repress it with drugs or anything, then it remains in the system.

After Tao, remind me again. If it has not gone, then I will take it out!

Nanda: I'm scared to let it out because I'm scared it's just going to explode...

No, no.

Nanda : ... incredibly, and I'll just freak.

You just wait. Just wait. You don't know what freaking is; when you see people here (laughter) — just wait!

Asheesh sits ready for his energy darshan. Instead there is a pause, then Osho says, A few things to be remembered...

This is a totally new phase of work, so you have to be totally available, as if you are not — only then can my energy penetrate to the very core.

And for the helpers, for the mediums who will be helping; they have to be utterly absent, merged into me — only then can their energy become part of my energy and move.

From today, slowly slowly, mediums, helpers, will be chosen. Only those will be chosen who can be with me totally, with no critical mind — not analysing what is happening, but simply going into it, whatsoever it is. Any analysis and it becomes a disturbance.

Energy can go to tremendous heights, it can simply bloom into a lotus. Within minutes it can happen, but just total availability is needed, and more so on the part of the mediums.

24

Osho is addressing Lars....

Osho : This is your name : Swami Deva Lars. Deva is Sanskrit, it means god. Lars is Scandinavian, it means symbol of victory — god, the symbol of victory. Remember, unless god is achieved, nothing is achieved. Unless god is realised, we are failures, utter failures. It is only with the realisation of god that victory arrives; there is no other victory. All are cover-ups for defeats. One can have all the money of the world and all the power and all the prestige and fame, but they are all cover-ups, cover-ups to hide the wounds — wounds of continuous defeats, wounds that every desire and its disillusionment have left behind.

Let this become your only longing — that god has to be attained, that everything has to be sacrificed for this search.

Sannyas is a commitment to this ultimate victory.

(to Michael) This is your name : Swami Anand Michael. Anand is Sanskrit; it means bliss, the ultimate state of consciousness where no duality exists, where nothing is good, nothing is bad, where nothing is happiness and nothing is unhappiness, where darkness is light and light is darkness, where all dualities have disappeared into one. That state of serenity where the conflict, the constant conflict of dualities has disappeared — that is bliss. That is the goal, and unless a man achieves it, he remains hollow, empty, and goes on feeling that something is missing.

Michael is Hebrew; in Hebrew mythology, Michael is the

chief of the angels. To be blissful is to become an angel. Man has to surpass himself — that is the meaning of being an angel. Below man is the animal, above man is the angel; man is a tension between these two. There is a great pull from the animal, but also there is a great desire, a longing, to go upwards.

If you co-operate with down-going energies you start behaving like the animal. If you co-operate with the upward-going energies you start behaving like the angel. The angel simply means that energy has started moving upwards.

Become a blissful angel!

(to Janine) This is your name: Ma Sat Janine. Sat is Sanskrit. It means truth, the ultimate truth — not as we know it, but as it is, as it is in itself. And janine is Hebrew; it means a gracious gift of god — truth, a gracious gift of god. Truth cannot be manufactured, cannot be invented: it can only be received with a grateful heart. Truth is a gift of god. One cannot speculate about it, guess about it.

That's what philosophy goes on doing — guessing, inferring, thinking; it never arrives at any conclusion, it cannot. In the very nature of things, truth is not a by-product of a thought process; it is a gift. The mind knows nothing of it; only the heart can open up to receive it, only the heart can become the womb, can receive the seed of truth and give birth to a new life — but it is the heart.

That's the difference between philosophy and religion: philosophy remains thinking, religion is experiencing. Philosophy tries to find out truth, religion prays so that truth can be given to us.

Rose is German. He keeps her name, adding to it, Divyo, and goes on to explain:

In Latin, rose means rose, the flower; but in German it has a very strange meaning, it means horse. It comes from...

He pauses and turns to Haridas.
How do you pronounce it?

Haridas : Ross — it's a double 's'.

Good (laughter)!
In the past, the Germans used to worship the horse, they thought the horse divine — just the same foolishness as Hindus thinking the cow divine (laughter). Either all is divine or nothing is divine! So forget the German meaning; don't be a horse, there is no need. Stick to the Latin meaning. Your full name will mean : a divine flower.

Man is born as a bud. We have to help ourselves to open up and to become a flower. And unless the fragrance is released to the winds, one remains unfulfilled, one remains meaningless. It is only by sharing your fragrances with existence, by singing your song to the world, by dancing your dance to the stars, that you will find meaning.

Meaning is a by-product of sharing.

(to Benjamin) What is the meaning of your name?

Benjamin : I know that Ben means the son of, and that's all.

The son of? Mm, dictionaries say something which is very strange : they say 'son of the right hand'. Have you any idea what it means?

Benjamin : Possibly that I'm useful (laughter)!

Mm, that is possible.
Come close to me.
This is your name : Swami Deva Benjamin. Deva means god, and benjamin, the son — the son of god. We all come from god, we all live in god, and finally we all disappear in god. It is the same energy that is born, that lives, that disappears in death.

To think of ourselves as separate from this universal energy is the cause of all misery, and to drop the idea of separation is the beginning of joy, is the beginning of celebration. In fact that is the meaning of being a son of god : godfathers, mothers, everything. God is just like the ocean for us; we are just the fish in the ocean. He is our life, our being, our very breath.

Slowly slowly start dropping the idea of separation, and as the idea of separation disappears you will be surprised that a totally new being has come into existence — something that you had never known before, something that you had always been but were unaware of.

How long will you be here?

Deva Benjamin : At least two months.

Good. Have you done any groups?

Deva Benjamin : Not yet, but I'm booked for Centering, Satori, Tantra and Primal.

Good. Do these four and then I will give you a few more. Anything to say to me?

Deva Benjamin : Yes, Osho. After just my first day here I realised that I had been a sannyasin at heart for much of my life.

You *have* been — not only in this life but in other lives. I can feel it, I can see it. It is a long, long relationship; it is not new.

It is just the renewing of something very ancient. Good, Benjamin!

(to Suse) This is your name : Ma Prem Suse. Prem is Sanskrit, it means love. Suse is Hebrew, it means a lily flower — love, the flower. Love is the only way to flower; it is only the juice of love that helps one to flower. It is only when the spring of love has come that one starts blooming. Without love, all that is significant starts dying. Without love, the soul remains unnourished. Just as the body needs food, the soul needs love; and just as the body can be healthy and blooming and radiant, the soul can be.

The radiance of the soul, the flowering of the soul, the health of the soul, is what I mean by flowering. And when one has come to flower in the innermost core of one's existence, one knows who one is. That knowing triggers an infinite sequence of knowing; then one goes on knowing more and more about the mysteries of life and death. Just open the first door of self-knowledge...

His hand turns the lock...

...and many doors start opening on their own...

...and then indicates the unfolding of the veil behind the veil behind the veil.

But self-knowing is possible only when we nourish our being with love. So love as much as you can, don't be afraid of love. When it knocks on your doors, receive it; and whenever you can share, share it. Take as much as possible and give as much as possible. This is my basic message for my sannyasins : love is my religion.

This is your name : Swami Deva Luigi. Deva means divine, and luigi is a very strange word. It is from the Teutonic; it has many meanings, but only one is worth choosing. It means battle, fight, hale, wild, etcetera, etcetera; but there is one meaning that is glory : I choose that.

Your full name will mean divine glory, divine splendour. We may not be aware of the treasures that have been entrusted to us. We have completely forgotten our real identity, hence we look like beggars. Otherwise the whole

Won't You Join the Dance?

kingdom of god is ours; our glory is infinite, our splendour is eternal.

Sannyas is only to remind you that you are not a beggar, that you are an emperor. And this has nothing to do with the ego, because in reminding you that you are an emperor, I am reminding everybody else too that the same is the case with them — not only with man and woman, but with animals, birds, trees.

Everyone in his own right has this whole kingdom as his own. Once this is understood, a great explosion happens; consciousness starts expanding. Then you cannot remain confined to the small body and to the very small mind; they are small keyholes through which we are looking at the sky — and the whole sky is ours.

How long will you be here?

Deva Luigi: Only two weeks.

Good. Have you done any group here?

Deva Luigi: Yes, I have done Intensive Enlightenment and I'm doing Centering now.

Next time come for a longer period so that much more can be done.

Would you like to say something to me?

Deva Luigi: I have a question.

Mm mm — tell me.

Deva Luigi: I feel I can gain an enormous amount of energy; I feel as well that I can give it to other people.

Mm mm.

Deva Luigi: The only thing is, I don't know how.

Mm mm.

Deva Luigi: What can I do?

Mm mm (a pause). Just lay your hands on the needy part of the person. If the person has a headache, lay your hands on his head, close your eyes, start feeling energies pouring, and you will have a tingling sensation in the hands, they will become electrified. Or if the person has some trouble with the stomach, put your hands on the stomach. The needed part has to be touched. If it can be touched bare, without clothes, it is better, it will be more effective. But don't touch the needed part for more than one minute. If you touch the needed part for more than one minute, then sometimes the disease can start flowing towards you.

Energy is a rhythm : one minute it goes outwards, another minute it comes inwards. So make it a point that when you put your hands on somebody's body, exhale; it synchronises with inhalation, exhalation. When you put your hands on them, exhale, and go on exhaling; and when you see that you cannot exhale any more, take your hands off and then inhale. If you inhale while laying your hands on, you can be affected by the illness. The person may be healed but you will suffer, and that is meaningless. Just lay your hands with exhalation, and the moment inhalation starts, withdraw.

You will be able to do it. You can be of immense help to people.

(to Palma) Raise your hands! Feel like a palm tree — that is the meaning of your name, Palma.

Palma is a movie actress from Italy, and she is already smiling at the idea as she closes her eyes.

It is raining and it is windy and the tree is delighted. Enjoy the dance in the wind and the rain, and allow the body to move like a palm tree.

When he calls her back to place the mala over her head, he holds her, caught in a lasso, and seems to gaze into her.

This is your name : Ma Prem Palma. Prem means love,

palma means palm tree — a palm tree of love. Man is also a tree, man also has roots in the earth. They are invisible, but they are there. We are continuously nourished by the earth. We *are* in its gravitational energy-field. We are pulled by it; just as trees are caught by it, we are caught by it. And we have also to grow branches in the sky, we also have to whisper with the clouds.

The tree is a bridge between the earth and the sky; the tree is a longing of the earth to meet the sky. The tree is a hand stretched towards the stars. It is a tremendously significant symbol.

Sannyas is also a longing for the distant star of god — a tremendous desire to know, to be, to love, to sing the song of life in all its multi-dimensionality, to bloom.

Good, Palma. How long will you be here?

Lalita (translating): She doesn't know.

Be here... be here. Have you done any group?

Palma: No.

Would you like to do a few groups?

Palma: It's all the same to me.

Mm? Do a few first — it will never be the same (laughter)! The first group you do is Centering, the second group is Intensive Enlightenment and the third is Gestalt Art. These three, and then I will see what else you need.

Good, Palma!

Niraj leaves for Holland tomorrow.

Something to say to me?

Niraj: I only wanted to say thank you.

When will you be coming back?

Niraj: I don't know.

Whenever it is possible, come back to say thank you to me again (laughter)!

Hasya is leaving too, returning to America for three months she says (she has been assisting Santosh in the Hypnotherapy group).

Then you are coming forever?

I don't know!

Think about it! I'm just giving you the idea.

Then he calls her close to touch her head.

Good! Come back — I need you here!

Hello, Arhata. When are you leaving?

Deva Arhata : Monday.

Something to say to me?

Tears spring to her eyes and her nostrils quiver like a bewildered little rabbit.

Deva Arhata : Yes, that I'm very frightened... I'm very afraid of going home.

What exactly is the fear?

Deva Arhata : That I have to say 'no' to them, to come back here. It's difficult; it's not only about them, it's also because I live my whole being in my mind and I don't know if I'm strong enough.

I will make you strong enough; don't be worried at all. Just go and you will be strong enough; I will see that you are strong enough. You will be able to come.

You are trapped; don't be worried!

Her eyes open wide and she looks to Lalita, alarmed...

Deva Arhata : I'm what?

...and bursts out laughing as Lalita translates.

Keep it (a box) with you and whenever you need me just put it on the heart — and come back!

Taro, returning to France, explains to Lalita that very often she feels frightened, and she doesn't like it.

One has to learn to accept, and the miracle is : if you accept it, it will disappear. Fear can exist only if rejected; fear dies the moment you welcome it. If you want to have it forever, go on rejecting; if you want to finish, it can be finished right *this* very moment. Just accept it as a part of life.

What is wrong in it? It is natural, it is human. You are not a rock; you are a human being! And the heart is so delicate, more delicate than the rose. Life is so hard, and the experiences of life are so bitter and so poisonous, that it is simply natural that the fear arises. But if you can accept it, it will be gone. Give it a try!

25

Come close! and Osho malas Vincent.

Osho : This is your name : Swami Prem Vincent. Prem means love, vincent means victory — victory that comes through love, the victory that love is. Any other kind of victory is only apparent, only love gives you the real thing, because every other kind of victory is forced, violent; sooner or later there is going to be vengeance, revolt, reaction. Only love knows no revolt, because love is not an enforcement : it is a gift.

And love is a paradox, because it becomes victorious — not by becoming victorious but by surrendering, not by conquering but by surrendering. It allows itself to be defeated; that is the mystery of love. And in that very thing is the secret of victory. That victory is eternal which comes through love.

Come back again. When are you leaving?

Vincent : On the 27th.

Something you would like to say to me?

Vincent : No.

Come back! Keep this (a box) with you and whenever you need me just put it on your heart.

And Megha, when are your leaving?

Megha : On the 27th.

Something for you, some music.

Vivek has slipped into Laxmi's room, and passes something to Osho; it seems to be a record of classical music. Osho leans forward to Megha.

Whenever you want to remember me, listen to it.

Megha : Yes.

Something you would like to say to me?

Megha : Many things ... but seeing you is enough.

Just remember that life knows no death. Remember that you are not the body, not the illness. Remember that you will be forever and forever.

Once this is understood, all fears disappear. We are part of god, we are gods. We have been here forever and we are going to be here forever; only forms will change. And it is good that the form changes; when one form has been used, it has to be thrown — another form, another life, another dimension. Each end is a new beginning.

And remain rejoicing. Whatsoever happens to the body, don't be worried : it is not happening to *you*. And I will be with you!

You have a box with you?

Megha : Si!

Good... good.

This is your name : Ma Sat Jani. Sat means being; jani is Hebrew, it means god's gracious gift. The greatest gift has already been given to us — that is our being. The greatest gift is that we are; nothing more can be greater than this. Everything else becomes possible only because of this. This is the opportunity for everything else; without it nothing is possible. But there are millions of people who never think to thank god for life, for being, for existence. On the contrary, they go on complaining about small things, trivia.

The turning point in life comes only when complaints disappear, and instead of complaints, gratitude arises — that is conversion. And sannyas has to be that conversion. From this moment, think of life as a precious gift and remain thankful each moment for it.

Close your eyes! he instructs Hyklya (she is from Holland). Then, his eyes to the paper on which he is writing, What is the meaning of your name? He looks up; she's obediently sitting, head bowed.

Open your eyes! Do you know the meaning?

She smiles : No, she doesn't.

I think nobody knows about this name!

We laugh.

Close your eyes again!

So this will be your new name : Ma Anand Sonal. Anand means bliss, sonal means golden — golden bliss. Man can live in the dark valleys of life, but he can also climb to the sunlit peaks. Man has both the alternatives open. Man is a ladder. You can go to hell on the same ladder as you can go to heaven. All depends on the direction; the ladder is the same. Man can be just dust unto dust, and man can also be divine.

Life is an opportunity to transform the lower into the higher, to transform the darker into the lighter, to transform dust into the divine. Sannyas can make it possible. Sannyas is nothing but an alchemy.

Premhari's father and Sagara's husband, Dutch Cornelis, joins the orange family.

This is your name : Swami Prem Cornelis. Prem means love; in Latin cornelis is the name of a tree — tree of love. Man is only a seed, he has to become a tree. The seed we bring with us, but very few people ever make any effort to find the right soil. Very few people really are aware that they

Won't You Join the Dance?

are only seeds, potentialities, not actualities. Ninety-nine point nine percent of people take life for granted, as if it has already happened — it has not happened yet! It has happened to a Jesus, to a Buddha, but it has not happened to everybody. It *can* happen, but it can be missed also.

Each step has to be taken very carefully, because the true door is one and the false are many. To reach the goal is almost an impossibility, because it is so dark and we are so blind and we have no idea of who we are, from where we come, to where we are going, or why in the first place we are here. We have no idea, no notion; it is groping in the dark. But the groping can be done with more alertness, with more attentiveness, with more totality, with more intensity — and then, slowly slowly, the darkness is not so dark; a little light starts arising.

Out of our own intensity, light is born. Out of our own totality in any act, a certain luminosity arises; and those small acts which become luminous become lamps on the way. Even to have a small lamp is enough. One should not be worried : 'How am I going to travel such a long journey with such a small lamp? — because it throws light out only three feet ahead.' That is enough; when you have moved three feet, it again throws light three feet ahead.

Lao Tzu says that with a small lamp the distance of ten thousand miles can be crossed.

Sannyas is a small lamp, a small step, but it carries within it the infinity.

How long will you be here?

Prem Cornelis : Till the seventh of March.

He'll do a group if Osho thinks there's time. Time enough to do Intensive Enlightenment, Osho suggests, and adds :

It will be very helpful; it will give you a deep insight into meditation, into your own being.

And next time come for a longer period. Much has to be done!

Nicolee bends forward to listen,

This is your name: Ma Anand Nicolee. Anand means blissful; nicolee is Greek, it means victory — blissful victory. Life *can* become a blissful victory. Ordinarily it becomes only a miserable defeat. If we don't do anything, it is going to become a failure. The failure comes of its own accord. One need not be very intelligent to bring it, one need not make any effort to arrive at the failure. It comes searching for you. It is easier to fall, because it is downhill. It takes a little effort, risk, courage, to go uphill — and victory is uphill; it is going to the sunlit peaks of life. And the higher you go, the lonelier you will feel. The lower you are, the more you will feel surrounded by the crowds.

Life is like a pyramid.

His hand deftly cuts a pyramid in the air — the sides, the base — his eyes following its outline.

The base is very big; as you go higher, at the highest point you will be alone. That's why much courage is needed to be victorious — the courage to be alone, the courage to be free, free from the crowd, free from the crowd-mind, free from the psychology of the mob. One has to be a lion to be victorious, not a sheep. But each step towards victory is a blessing. Only those who reach to the highest peaks of life know what a precious gift has been given and how people are wasting it.

Anything to say to me?

> *Anand Nicolee:* Yes, Osho. Two months ago when I was meditating, the thought arose to come here, and I was here a month later!

Very good!

Anand Nicolee: There were no complications; it was as if you had taken me by the hand, and with total ease you brought me here.

I am going to take you by the hand to so many new dimensions too — so many new lands.

Anand Nicolee: I felt very much here like I'm becoming a child...

I see it.

Anand Nicolee: ...and I feel all the danger in me and I'm learning how to rest with it, to rest with my child.

Come back; the danger will disappear! Next time come for a longer period, much has to be done — but you have been chosen already!

Anand Nicolee: Thank you, Osho!

From Germany, Nikolaus is a student.

This is your name: Swami Deva Nikolaus. Deva means divine; nikolaus is Greek; it means victory — divine victory. Remember, all victory is God's victory, and all defeat is our defeat. All that is good is his, and all that is bad is ours.

Evil is our creation, it is man's invention. We have created a very ugly and miserable world, but God is not responsible for it. He gave us paradise; we refused it. We refused for a stupid reason: we wanted to eat the fruit of the Tree of Knowledge. So we have enough knowledge and no life, enough knowledge and no love, enough knowledge and no wonder, enough knowledge and nothing worth living for or nothing to live for.

This is something very fundamental: whatsoever reason, intellect says is real, is not worth living for; and whatsoever the heart says is worth living for, reason says that it is unreal, it is imagination and nothing else. This is the dichotomy of man. Those who listen to the head go on living a life which is more like a wasteland than a garden. Listen to the heart, and slowly slowly the desert is transformed into an oasis. But whatsoever happens, thank God for it; and whenever you go wrong, feel responsible for going wrong. All good is his, all bad is ours. Let this be your work upon yourself.

Savita's mother has been here five days or so, and on the twelfth of this month submitted a question for the discourse, saying that she felt in accord with Osho and inspired by him, but why was he against the mind and why the insistence for orange? She felt she could simply visualise him whenever she felt the need, so why the outer gestures of being a sannyasin?

Joyce Brandt, dear lady, it must have been a coincidence that you felt in accord with me, Osho began. He said she had great ideas, she was very knowledgeable, her question was not out of innocence.

What do you mean by inspiration? he'd demanded. I'm not here to support your beliefs — and all inspiration creates slavery.

Sannyas is for the chosen few, he went on; the orange and the mala to keep unwanted people out.

You say 'I can have you in my heart, deep in my being' as though you know what being is, what depth is. You say that you can conjure me up, but whatsoever you conjure will be a figment of your own mind; it cannot be me. You can have me only unconditionally...

Osho greets her.

So finally you have come (laughter)! Good. You *had* to come — I was certain from the very beginning! Just close your eyes, feel me...

Good! Come closer to me. Just look at me. I have been waiting for you!

Joyce : I've been waiting too.

And this is your name : Ma Prem Joyce. Prem means love; joyce is Old French, it means rejoicing. Rejoice in love, and that is all there is to prayer. Rejoice in love, and that is all there is to god. Those who can rejoice in love need no other religion. Love is the highest religion, in fact the only religion.

But, down the centuries, the priests have made people very sad — because they based their religion on a kind of paranoia, fear, they based their religion on pathology. They did not create a holy man, because they did not create a *whole* man. They created saints but they were not wholly, they were partial. They were not perfect circles; much was denied. And when you deny much, the life juices stop flowing in you. When you deny much, you have to cut many roots, you have to depend on fewer roots than you needed. When you deny much, you become uprooted, and life becomes sad, loses joyousness — the song, the poetry, the music. Religions created a sad earth.

My effort through sannyas is to bring rejoicing back to religion, so people can again dance for god, in god, through god — so god is no more a sad concept but laughter, is no more theology but poetry. Then a totally different kind of life arises out of it.

And remember one fundamental fact. Jesus says 'Those who have, more shall be given to them; and those who don't have, even that which they have will be taken away.'

It is one of the greatest sayings ever. In fact I have not come across any other saying of any other enlightened person that can be compared to this statement. It is a very strange statement. On the surface it looks unfair, unjust : 'Those who have, more shall be given to them; and those who don't have, even that which they have will be taken away.'

But what can Jesus do? It is so : if you rejoice, more and more joy will be showering on you. If you are sad, all the sadness from every nook and corner of life will start flowing to you. We attract that which we become.

So let it not only be your name : now let it become your very existence.

How long will you be here?

> *Prem Joyce:* Only till next Saturday.

Come again whenever you feel like coming, otherwise I am coming with you!

> *Prem Joyce:* I want to come again.

Something to say to me?

> *Prem Joyce:* Thank you. You've helped me.

Good!

Sambhava is returning to Australia tomorrow morning.

Good! Something to say to me?

> *Deva Sambhava:* There's something in me that keeps fighting, and I'm just wondering if you have any suggestions.

Just tell me.

> *Deva Sambhava:* Well, yesterday I was supposed to have an energy darshan but I felt my head was exploding, I got feverish and the doctor said I couldn't come. Now I think it was just something in me fighting.

You — fighting it?

> *Deva Sambhava:* Yes.

You don't want to have it?

> *Deva Sambhava:* I don't seem to be sick today; I feel alright.

Mm?

Deva Sambhava: I seem to be alright today, the doctor said I'm alright. It's as if I really want to surrender totally, but something prevents that.

Don't ask for the impossible. You cannot do *anything* totally at this moment, at this stage. Whatsoever you do, if it is sixty, seventy percent, that is almost perfect. To be one hundred percent total means to become enlightened. Nothing is remaining then; what will the barrier be?

At the most, right now do whatsoever the major part of your being wants to do. So what do you want? If you want an energy darshan you can have it. Or if you are still afraid and more afraid, then...

Deva Sambhava: Yes, I want it.

So wait, mm?
(to Mukta) Call him for energy darshan.
(to Sambhava) Just wait...

He returns to his place in the group, then about fifteen minutes later is called back and charged up...

You were unnecessarily afraid. Things are perfectly good. Next time I will give you a bigger dose (much laughter)!

Osho spoke about the come-close darshans in the discourse this morning. He had been talking about energy...

Energy is delight. Desire is energy, energy is delight. Contemplate over it — just pure desire, just overflowing energy, for no particular object, with no destination. That's what you have to remember when you come to me for an energy darshan, for a close-up. Just become pure desire, just an overflowing desire for nothing in particular. Don't wait for any experience. Experiences will come, but don't wait for them. If you wait, you will miss, because when you are waiting for the experience you are no more in the herenow.

You have already missed the point; the mind has come in. The object has obstructed the purity of the desire.

When you are in an energy darshan with me, when you are partaking of something of my energy, just be pure desire — going nowhere, moving nowhere, just thrilled for no reason at all, just madly ecstatic for no reason at all. And in those few moments you will have the contact with me, because those few moments are my reality.

But if you are sitting there, waiting to have some great experience of light inside you, then maybe you may experience some light, but you missed : you threw the diamonds away and gathered pebbles on the shore. You may be waiting for your kundalini to rise : you may have a certain sensation rising in your spine, but what is it? It is pointless! It may give you a kick, a spiritual kick, but then it is gone.

With me, be just pure desire — swaying with me, moving with me, dancing with me, allow me to penetrate you to your deepest core, to the deepest core of your desire, to the very seed. Then something immense, something incredible, something you cannot imagine, is possible : and entry of the beyond into you, the meeting of the earth and the sky...

26

Sumati is back from Australia with Tao (he's seven), Casey (who is four), and Lucy (a two-year-old), in tow. Manshar, her husband, who has been here for some time, sits beside them.

Lucy, perched on Sumati's lap as Osho writes her name, occupies herself with pulling down and straightening her dress. With that under control, she picks herself up and proceeds to play bouncing onto and then slithering off her mother's lap, until her big brother is called forward.

Osho hands Tao his name, and says to Manshar:

Osho : His name is good : Swami Prem Tao. Prem means love, Tao means the ultimate law — the ultimate law of love. Keep your name, Tao. Good!

He turns to Tao's brother.

Come here. What is your name — Casey?

Casey : Yes.

That's good (laughter)! Just look at me.

Osho's finger is on his diminutive third eye, and he smiles into Casey.

Good, good, Casey.
Your name will be : Swami Prem Casey (laughter). Prem means love, casey means pure — pure love.
Come here, Lucy! Your mala!

She hesitates, then understands that the proffered loop of beads is hers. She trots forward and dips her head into the noose, then makes to retreat...

Come here! First look at me!

---

262 ≈ *Won't You Join the Dance?*

...and returns, disciple to her master's voice, to be gazed into, a little hand on the way to somewhere, poised by her face. She turns away to make for her mother and brushes her eyes with the back of her hand as if to wipe away the fairy dust of that exchange! Osho chuckles, and holds out the sheet with her name on it.

Your name (much laughter). You will have to come again — your name!

She trots up to Osho a third time and takes it from him. He turns to Manshar.

Her name is good: Prem Lucy. Prem means love, lucy means light — light of love.

Something to say to me?

Manshar: No.

(to Sumati) You have something to say to me?

Prem Sumati: No.

Sumati says she has only just arrived from the West.

So just be here. You will have to take care of these people.

He gazes affectionately at the little trio.

Good!

This is your name: Swami Prem Regis. Prem means love, regis means wise. Love brings wisdom. Wisdom is the shadow of love; without love there is no wisdom. Without love knowledge is possible, much knowledge is possible, but wisdom impossible. Wisdom is the function of the heart, and without love the heart remains dormant. It is the force of love that moves the dynamo of the heart, and once the heart is stirred, the seed of wisdom that we are carrying within us starts growing. Sooner or later there is a tree of great wisdom.

The tree of knowledge is not the tree of wisdom. In fact the tree of knowledge should be called the tree of ignorance, because nothing keeps man more ignorant than knowledge. It is only by dropping knowledge that someone comes to wisdom. The day one realises 'I don't know anything' is a great day in life. From that moment the heart starts functioning.

Jenny is a picture researcher.

This is your name : Ma Prem Jenny. Prem means love, jenny means god's gracious gift. Love is the greatest gift that god has given to us. It is greater than life, because life itself without love is meaningless. Life becomes significant only if it starts growing towards love, if it becomes love.

Life is only an opportunity; love is the fulfilment. Life is a seed; love, the fragrance.

Alva is from the States where she works as a hotel maid.

This is your name : Ma Deva Alva. Deva means divine, alva means white, whiteness — divine whiteness. White is a symbol of purity, of utter cleanliness, not even a particle of dust in the soul. When the mirror is so clean that not even a particle of dust is on it, it reflects that which is. The heart has to be also that purity, mirrorlike, only then can god be known.

God cannot be known by logical thinking and cannot be known by stupid rituals; it is not that cheap. God can only be known by the purity of the heart. What is the purity of the heart? The purity of the heart is the silence undisturbed by thought, stillness uncontaminated by the mind. The mind is the impure thing. The heart is naturally pure, but the mind is imposed on the heart. The society has put the mind as the master. The master is chained and the slave is ruling : this is the situation.

Sannyas means changing everything from topsy-turvy, putting the master back into its place and reducing the servant to its own work. The mind is beautiful if it is a servant, but not beautiful as a master; then it is a tyrant. The heart is beautiful when it is the master, because it can see what is, and it can live according to that which is, it can follow reality and god.

If the heart follows god and the heart is followed by the mind, your life is religious. But right now the situation is that the mind is the leader, the heart has to follow the mind, and god has become completely disconnected from us.

Let the mind follow the heart, and the heart will *automatically* follow god. Its very purity is the guarantee.

He suggests groups for her — Centering, Intensive Enlightenment and Vipassana.

These three groups, and they will take you deep into meditation!

Anything you would like to say to me?

Deva Alva : No... happy to see you!

Good, good, Alva!

(to Arne from Denmark) This is your name : Swami Prem Arne. Prem means love, arne means black or dark. Darkness has something beautiful about it, it has depth. Light is always shallow because light is always defined. Darkness is undefined, unbounded. Light /makes everything de-mystified, and the moment things are de-mystified they lose all beauty. Darkness mystifies everything. It makes everything look tremendously enchanting, wonderful; it creates the mysterious. Darkness is also of immense value, because to grow the seed has to go into the dark soil, and to grow the child has to go into the darkness of the mother's womb. Everything grows in darkness, all energies grow in darkness. Only when they have become mature can they come into the light, otherwise not.

Love also grows in darkness. One day it comes into the

world of light, but the roots always remain in the dark; only the flowers come into the light. To be total a man has to be both, the roots and the flowers. He has to be both rooted in deep darkness and yet looking at the farthest star. In that totality is benediction, that totality *is* benediction.

Frank is Australian but lives in London where he works as an acupuncturist.

This is your name : Swami Sat Frank. Sat means truth, frank means free, freedom. Jesus says 'Truth liberates.' That's exactly the meaning of your name : truth *is* freedom. Not to know is to be in bondage. Our chains and imprisonments consist of ignorance, and the greatest imprisonment is self-ignorance. To know is to be free, and the first and the greatest freedom is self-knowledge; then everything else follows of its own accord.

The essential core of all religions has always been the same : Man, know thyself. Modern psychology has stumbled upon the fact that if you can know a certain thing that has been crippling you, the very knowing of it becomes its disappearance. If a dream has been persisting in your life again and again and again, if it is analysed, understood, it disappears; then it never comes. The message has been understood; there is no point now for it to come again. If you understand why you are afraid, you are no more afraid. To know the cause, just to know the cause, brings freedom without any other effort.

This has been the greatest discovery of religions; now psychology has again discovered an ancient truth.

Upageya, leaving for Germany, has had a beautiful time here...

> *Upageya :* ...but every time I'm here I'm totally closed up when I look at you; I can't relax. I don't know... I'm sweating now.

Yes, some fear is there, and the fear has some meaning.

The meaning is really good, it is not bad news. People who are really so afraid of me are simply saying that their mind is giving them a signal : no more movement towards this man — there is danger!

That's true, Upageya murmurs, and grins.

But now you cannot resist. The temptation is greater than the fear, so just wait!

Ashramite Chinmaya has been ill again, so much so that he's been confined to his room and you can visit him only if you have no infections yourself and are wearing a mask. He's got both T.B. and Hodgkin's Disease, and he feels in need of a dose of divine energy!

Osho has him turn to face Shiva, and rather than having his special team to work on him, calls up Pradeepa (who is here with her Zazen group) to support him. He seems to fill Chinmaya very slowly, very very gently. Anyway, it leaves Chinmaya beautifully loose and floppy, and he lolls against Pradeepa's chest as Osho talks to him.

Good, Chinmaya, very good! You are doing so well, defeating death! Don't be worried. You are almost doing the impossible. Anybody in your place would have been born at least nine years before (laughter). They would have been nine years old by now! (much laughter).

Things are good!

Rammurti is called. Osho greets him, then turns to his mediums.

All the mediums come here. There are just a few things I have to talk to you about.

The first thing to be remembered is that the work that is now given to you is of immense importance, it is no ordinary work. And this is only the beginning; it will have many many dimensions soon. So only those who really surrender totally will be chosen for further dimensions.

The function of the medium is to be utterly absent so that I can penetrate your being totally, so that my energy can start flowing through you. Your energy has to become attuned

Won't You Join the Dance?

with my energy. The energy that you have is stored at the sex centre; *all* energy is stored at the sex centre, all energy is basically sexual.

So the first arousal of the energy will have a sensuality about it. You are not to repress it, you are not to suppress it; you have to help it to go up. It is the same energy that at a certain point becomes spiritual, divine, but only at a certain point, at a certain intensity. But our minds start repressing it before it reaches that intensity. So many taboos, so many inhibitions, so many stupid ideas, have been taught down the ages that they function automatically. It is not that you repress; just as the sexual energy starts moving, an automatic repression comes in. You have to destroy that automatic reaction in yourself. You have to enjoy the sensuous feel of the energy rising, with no fear, with great welcoming and receptivity.

When I say that the energy is rising up in you, you have to start moving and swaying with the energy. It has to be very graceful, very subtle, very aesthetic. You have to be sensitive, because you are moving on very subtle planes; grossness is not needed. But you have to be available to me on all levels, from the lowest to the highest, the whole ladder of your being, so that I can help your energy to reach to the highest peak.

So when the energy starts moving it will almost feel as if you are making love. And in fact it is so : you are making love to existence itself. So start moving, swaying, in the same way that you will move while you are making deep love, while you are in deep intimacy with somebody. Abandon yourself and go totally into it. The same thrust will be there, the same movements, the same sounds of joy will start coming. Don't repress them; let them, allow them, help them. Meaningless sounds and words will come, sometimes from your past lives, sometimes when you were animals, sometimes when you were birds, and sometimes when you were trees — the past is infinite. Like clouds, fragments will start coming; you have to allow them.

When I say 'Go ecstatic' you have to allow everything; you have to be totally in a state which will be thought of as mad. All this time the light will remain off, because the energies can grow only in darkness. And the moment I put the light on, three are the possibilities. One : I may put the light on while you are in that mad ecstatic state; you are not to repress it. If I put the light on, you have to continue in your mad ecstatic state. The second possibility is : before putting the light on, I will say 'Cool down and let the energy disappear into the earth.' Then you cool down and let the energy disappear; then you will become very silent, very still. No wind, and the trees are just still. But still your face will have the fragrance of ecstasy. It will not be like a laughter; it will be like a smile, very subtle — a grace, a joy, a rejoicing, but not loud, not wild. Your hands will be in a receptive mood, your body will be in a graceful posture. Then I will put the light on.

The third possibility is that I may put the light on and you are in a wild state and suddenly I say 'Stop!' Then without relaxing the energy and letting it go into the earth, stop as you are : if your hand is raised then your hand is raised, if your eyes are turned upwards then your head remains that way. Whatsoever the state, immediately become frozen. These are the three possibilities. It will depend on the person who has come for the close-up. I will call the person the guest.

He is a guest in my energy-field. I am the host; you are my bridges to him. So it will depend on the guest what kind of situation will be more helpful to him — wild, ecstatic, sudden stop; or a very very cool, slow settling. Good.

27

*M*aya *has just got back from Australia. This time she's got her children with her — Madyam, five, and, her face hidden in the folds of Maya's dress, Shreyas, seven.*

How long will you be here? Osho asks Maya.

> *Maya :* I don't know.

Osho : Be here. There is no need to know! Just be here. This is not a place to know anything (laughter)! This is a place to become as ignorant as possible.

There is a knowledge which is ignorant, and there is an ignorance which knows. Just be here, available to me, open.

Would you like to do a few groups?

> *Maya :* It's up to you, really. I came here prepared either to work or to do groups.

You used to do groups?

> *Maya :* When I was here last time I did groups.

What groups have you done?

> *Maya :* Encounter, Intensive, Kyo ... I did nine groups then.

Nine? Very good. So this time just be here, meditate and enjoy. Would you like to work?

> *Maya :* Yes, when I get settled I'd like to work.

First settle and then start working. And anything about you?

Shreyas ventures to peek out in response to the question, then like a little mole buries herself again.

This is real ignorance (much laughter)! Good, good.

(to Birgit) Close your eyes ... just look at me.

This is your name : Ma Prem Birgit. Prem means love; birgit is Celtic, it means strength. The strength of love — that will be the meaning of the full name. And love has a very paradoxical strength : it is soft, soft as a rose, and yet hard, hard as a rock. It is delicate, very fragile, and yet the very source of all strength of life.

Love is the strength of feminine energy, non-aggressive, non-violent, non-conquering, yet it conquers, yet ultimately it becomes victorious. It defeats all — it defeats even death. Only in moments of love does one come to know the immortal, the deathless.

Diana is a singer and is from the States.

This is your name : Ma Anand Diana. Anand means blissful, diana means moon goddess — blissful moon goddess. The moon is symbolic of many things — basically of coolness, of light, but a light with a difference. Sunlight is hot, moonlight is cool; sunlight is more like passion, moonlight is more like compassion. Sunlight is male, moonlight is female : it has grace, tranquillity, silence, beauty.

All these things should be the qualities of a sannyasin; every sannyasin has to become a moon. That's exactly the meaning of my name : the moon.

How long will you be here?

Anand Diana : Tomorrow is my last day.

Something you would like to say to me?

Anand Diana : Just that I love you, and thank you!

Come back again for a longer period.

Anand Diana: I will!

And help my people there. I will be with you.

Anand Diana: Thank you.

Good, Diana.

He adds Deva to Sigrid so that her name means divine beauty.

All beauty is divine. To worship beauty is prayer, to be sensitive towards beauty is to be religious. As one grows deeper and deeper into the feel for the beautiful, one comes closer and closer to god, because god is the ultimate experience of the beautiful. He is reflected in the rose, in the moon, in the birds, in people's eyes — but these are reflections. Search for the one that is reflected in all : one moon reflected in millions of lakes.

It is beautiful when you look at even the reflection of the moon, but don't be lost in the reflection. Let the reflection just become a longing for the search of the original, then every beautiful experience leads you towards god.

This is your new name : Swami Premdas. Prem means love, das means servant — a servant of love. And that is the way to become a master. The kingdom of god belongs to the servants of love. The deeper you go into love, the more you disappear, and the more your life becomes that of service, of compassion, of sharing. You are not there any longer; you become instrumental to god. You become his hand, his voice, his eyes. He starts looking through your eyes into the world, he starts working through your hands in the world.

That's exactly the meaning of becoming a sannyasin : to be so surrendered to love that one becomes a vehicle of the divine.

How long will you be here?

Premdas: I don't know.

Be here as long as you can.
Have you done any groups yet?

> *Premdas*: Not yet.

Would you like to do a few?

> *Premdas*: I'll think about it and choose one, because I can stay as long as I want.

You choose ... you think. Good.

Clive is from England.

This is your name: Swami Anand Clive. Anand means blissful; clive is a very beautiful name, it means a cliff-dweller. The search, the whole search of human consciousness, is to reach the ultimate peak of existence. It is dangerous, hazardous, in fact almost impossible, because the hindrances are so many, the difficulties millions. And to remain in the safety and the security of the plains is very tempting. To move towards the cliffs is to take risks, and to become a cliff-dweller is to become a sannyasin.

Man can live on many planes, man has many levels of being — seven, as Eastern insight has found. We live on the lowest, the first; we live on the ground floor.

As you move higher, joy arises, but insecurity also. You feel more and more freedom, but more and more danger too. Hence the statement of Friedrich Nietzsche: Live dangerously. Unless one lives dangerously, one cannot live on the mountains, one cannot live beyond the clouds — and that is where our real home is, beyond the clouds.

To become a sannyasin means to become part of a commune of seekers, of searchers, of people who have already decided to go on the ultimate adventure, of people who have already decided that the ordinary life, the so-called ordinary life, is not worth living at all, and that there must be more to life. And there is, but it is available only to those who risk for it.

How long will you be here, Clive?

Anand Clive: About six months, Osho.

That's very good.

He'd like to do groups, he says, and has already booked for five.

Do these five. Anything to say to me?

Anand Clive: My questions have dropped!

Good!

This is your name: Ma Anand Barbara. Anand means blissful, barbara means a stranger. Be a blissful stranger in this world. It is not our home; to think that it is a home is to remain in an illusion. We *are* strangers here: today we are here, tomorrow we are gone. Don't make too much fuss about this small time that is given. Rather, use it in being more blissful, more peaceful, more silent — because when the body drops, you can still carry the treasure of silence, love, bliss. There are treasures of the outside: diamonds and money and power and prestige. There are treasures of the inside: love, compassion, silence, meditation.

Once this is understood, that we are strangers here, the gestalt changes; then we are not concerned too much with outer things. If they are there, good; if they are not there, so what? Our concern becomes inner, we become more concerned with our state of consciousness. And that concern is the ultimate concern: once that starts growing, a person starts moving towards the real home.

God is the name of that real home. Unless we live in God we remain strangers.

Atten and Udgeya are going back to Germany.

Udgeya : Since I've been here I've felt so many changes and so much opening.

It is there — I can see it! Mm?

Udgeya : It's like I'm one now.

It is the beginning of a new life. Don't close back home : just remember that for a few days, and then there will be no problem. Otherwise old situations, family, acquaintances, they all expect you to be the way they used to see you, and just to fulfil their expectations you may fall back. There is no need to fulfil their expectations, because these expectations are ill, not healthy expectations. And soon they will enjoy your openness — because an open person is more loving, more friendly, is capable of more intensity in everything, with more totality, intimacy.

If for three weeks you can remember not to fall back into the old pattern, then there will be no fear; then this opening will go on growing. There is no end to it : one can become as open as the sky and can contain all the stars within.

Continue to meditate and help my people there, and whenever you need me just put it (a box) on the heart.

Ajana is returning to England.

Something to say to me?

Ajana : It's hard to leave.

It *is* hard.
When will you be coming back? Mm?

Ajana : Soon, I hope.

Come back soon. Make it less hard! Come back soon. And then are you thinking to come forever?

Ajana : Yes.

Come forever, mm? Why suffer unnecessarily? Mm — going will become more and more hard every time.

Your home is where I am.

Niyati is back from Germany.

Hello, Niyati. When did you arrive?

Niyati : A few days ago.

Her voice breaks.

Good! Something to say to me?

Niyati : I'm afraid of going back to the West and I'm also afraid of staying here.

That's the situation that almost everybody is in. Fear is the state of the normal human mind; one is afraid, simply afraid. It is not a question of what one does; all are excuses, just pegs to hang your fear on, that's all. So if you are here, you are afraid of that; if you go there, you are afraid of that. If you do this, you are afraid of this; if you do something else, you will be afraid of that. So rather than thinking about *why* you are afraid, go deeper into this state of fear. Don't be bothered by the excuses, they are irrelevant. Go into this fear, just be afraid — why find excuses? If fear is there, then why not be simply afraid? And you will have a tremendous experience.

From tonight, every night for one hour before you go to sleep, sit in the darkness of your room and just be afraid, for no reason at all. Tremble, shake, be afraid — and remember, don't try to find any reason for it. There is no reason really.

Man *is* fear, and if we can go deep into fear without finding any explanations, then the fear can be transformed into love. It is the same energy that becomes love. But first you have to go into it, to the rock bottom of it. So this has to be your meditation for a few days, and after six weeks report on how you are feeling.

Would you like to do a few groups? What have you done before?

> *Niyati :* Oh, many groups; I don't remember the names.

Would you like to work? You have done some work before also?

> *Niyati :* Yes.

Then start working, and just join the music group in the night. Then in the late night. Then in the late night when you are going to sleep, the fear meditation. Good.

Harida is the first for an energy darshan. Once he is seated, Osho motions the mediums to sit in front of him....

Three things. The first : two consciousness can relate in three ways. The first way is the way of I-it. That's how millions of people relate : they reduce the other to a thing. Somebody becomes a husband or a wife; then it is an I-it relationship. Then the other is not respected as a person but used as a commodity. And I-it relationship means a relationship of possession; it is the ugliest relationship. Science functions in the world of I-it, that's why science cannot believe that there is a soul, that there is God. There are only things, matter; it reduces everything to matter. I-it is the world of the scientist.

The second relationship is of I-thou. That's how lovers relate. The other is respected, respected tremendously. The other is not reduced to a thing, the other is not used; in fact both enhance each other, both enrich each other.

In the first, the I-it relationship, you take; your whole concern is how to take more and more. In the second, you give; the whole concern is how to give more and more. It is not that by giving you don't get — you get a thousandfold, but that is a different matter, that is not your motive.

The second is the world of art; the artist lives in the world of I-thou. And many religions of the world, particularly religions born out of Judaism — Judaism, Christianity, Mohammedanism — have not gone beyond I-thou. Hence they have not been able to develop meditation — only prayer. Prayer is an I-thou relationship; god is the other. Great respect is there, but still the other is the other; there is a separation. There is closeness, but not bridged yet — very close, intimate, but not one yet.

The third relationship is really not a relationship at all. It is very paradoxical; it is neither I-it nor I-thou. The two persons don't exist in it as two, they start functioning as one. They become one organic unity, they become one orgasmic joy. That's the state the mystic lives in, and that is the state the meditator tries to attain.

All of my mediums have to attain to the third. With me you have to be in a relationship which is not a relationship at all. So if I put my hand on your head, it is not somebody else's hand, it is your own hand. And when I put my head on your head it is not somebody else's head, it is your own head. That feel has to grow. As it grows, you will become more and more open vehicles for my energy. That has to be remembered, then your being mediums will become your great meditation. It will not only be helpful to the guest, to the person who has come for the close-up; it will be a tremendous upsurge in your being too.

The second thing : this is the beginning of a new phase of work. I will relate many more things to you — many more that you cannot imagine, many more that you have never dreamt about — but the first basic you have to learn before that can be conveyed to you is : let this relationship with me be absolutely exclusive. This has not to become your gossiping.

The temptation will be there, because when you know

something and somebody else does not know about it, there is great temptation to play the role of the knower, and to say it. It is a human temptation. But this has to be remembered, that whatsoever transpires between me and you is an absolute secret.

And remember, it is not the matter that is important; the matter may not be important at all. It is your capacity to keep it secret that is important. I may have simply told you that two plus two are four — that is not the point. It is immaterial whether you convey it to somebody or not; that is not the question. The content is not the question, the question is : your capacity of keeping it absolutely to yourself, your not revealing it even to your own spouse, your friend, your love.

There is an ancient Sufi story....

A man who was a great seeker heard of a mystic who had attained to the ultimate secret. But he lived far away in the dark desert and nobody knew the way to him — he hid himself. The man tried : he sold everything that he had, he renounced his family. It took him three years to find the old master. He was utterly happy when he touched the feet of the master, and he said 'So I have come. Now reveal the secret to me.'

The master said 'if you want the secret, then you will have to pay for it.' He said 'I have nothing left. I have already paid.' The master said 'No. That is not the question You have to just be here for three years, utterly silent; not a single word has to be uttered. That will be the payment, and then I will reveal the secret to you.'

The three years were long, living in that desert — nobody else there but the master and the disciple, and the disciple was not allowed to utter a single word. It was really hard; he was going crazy inside, but he waited and waited. Three years passed, and he said to the master 'Now three years have passed : reveal the secret to me.' The master said 'Now the condition. You have paid, true, but now the condition : you have not to reveal this secret to anybody else, it has to be kept absolutely secret.' He said 'Agreed — but reveal it to me.'

The master started laughing. He said 'How can I reveal it to you? If you can keep it secret, why can I not keep it secret? In fact my master told me the same thing : "Keep it secret — don't reveal it to anybody" — and I don't know what *his* master said to him. Whether there is any secret or not, that is not the point at all!'

So that is not the point — the content, or any secret — but your capacity to contain it. That you have to remember. If any of you starts gossiping, it is bound to reach me, remember : gossip has wings! And those who do that will automatically be dropped, slowly slowly. The higher work is not for them; they are childish.

And the third thing : Vivek will be your chief, so you have to listen to her, to whatsoever instructions she gives to you. I have been working on her for seven years; now she is ready.

So you have to surrender to her, you have to listen to her; whatsoever information she conveys to you, you have to follow.

And I am in search of creating a big group of mediums, because as the commune grows I will need much bigger groups of mediums to help people. Thousands are going to come, and they are going to come so fast that you will not be able to manage them!

So remember these three things.

28

Osho : This is your name : Swami Prem Eberhard. Prem means love, eberhard means brave. Love is the most courageous quality of human consciousness, because love can risk all. It is the very centre of courage, because it can even encounter death. The man of fear cannot love and cannot even allow anybody to love him. The man who can love *and* can allow himself to be loved, slowly slowly forgets what fear is; fear becomes a forgotten language. It *should* become a forgotten language, but that very rarely happens. What happens is that *love* becomes a forgotten language. For the majority of human beings, love means nothing; it is an empty word. Fear means all; it is very substantial.

For the sannyasin, there is needed to be a total conversion. Fear becomes nothing, an empty word, and love becomes all. Then god is not far away, because love is god.

Alf is from Germany.

This is your name : Swami Deva Alf. Deva means divine; alf means wise, wisdom — divinely wise or divine wisdom. Knowledge is human, hence knowledge never becomes wisdom. Knowledge is a creation of your mind; it always remains so-so, arbitrary, hypothetical. Wisdom descends. It is not a creation of the mind — on the contrary, when the mind ceases to function, when it gives way for the divine ray to enter in you, then only does it happen. It is a gift from god, hence it is infallible. And it is not a hypothesis, it is absolute. The whole world will go on changing but wisdom remains the same. All Buddhas say the same thing. The languages differ, obviously, the expressions differ, certainly, but what is expressed, what is indicated, is exactly the same. It may be Jesus or Confucius or Socrates; it makes no difference at all. All those fingers are pointing to the same moon.

Don't be confined to human knowledge and inhuman knowledge. Strive to be open, surrendered, for the divine to descend in you. And the moment one is open, it immediately happens, instantly happens. It is just for the asking or just for the taking.

Christian is from France; he's a chef!

This is your name : Swami Christian. Christian means to be with Christ. And that's exactly what sannyas is all about — to be with Christ. Christ is not the name of any person. Jesus is only one of the Christs; there have been many, there will be many.

Christ is not a personal name, it is a state of consciousness. Lao Tzu is a Christ, Jalaluddin is a Christ, and the day you become enlightened *you* are a Christ. But meanwhile, when you are not enlightened and you are not a Christ, the best thing to be, the next best thing to be is to be a Christian, at least — to be with Christ, to aspire, to long for the Christ-consciousness.

Meditation is the bridge which will make you a Christ. Never be satisfied with being just a Christian. That is the beginning, and it is beautiful as a beginning, but it is not the end : the end is to be Christ. And each human being has the potential to be Christ. If we don't fulfil it, we will remain in discontent. It *has* to be fulfilled. Once it is fulfilled there is all contentment, all joy, all celebration.

From Germany, Thomas is a psychologist.

This is your name : Swami Veet Thomas. Veet means beyond. Thomas is one of the apostles of Jesus, but because he was of a doubting nature, full of doubts — which is very natural, human — his name has become a symbol of doubt :

Doubting Thomas. But one thing has to be remembered: doubt arises only when one tries to trust. It is not necessarily a calamity. It never arises in people who are not searching for trust. There are millions of people who have no doubt; that does not mean that they have trust, that simply means that they don't care, that they are not bothered. They are not searching for truth, hence there is no doubt either.

When one starts searching for trust, when one wants to trust, doubt arises. So, doubt is not necessarily evil; it is a by-product of the searching, enquiring mind. But I am not saying that it is something to be protected, saved, treasured, no. One has to go beyond it. One has to go through it and one has to go beyond it. So there are two steps: one of doubt, and another of trust.

Veet means: go beyond the doubting mind, transcend it. To be in trust is a tremendously blissful state. Worries simply disappear, hesitations wither away, darkness is no more there. All those things are created by doubt; doubt starts eating the very roots of your being.

There are three kinds of people. The first one has no doubt but no trust either — that is the state of the majority of people, a very ugly state; the desire for truth has not arisen yet. Then the second person, in whom the desire has arisen, and with the desire, the shadow of doubt; it is far better than the first. And then the third is one who has arrived in trust; the shadow has disappeared, it is all light.

It is said that in heaven, people walk but no shadows are created. It is a beautiful symbol: When trust is total there is no shadow of doubt. Trust is so transparent that it is like glass, so transparent that it makes no shadow. That is the goal.

Another lady farmer, Christine is from Germany.

This is your name: Ma Prem Christine. Prem means love,

christine means a follower of Christ. Love is the message of Christ. Moses is more a law, a commandment, a code of conduct. He was more concerned with what to do, what not to do — but that was the need of the people in those days. That was the first step, to create character. Once character is created, then the shift is possible from character to consciousness.

Jesus is the second step. Moses brings law to the world, Jesus brings love. Love does not think in terms of what to do and what not to do, but in terms of what to *be*. It is a deeper quality. Action is on the surface, being is at the centre.

Somebody asked Saint Augustine 'I am very ignorant, I don't know anything of religion and the scriptures; but can you tell me in short, very short, the essence of all religion, so that I can follow it?'

It is said that Augustine closed his eyes, meditated for a time, then opened his eyes and said 'Love. That is the very essence — and if you love, then whatsoever you do is right. Out of love, wrong is impossible; and without love, right is impossible.'

So if one really wants to attain to Christ-consciousness, then love is the way.

Rheba is a teacher.
What is the meaning of your name? Osho wants to know.

Rheba : I don't know. It's short for Rebecca.

Rebecca? Mm mm. Close your eyes!
This is your name : Ma Anand Rheba. Anand means bliss — and I also don't know what rheba means, but that is irrelevant (laughter). Be blissful, that is the point. Be a blissful Rheba, whatsoever it means (laughter)! And you can be very blissful, you have the quality, and it is easily available.

There are people who have the quality, everybody has the quality to be blissful, but it is hidden behind so much rubbish that if you go on digging and digging and digging, only then one day, maybe after years or after lives, will you find the treasure.

But your treasure is not very far away. Just a little cleaning — not digging, just dusting, even a vacuum cleaner will do (much laughter) — and the bliss will start!

Vidhano is returning to Norway. He wonders what method is best for him.

> *Vidhano:* I'm not sure if I'm going to be more remembering or forgetting myself.

Mm mm. Just come close to me.

From where I sit I see a Osho foot gently placed in Vidhano's cupped hands, and a finger on his third eye.

Good. Go into absolute forgetfulness. Forget remembering; that won't help you. Your eyes are already turning upwards, mm? That is a sign of forgetfulness, and that is going to help you.

These are the two paths: either remember totally or be drowned totally; and the eyes immediately show what exactly will be helpful to you, what will be natural to you. Don't try to remember, try to forget everything — forget yourself, forget everything. Just be a forgetfulness, and in that very forgetfulness you will start feeling god. God will not come to you as truth; god will come to you as beauty, as love. God will never come to you like a concept, but it will be a feeling.

So you can choose easily, and there is no problem in it. Don't create a confusion.

Something to say? he asks Christina before she leaves for Sweden.
I had a thousand questions but they've all gone now!
Come back soon; this is your home now. Always think of me as your home!

Won't You Join the Dance?

Raga is called. She has come back from England.
Osho asks her how long she will be here.

> *Prem Raga:* I have to decide whether to have my baby here or in Japan.

How old is the pregnancy?

> *Prem Raga:* Nearly six months. I felt very very strongly that I wanted to keep the child.

Mm mm, keep the child, and have it here. When I am here, why go to Japan? Let the child be here.

> *Prem Raga:* I'm with Agar ... I thought we were going to come and see you together just now.

Call him, Osho says to Mukta, and Japanese Agar comes up to sit by Raga.

You have something to say?

> *Agar:* I'm very glad to see you. I travelled in Europe for six months...

Mm mm.

> *Agar:* It was the first trip to Europe and I had a very hard time, especially in England, because I felt ... I still have a very traditional...

His efforts are terribly earnest, but finally his English fails him.

Use Japanese; that will be easier for me too (much laughter)!

> *Nartan (translating):* He feels that what is preventing his heart being open is that he somehow clings to something Japanese, traditional. On the other hand, he feels it is a very good thing.

Mm?

Agar: On the other hand I feel that my Japanese is very good.

Mm mm.

Agar: That's why I feel that I cannot open myself to anything Western.

If something is really good, clinging is not needed, one can be simply open. If something is really good, it does not require clinging; you can be open because you know that the thing is going to remain there. In fact it is the fear that keeps you clinging and closed. Deep down you are afraid that what you call good is not good, may not be good. Deep down you are afraid that if you open up, your cherished tradition may disappear. It is fear and doubt. If you really love something and you know it is good, you remain open — what is the fear? You remain vulnerable, you can face it. And if something is wrong and drops, it is for the good; nothing is wrong. Even if it is Japanese and is wrong and drops, good!

But be open. To be open is very decisive — because when you are open, then only that which is really good can remain with you, and that which is not really good automatically disappears.

It is hard, I know. It is harder for a Japanese than for anybody else : he has been brought up very traditionally, and he is very proud. But you will have to be open. If you really want to decide what is good and what is not good, it can be decided only by being open. This is the miracle of openness : the false disappears and the true settles. So if something is good in the Japanese tradition, and there *is* much good, that will remain, that will abide with you. So drop fear.

I have lived totally openly, but anything that is good anywhere has not left me — in fact it has become more and more deeply rooted in me. Not only the Indian, but all that is good, anywhere, in any culture, in any race, in any country, has become part of me. The more open you are, the bigger is your heritage; you can contain the whole universe.

Open up! Good.

(to Raga) So would you like to have your child here or, because he is so attached to Japan, would you like to go to Japan?

Prem Raga : Yes, I want to be with you.

That will be better, and it will be better for the child, otherwise the child will have the same problem as he has!

Agar laughs good-naturedly.

Then the two of them are replaced by the first candidate for a come-close, Krishna Prem.

But first Osho indicates that the mediums move around behind Krishna Prem for a talk.

The first thing : to be a medium means a shift of energy from the left-side hemisphere of your brain to the right-side hemisphere. People are living only fifty percent of their life; only half of their mind is functioning — and the mind that is functioning is the mundane mind that calculates, that is cunning, that does all the business. The mind that is functioning is not of any worth. At the most it gives you a living but not a life.

The other mind, which is far superior, the right hemisphere, is completely blocked. The right hemisphere contains all poetry, all music, all love, all that is beautiful, all that is worth living for, all that makes life meaningful and significant.

To become a medium means to shift the energy. And the only possible way to shift the energy, I say the *only* way, is through your sexual energy. Your sexual energy is still part of the right-side hemisphere. That is the only possible hope left for humanity. That is the only thin thread through which you can move to the right-side hemisphere, otherwise everything has been taken possession of by the left side.

So while you are absorbing my energy feel utterly sexual, sensuous. In the beginning it will look very sexual. Soon there comes a point of intensity when it starts changing, when it starts becoming something that you have not known before at all, something that can only be called spiritual — but only later on, and only if you go totally into it. If you inhibit, your taboos come in and you stop yourself, then it remains sexual, it never becomes spiritual.

All taboos, all inhibitions, have to be dropped; only then at a certain intensity does the transformation happen. Suddenly you are thrown from the left hemisphere to the right hemisphere — and the right hemisphere is the hemisphere of the mystics.

There is an ancient fable of a Hassid mystic. He asked one of his disciples "What do we mean when we use the word 'god'?" The disciple wouldn't answer. Thrice the master asked and the disciple wouldn't answer. The master was really angry and he said "Why don't you answer me?" And the disciple said "Because I don't *know* god!" The master started laughing and he said "Do you think I know?"

God is not a question of knowing at all, it is a question of feeling. Nobody has ever known god. Those who think they have known, have not really known but felt. It is the function of the right hemisphere of the mind. So the deeper you enter into the right hemisphere, and as your energies start moving in the right hemisphere, you are more and more close to me, to god, to yourself, to everything that is.

This is the first thing to remember. The second thing to remember is : when you are joyous your energy flows into the other; when you are sad you start sucking energy from the other. So while functioning as mediums, be as joyous, ecstatically joyous, as possible; only then will your energy start moving into the guest. Only then will you shower your energy into the guest, only then will *he* start overflowing. Joy is contagious. So you are not to be a medium out of duty; it has to be a joyous celebration.

The third thing: your bodies are musical instruments. The medium has to be just a harp in the hands of the master, so I can play on the music of your body, so I can help the music become awake in you. It has to be a very musical process, very graceful, very caressing, loving. When you play upon a musical instrument, you caress it with each touch. You have to become my harps, and you have to remember that — to be very very soft, open, vulnerable, available.

A little resistance from your side and the music will disappear. Then you can go on moving in an empty gesture. It will be empty, of no use; it will make you tired. If you are not making an empty gesture, the guest is going to be helped and you are going to be helped; both are benefited. In fact the mediums will be benefited more, because they will be available every day.

The fourth thing: the first medium, on whom I will be working more, has to function as a triggering point. So whatsoever starts happening in the first medium, you have to fall in tune with her, you have to just move with the first, you have to be just one with the first. And you will be surprised: what is happening to the first will start happening to you all, exactly the same, because it is not a question of the physical body, it is a question of an energy-field. I am just creating an energy-field: if you are ready, the first will be the triggering point and soon you will be taken possession of. So wherever you are — a few people will be standing here behind the guest, a few mediums will be sitting.... Those who are sitting, they can also participate just by sitting there.

The fifth thing: this is not only a small experiment to help the guest; this is to transform the whole energy-field of the commune. Right now it is a small commune. I was waiting for the new commune, but I think it will be delayed a little more, hence I decided that the work has to start. But in a way it is good : if you can fill these six acres of land with your energy, then it will make you able to fill the new commune. The new commune will be big, at least three square miles. But if you can fill six acres of land with your energy, it will not be difficult to fill the three square miles. It is not a question of how big the place is; the question is whether you have got the knack of it.

So before the new commune happens I am trying to give you the knack of it. And it has started happening : the whole commune is affected. Even people who have not participated, who have not been here at all, even in their rooms they are affected.

I'd heard talk to that effect too. The first night that these special energy darshans began, the Encounter group (that happens to be here in darshan tonight) had had a particularly potent session, exactly at the same time as the come-close-ing was happening, though none of the participants or the group leader knew what was transpiring at darshan. But the energy had found its way to them anyway!

From tomorrow, the time for energy communion will be the time when all the lights in the ashram will go off. All activities will stop; for that half hour or forty-five minutes there will be utter darkness and all activities will stop.

People, wherever they are, have to sit silently and be in a receptive mood, and whatsoever starts happening to them — there in their room, in the garden, wherever they are sitting, on the roof — they have to allow.

So this will be the beginning, and once the experiment succeeds here, then I can prepare a bigger group for the new commune, because then there will be the need of a bigger group.

The sixth point : the people who are sitting here in silent darshan, they can also participate. But they have to be aware : when the group is ecstatic, they can be ecstatic; when the group falls silent, *they* have to fall silent; when the group becomes absolutely quiet, they have to become quiet, otherwise they will be a disturbance. But when the group is going into ecstasy, into movement, into wild laughter, they can also. So you can also participate with closed eyes.

Just two things to be remembered : when the group stops, you have to stop immediately; and the second thing, you are not to disturb somebody else who is sitting by your side, you are not to touch somebody else by your side. You have to be alone, on your own.

So these things to be remembered. Good.

The mediums move back to their place, and Krishna Prem is instructed to hold Vivek's hands, Divya, then Chetana, behind him, and Vasumati gently holding them together. Feel the energy slowly moving, Osho begins...

Good, Krishna Prem. Good, Divya. Come back!

About the Author

Osho defies categorization, reflecting everything from the individual quest for meaning to the most urgent social and political issues facing society today. His books are not written but are transcribed from recordings of extemporaneous talks given over a period of thirty-five years. Osho has been described by The Sunday Times in London as one of the "1000 Makers of the 20th Century" and by Sunday Mid-Day in India as one of the ten people – along with Gandhi, Nehru and Buddha – who have changed the destiny of India.

Osho has a stated aim of helping to create the conditions for the birth of a new kind of human being, characterized as "Zorba the Buddha" – one whose feet are firmly on the ground, yet whose hands can touch the stars. Running like a thread through all aspects of Osho's talks and meditations is a vision that encompasses both the timeless wisdom of the East and the highest potential of Western science and technology.

He is synonymous with a revolutionary contribution to the science of inner transformation and an approach to meditation which specifically addresses the accelerated pace of contemporary life. The unique OSHO® Active Meditations™ are designed to allow the release of accumulated stress in the body and mind so that it is easier to be still and experience the thought-free state of meditation.

OSHO International Meditation Resort

Every year the OSHO® International Meditation Resort™ welcomes thousands of people from over 100 countries who come to enjoy and participate in its unique atmosphere of meditation and celebration. The 28-acre meditation resort is located about 100 miles southeast of Mumbai (Bombay), in Pune, India, in a tree-lined residential area, set against a backdrop of bamboo groves and wild jasmine, peacocks and waterfalls. The basic approach of the meditation resort is that of Zorba the Buddha: living in awareness, with a capacity to celebrate everything in life. Many visitors come to just be, to allow themselves the luxury of doing nothing. Others choose to participate in a wide variety of courses and sessions that support moving toward a more joyous and less stressful life, by combining methods of self-understanding with awareness techniques. These courses are offered through OSHO® Multiversity™ and take place in a pyramid complex next to the famous OSHO® Teerth Park™.

People can choose to practice various meditation methods, both active and passive, from a daily schedule that begins at six o'clock in the morning. Early each evening there is a meditation event that moves from dance to silent sitting, using Osho's recorded talks as an opportunity to experience inner silence without effort.

Facilities include tennis courts, a gym, sauna, Jacuzzi, a nature-shaped Olympic-sized swimming pool, classes in Zen archery, Tai chi, Chi gong, Yoga and a multitude of bodywork sessions.

The kitchen serves international gourmet vegetarian meals, made with organically grown produce. The nightlife is alive with friends dining under the stars, and with music and dancing.

Online bookings for accommodation at the OSHO® Guesthouse which is inside the meditation resort can be made through the website below or by sending an email to guesthouse@osho.com

Online tours of the meditation resort, how to get there, and program information can be found at: www.osho.com/resort

For More Information
www.OSHO.com

In this multi-lingual OSHO website you can experience meditation, explore the OSHO International Meditation Resort, enjoy an online magazine and take an online OSHO Zen Tarot reading. You can also browse the meditation and self-discovery programs available in the OSHO Multiversity.

All OSHO audio talks and e-Books are available for download from the shop section and complete OSHO Library is now online for your reference and research.

To contact OSHO International Foundation go to www.osho.com/oshointernational

OSHO International Meditation Resort
17 Koregaon Park
Pune 411001 MS, India
resortinfo@osho.net

Recent Full Circle Books by
OSHO

Die O Yogi Die

Gorakh is one of the four people whom Osho calls "the foundation stones of Indian mysticism". Gorakh is direct and to the point, earthy, an "unpolished diamond" who doesn't allow any detours or side-stepping on the path to self-realization.

This book is about the death of the ego and the practical steps everyone can take to live a full, aware and joyful life.

Behind a Thousand Names

Osho loves the Nirvan Upanishads because it is so revolutionary – revolutionary because it insists that the only way to experience true awareness is to go beyond all systems of morality. Maybe this startling message is the reason why Osho's commentary on this Upanishad is the first that has ever been made.

Available at all leading bookstores.